Politics, Theory, and Contemporary Culture

D1569544

EDITED BY
M A R K P O S T E R

Politics,
Theory, and
Contemporary
Culture

Columbia
University
Press

NEW YORK

Columbia University Press
New York   Chichester, West Sussex
Copyright © 1993 Columbia University Press
All rights reserved

Library of Congress Cataloging-in-Publication Data

Politics, theory, and contemporary culture
Mark Poster, editor.
p.   cm.
Includes bibliographical references and index.
ISBN 0-231-08056-5 (alk. paper.)
ISBN 0-231-08057-3 (pbk.)
1. Politics and literature.
2. Politics in literature.
3. Literature and society. 4. Criticism.
I. Poster, Mark.
PN51.P557 1993
809'.93358—dc20   92-23573
                                CIP

∞
Casebound editions of Columbia University Press books are
Smyth-sewn and printed on permanent and durable acid-free
paper.

BOOK DESIGN BY KATHLEEN SZAWIOLA

Printed in the United States of America

c   10   9   8   7   6   5   4   3   2   1

Contents

Politics, Theory, and
Contemporary Culture

M A R K   P O S T E R

Introduction

From the fall of 1988 to the spring of 1991 the Critical Theory Institute at the University of California, Irvine, worked on the topic "Critical Theory, Contemporary Culture, and the Question of the Political." This volume reflects that work and consists largely of essays by members of the group and invited guests that were presented, discussed, and revised during that period. When we decided on the topic, we had no inkling of the enormous events that would unfold on the world scene during the period of our work: the Tienanmen Square massacre, the collapse of East European communism, the fall of the Berlin Wall and reunification of Germany, the end of the cold war and the beginning of the reform of Soviet socialism, the war in the Persian Gulf and its representation on CNN. In different ways, these events heighten the sense that the world is undergoing fundamental reordering and that the perspectives of the past may not suffice to grasp the present or serve as a point critical judgment in relation to it.

The hypothesis we developed as a focus for our discussion is that the great traditions of Western political thought are exhausted; that liberalism and Marxism no longer serve as effective frameworks to make political experience intelligible and no longer function as spurs to the Enlightenment project of emancipation, to the extent that that project may still coherently organize political thought and action. In short, traditional political metanarratives do not effectively frame the play of power. At the same time the particular intervention of theory in the field of disciplinary forces has not yet adequately drawn coherent paradigms of politics, and at times calls into question the value of such an endeavor. Despite the efflorescence of theory in the humanities and social sciences, especially in the past decade, and despite many gestures in the direction of the political, few contributions have been made to the political scene, although many important new possibilities of political theorizing have emerged.

The intent of our hypothesis is to show not, once again, that each of the "fields" is "political" but rather that our contemporary sense of what constitutes "the political" has been dramatically shaken by the events (political, historical, theoretical, aesthetic, and literary) of the twentieth century and that a critical questioning of politics cannot occur if the traditional (for us, post-Enlightenment, positivist, liberal or Marxist, and so forth) teleologies are not challenged. Our focus is on the challenges that specific forms of history, art, and literature (also sociology, psychoanalysis, and anthropology) constitute for political theory.

The issue of the political raises the related question of self-reflexiveness. The clarification of the political as a theoretical question implies a taking stock of the place and role of theory; it demands an accounting of the manner in which theory inserted itself into the contention of discourses and especially into what might be called the hidden university, those marginal programs or groups where these issues are played out with special intensity. The important question here is how nondisciplinary interpretive strategies have been able to insert themselves into a texture of discourse characterized by sharp disciplinary boundaries. What are the implications of this insertion, and what are the challenges to the institutional framework of these disciplines and to the social framework of this institution? How does the absorption of theory by the interrelated levels of society, institution, and discipline (down to the microlevel of teacher-course-student) not only subvert those levels but also transform the contours and the direction of theory?

At this point the second question about self-reflexiveness turns around and faces the first concerning the political: Is the very turn to the political a sign of the recalibration of theory through its "successful" dissemination into institutional discourses, paradigms, procedures? Is the actual question of the political an indication of uncertainty or hesitation or worry that theory may be or may have been "co-opted," or is it instead a sign of the continuing vitality of theory, an indication of its extension into new terrain—terrain that may provoke a restructuring of the disciplines?

These were the kinds of questions that originally motivated our turn to the topic of politics, theory, and contemporary culture. The papers gathered here address these issues but from a great variety of standpoints. Our group and our invitees share no common theoretical or political protocol but instead represent, I think, the broad range of positions that characterize contemporary discussions of the issues. In terms of methods, some of the papers proceed by reexamining the great texts of the past—Kant, Marx, Freud, Benjamin, and so forth. Others attempt to theorize along new paths; still others inscribe theoretical investigation and its questions within genres not commonly associated with such investigations, such as the fable and the travel report. The result is a volume containing considerable diversity but one that nonetheless intensely pursues the original hypotheses. To complete my introduction I will discuss each essay's relation to our general intent and trace some links between the individual pieces.

Catharine Stimpson asks about metanarratives from a particular locus of discourse, that of reception. She asks about the "we" of feminist theory. And she asks about it in relation to the theory and politics of difference. What is the substance of the "we"? Does feminism as a theory and as a politics have—if it had in the past, in the 1970s, for example—the force of a "we"? Have theory and practice so diverged that the "we" serves as a false unifier, dissembling a medley of antagonisms, disputes, differences within difference? Does feminist theory restrict the "we" to a coterie of those informed by the abstruse languages of criticism? Does feminist practice maintain a presence on the diverse scenes of politics powerful and effective enough to warrant the collective referent *we*? In these ways Stimpson raises important theoretical concerns about unity within difference.

In *Technologies of Gender*, cited amply by Stimpson in these pages, Teresa de Lauretis suggests that feminists need to reconsider the essentialism implicit or explicit in the grounding of their theory in difference. Such a reliance on difference might well imply a new form of grand narrative, a troubling reinscription of a totalizing element within a theory and a politics that seeks to avoid this strategy, since it mimics the foundationalism of theories that feminism wishes to dispute. Stimpson provides a welcome and insightful overview of feminist positions in the age of theories and politics of difference, including an excursis on the fate of some of those positions in the discourse of one male theorist. We have, as a result, a kind of "state of the studies" on feminism that suggests many comparisons with Jean-François Lyotard's essay and foreshadows themes and positions in the essays of John Rowe and Gabriele Schwab. As a depiction of the current state of theory, Stimpson's essay also suggests the cautious position of Carroll, as we shall see.

In "The Writing Class" John Carlos Rowe confronts the theoretical issue of Marxism in postmodernity. As a starting point he examines the question of class in Marx's writings in relation to the problem of language. He then examines recent attempts, such as those of Bourdieu and Lyotard, to redefine class in cultural terms. With the institutions of education and science now so thoroughly inscribed in the economy, older treatments of class in terms of the relation to the means of production no longer suffice. The theoretical issue of prime significance has become the manner of determining class hierarchies through highly rhetorical language practices without losing the advances of materialist critiques. The enormity of the difficulty of politics in postmodern society is thus fully faced by Rowe: How does the performative force of the control of resources by an elite become a recognizable structure of domination when the practice of groups producing material objects is no longer the central dynamic of the social system?

The problem of the media becomes Rowe's central focus to approach this question. In particular, he links the issues of class and community to the representational power of electronic communication systems. The media, he argues, constitute the social identities of individuals in such a way that the concepts that articulated systems of control under industrial capitalism (exploitation, alienation, commodity fetishism, reification) no longer begin to unravel the complexity of postmodern forms of mystification. Today, Rowe contends, a "writing class" has emerged that includes everyone from corporate researchers and the service professions to the academic professoriat and participates, directly or indirectly, in the creation of images and discourses that stabilize the current order. These same groups, along with feminists, ethnic and racial minorities, and ecologists, may well hold the key to a new critical politics that would transform the hegemonic effects of the media into a means of liberation. Yet once uttered, these words boggle the mind with the problems they raise. Rowe's essay breaks with earlier traditions of social criticism by beginning an analysis of the rhetorics of capital in the postmodern age without blinking at the massive conceptual reorientation such a project raises.

A set of essays by Gabriele Schwab and Teresa de Lauretis takes up the problem of politics in relation to desire, pointing to the necessity of feminist theory for any theoretical understanding with a critical intent. Schwab reviews a series of texts that return to the vexed issue of the relation of Marx to Freud, politics to psychology, the social to the individual, the real to the imaginary. Turning her attention to the works of Fredric Jameson (*The Political Unconscious*), Gilles Deleuze and Félix Guattari (*Anti-Oedipus*), and Slavoj Zizek (*The Sublime Object of Ideology*), she argues that the Freudian interpretation of politics depends on a logic of connection and interaction, not one of substitution and opposition. Her aim is to promote an understanding of the interpenetration of politics and desire, the way politics is infused with unconscious fantasy and desire with political inscriptions. She finds Deleuze and Guattari and Zizek closer to this goal than Jameson; but since the case of the latter is instructive of the difficulty of the task, her essay is especially attentive to it, providing one of the rare sustained examinations of *The Political Unconscious* in relation to the politics of desire.

The absence of gender from Jameson's works, in particular *The Political Unconscious*, is striking. So egregious is this deficiency that the editor of a huge volume, containing fourteen essays devoted to Jameson's work, included none by women, and his extensive bibliography on Jameson contains but one book and only a few articles by women.[1] Pursuing this curious gap in the discussion of Jameson's work, Schwab explores the way Jameson's reference of the sexual back to the economic works against his theoretical project. She indicates how Jameson's critique of late capitalism is often forestalled by the way he positions the unconscious in relation to politics. His tendency to reduce the former to the latter understood as the mode of production, she contends, leads him to reintroduce the very elements he is criticizing back into his own text. With desire, fantasy, and gender submerged, Jameson slips back to a reliance on rational individuality that he is so determined to explain as a result of capitalist culture. Schwab carefully indicates how Jameson's readings of nineteenth- and twentieth-century novels exceed the limits of his theoretical prolegomenon, only revealing more urgently the need for a logic of connection and interrelation between politics and psychology.

If Schwab indicates how a theory of the political unconscious requires the introduction of the categories of gender and desire, Teresa de Lauretis attempts to develop this connection into what she calls "a theory of lesbian subjectivity." In this case the value of marginalized subject positions for a general reconfiguration of critical theory becomes exigent. Taking a stance decidedly in favor of the "other" (woman) and of the other of the other (lesbian), de Lauretis begins a reading of Freud that stresses his ambiguous attachment to Victorian norms and draws out those places in his theory that are inconsistent with or remote from them. Her thesis is that Freud's theoretical advances often went beyond his inscription within current conventional attitudes; his "science" struggled with his "ideology," if this Althusserian distinction may be invoked for purposes of clarification only. The vexed question of Freud's relation to feminism and to critical theory in general, then, takes on a different cast in de Lauretis's work.

De Lauretis points to certain inconsistencies in Freud's *Three Essays on Sexuality* and in his later metapsychological pieces such as "The Ego and the Id." She explores the ways in which for Freud the connection between desire and its object was at times unhinged, allowing a gap in which the process of normalization of sexual identity is not biologically determined and therefore opens the question of sexuality as a process of subject constitution, without any pregiven norms. In a different but related reading, de Lauretis shows how in places the connection between the ego and "normal" sexual identity is in doubt, how Freud *almost* unsettles Victorian heterosexuality in relation to the "perversity" of the id. If this ambivalent tendency in Freud can be developed theoretically, as de Lauretis hopes, the component instincts may be detached from any historical instantiation and the question of a normative sexual identity may be destabilized. The relation of politics to psychology is then placed in the register of resistance to normalizing gestures and the current *Kulturkampf* of the right may be resisted with new theoretical apparatuses.

Samuel Weber addresses the question of desire in psychoanalysis in relation to the field of ethics. If ethics is a question of a rule or limit under which one may make a judgment of a particular action, the problematic of desire destabilizes it. In a reading of Lacan's seminar on ethics, Weber argues that the psychoanalytic understanding of desire points to the uncertainty of any limit because the limit that establishes limits is not itself a limit and because all limits participate in this unfounded foundation. If ethics requires self-identical rules—stable limits—then psychoanalysis must open the field to a different understanding of ethics, one in which the movement of desire into action operates more like a fate than a calculated decision. Weber explores this theme through an analysis of Lacan's reading of *Antigone*, exposing the relation of tragic drama to a psychoanalytic comprehension of ethics.

As Weber reminds us, the issue of ethics is illustrated today by the politics of cultural repression that grows stronger and more ominous. Those who vociferously condemn writers such as Lacan are allied with those who preach a return to the ethics of the "Western tradition" to the exclusion of all others. Attacks on critical theory proceed in line with attacks on multiculturalism, feminism, and other protest movements. The connection among theory, politics, and contemporary culture is nowhere clearer than in the stentorian dicta of today's right-wing publicists. Weber connects these attacks with a form of ethics that wishes to retain some firm limit, like Creon in *Antigone*. Proponents of traditional courses on Western civilization want to require it of all students because it is the thing that allegedly holds us together as a culture and because it is simply the best. Such demands illustrate the way ethical formulations work to deny their contingency by repressing their own destabilizing moments. Those Americans who have cultural allegiances other than Western ones are repressed in the proposals of the right, and that repression is denied as it is uttered. Like Schwab and de Lauretis, Weber finds in the psychoanalytic concept of desire a basis for a critical theory that challenges this position.

David Carroll approaches the general hypothesis of our project from a different direction. Auschwitz is perhaps the ultimate referent of the collapse of the general political orientations of liberalism and Marxism. No other sign can so well indicate the failure of Western grand narratives to make sense of the past than this catastrophe. David Carroll insists on Auschwitz and, more generally, fascism as a fundamental marker of our age, a form of devastation that has not been overcome and still determines us, that continues to haunt our notions of community. Whatever relation we can conjure among politics, culture, and theory must, he argues, face the horror of twentieth-century history before moving on to what he considers perhaps the easier or more comforting traits of postmodernity, the hyperreal, or the age of information. A danger we face is that of a recurrence of the earlier devastation, a renewal of fascism—and this next time hardly, to allude to Marx, as farce. The recent intense discussion of Heidegger and his complicity with fascism, most noticeably in France, but also in Germany and the United States, is not for Carroll an odd serendipity but a reflection of the continuing force of Auschwitz in our time.

To theorize the relation of politics and culture, Carroll turns to Hannah Arendt, Jean-François Lyotard, and finally Jean-Luc Nancy. Although their positions are by no means homogeneous, he finds in them a manner of thinking about the issue of community that is consonant with the dire circumstances of our time, of its dangers and false promises. If in some of the essays here the claim is being made that politics needs to be rethought in relation to new or emergent social and cultural phenomena—consumerism, postmodernity, the media, the end of the cold war, global integration, feminism, postcolonialism—Carroll's essay is animated by those theorists who attempt to sustain the function of critical thinking against the ultimate threat to its demise. At this zero degree of politics, the point where freedom and critique are most in danger, Arendt, Lyotard, and Nancy offer diverse points of resistance. Through the discussion of their perspectives, Carroll emerges with a minimal requirement for rethinking community, rethinking it as a kind of insistent impossibility, a contradictory problem that is nonetheless unavoidable—community as a space that must be, to use his words, constituted and deconstituted at the same time.

Opposite the philosophical discourses of Arendt, Lyotard, and Nancy on the spectrum of political writing is travel literature, specifically that form of travel literature occasioned by great political events. The foreign traveler visits a place shaken by revolutionary upheaval. One thinks immediately of John Reed's *Ten Days That Shook the World*, but there are countless others. In these cases an interesting graft is made between socioanthropological tourism and politics, a hybrid of informal reportage on the exotic and the intensity of radical political change. Jacques Derrida visited the Soviet Union in 1990 in the midst of perestroika, an event whose effects on the entire world, have only begun to unfold but surely include the collapse of Eastern European Communist regimes and the reunification of Germany. In the United States, the cold war struggle has for so long been a framing element in political culture that the effects of the Soviet reversal on it are sure to be profound. The stable key to American politics has been our mortal enemy, the Soviet Union. As schoolchildren we crouched under desks in fear of their missiles; as adults we suffered the numbing stupidity of Cold War rhetoric, a pall on both foreign and domestic initiatives. And now, all of a sudden, it has practically vanished from the political horizon.

Derrida explores the difficulty of writing a travel report on Soviet life in the midst of perestroika. He evokes earlier attempts by Etiemble, Gide, and Benjamin to describe the Soviet Union, examining in remarkable complexity the pitfalls and the surprises of the discourse of the foreign witness. If we learn little of Derrida's personal experience of perestroika, we learn much about the type of writing such a report would entail. The issue of the narrative—its status today, its ability to frame, its foundational tendencies—is once again brought to the surface. If the grand narrative of Marxism, as Lyotard had argued, can no longer stitch the garment of political theory, then the narrative of testimony and of witness, Derrida warns, contains its own hazards. He points to the case of Benjamin, who, in his visit to Moscow, argued for the self-representationality of the city in social revolution and also that the events were so powerfully present that the witness need only point to them for their meaning to emerge. But can the city speak for itself, reducing language to a transparent mediation of expression, Derrida asks?

Alexander Gelley turns to the question of the city and explores various epistemologies of its representation. The question of community, as raised by Carroll, and the problem of the media for the writing class of late capitalism or postmodernism, as discussed by Rowe, hinge on the city and lead directly to the question of what forms of human association are now possible. Gelley stresses the difficulty of finding one's theoretical bearings in the topos of the city. In his classic study of the city, Max Weber defined it in relation to the process of modernization, the progressive differentiation of social structures and institutions on the basis of individual functions. As the space of the market, the city in the West was home to the first modern culture, a culture of "freedom," a space in which individuals were not bound to one another in relations of domination. Gelley examines the inheritors of this view—Raymond Williams, Michel Foucault, and Walter Benjamin. He problematizes the issue of the city as a knowable object by distinguishing between what he alternately refers to as the culture versus the fictive and urbanism versus representation. If the city is charted, its status as a knowable object is too easily assumed; if its knowability is in question, its charting is problematic. This is the aporia that Gelley attempts to elude with his strategy of "cultural semiology," what he sees as a middle path between the others.

Gelley opens his essay with a discussion of Godard's film *Two or Three Things I Know About Her,* in which he sees the representationality of contemporary cities as in doubt, as a partial consequence of the emergence of new means of communication. Like Rowe, Gelley discusses the media in relation to the city in terms of its reconfiguration. At stake is the question of how the media in general, and especially film, intrude into our very knowledge of the city. The particular issue of urbanity as a constructed entity, as fictionalized, was raised by Benjamin in the *Arcades Project,* which Gelley examines at some length. The flaneur, he contends, is the first consumer of images, a decidedly urban personage. But this "aestheticization" of the city, Gelley indicates, goes beyond its representation by romantics, thereby connecting the theme of the city with Rowe's discussion of the postmodern. Since for Gelley *any* thinking about the city must raise the problem of its refashioning, hence of utopia, the two essays converge around the issues of criticism, politics, and contemporary society.

Jean-François Lyotard discusses the impossibility of grand narratives in the present conjuncture. He reviews the situation in Central Europe and in the Middle East in order to show how a Marxist "analysis of the situation" can no longer provide a coherent, critical account. The proletariat is simply no longer a force on the world scene and the move to discover a proletariat in the third world produces unsatisfying results. Politico-cultural alternatives to Western liberalism are collapsing at a terrifying rate, Lyotard observes, and those remaining simply cannot match its technical superiority. Various "marginal" oppositional forces—feminism, ethnic minorities, ecology movements, gay and lesbian protest—continue to struggle but these, for Lyotard, either do not generate new grand narratives or are continuously co-opted by the system. This sobering portrait of the current political arena creates a fresh challenge for critical theory. It appears that the West has indeed developed a social order in which a certain gap or blank, as Lyotard calls it, anticipates—indeed invites—critique, only to domesticate it in one manner or another.

Faced with a seeming dead end to theory, Lyotard offers a surprising move. He tells a tale, a story of the condition of the cosmos, a grand narrative if ever there was one, but from a naive or child's point of view. He proposes a representation of reality today as seen not from a critical standpoint but from within the system of the West itself. The tale is very much a scientifico-technical one, almost a Hegelian narrative of the Earth's coming to save itself through the intervention of the social system of the West—not mankind's intervention, as he reminds us, but that by the system itself. Reading the tale, one considers its absurd logic; perhaps it is just this that Lyotard wants us to confront, if only as a beginning point for a new order of critique, a theoretical intervention that would be appropriate not to the conditions of modernity but to those of postmodernity. If Lyotard's analysis of the situation is correct, the failure of the grand narratives is a cause for a fundamental rethinking of the traditions of theory.

Related to Lyotard's analysis of the current situation as one in which the grand narratives of the past are losing their force of credibility is Ernesto Laclau's effort to renew democratic politics through a deconstruction of the opposition of modernity to postmodernity. Like Lyotard, Laclau searches for an alternative to modernity, the Enlightenment paradigm of rationality. He does so by disputing the nihilism attributed to the thesis of postmodernity by its critics. If postmodernity were, as these detractors argue, merely an opposite, a "beyond" of modernity, then it would indeed lead to a retreat from the political since it evacuates all contents of power, all forms of emancipatory movements, protest and revolution. Laclau's strategy proceeds along two lines of deflection.

The first is to deconstruct the logocentric visions of the social inherent in liberal and Marxist positions. Here the postmodern is the recognition of contingency in the hegemonized social field, the insistence on the incomplete, gap-riddled quality of determinate conjunctures, the analysis of political gestures as efforts to suture openings that are evidence of the openings more than genuine totalizations. The second is to argue for the specific feature of the contemporary world by which social identities are no longer fixed in relation to privileged terrains (the mode of production for Marxism and of representative democracy for liberalism). Today, Laclau contends, loci of identity construction proliferate to the point that the constructed character of identity becomes apparent to a degree not possible in earlier social formations. This impossibility/necessity of identity offers a line of flight for a new, "postmodern" politics, one that might recuperate the emancipatory aims of the Enlightenment without its logocentric wrapping.

In my view, one conclusion to be drawn from these essays is that a central problem for critical theory today, amid the crumbling of old political edifices across the globe and the recombination of a "new order" of national and international forces, is how to start initiatives from new cues, from emergent social formations and problems such as the media and ecology, from protest movements that had no serious bearing in hoary treatises of earlier generations; how to experiment with new forms of presentation that escape the procedures of established disciplines and find the means to experiment with new discursive patterns. In the United States, the political right, flailing out of control without the mad vision of the cold war to anchor its animus, blindly attacks theory along with feminist movements, ethnic challenges, and postmodern art. Perhaps the time for new affiliation and new initiatives has come.

Notes

1. Douglas Kellner, ed., *Postmodernism, Jameson, Critique* (Washington, D.C.: Maisonneuve, 1989).

CATHARINE R. STIMPSON

How Did Feminist Theory
Get This Way?

How did feminist theory get this way? So taken with herterogeneity?[1] So deeded over to diversities? Traveling so willfully from its commitment to "sexual difference" to "differences"? Not coincidentally, feminist theory developed during the same period as chaos theory in the sciences, the exploration of the "irregular side of nature, the discontinuous and erratic side . . . puzzles . . . or worse, monstrosities" (Gleick, p. 3). I now want to offer a story that might trace such an evolution in feminist thought. This reader's digest of a narrative will have three parts: First, "What Theories Suit?" is a sketch of the immediate past. Second, "Some Notes from the Jacket" is my response to Wayne Booth's *The Company We Keep*, one of his contributions to ethical criticism and literary theory. ("Some Notes" will be a case study in reading differences.) Third, "An Address to the Future" is a little slip of a section that glimpses some places where feminist theory might go.

Because national boundaries help to contain feminist theory and practices, I will tend to stay at home in the United States. Ideas, however, can travel without passports. United States feminist theoreticians range well beyond the borders of the state, sometimes imperiously, for their feed.[2] Feminist theories from the United States have also flown abroad. The word "feminism" will be a loose, admittedly ahistorical label both for formal movements organized for the sake of women and for informal gestures made for the sake of a woman's daily survival. Part of the difficulty in writing the history of feminism is that many of these gestures are subtle, muted, and coded. The historian must hear a grandmother whispering to a child as they pluck a chicken in a kitchen sink, "Men may work from sun to sun, but women's work is never done," a lesson in the preparation of a meal and the harshness of an identity.

What Theories Suit?

Women's history has many gifts for feminist theory: ideas and metaphors—such as Virginia Woolf's "room of one's own"; a humbling awareness of the limits and inadequacies of most ideas about women; a sense of the strength and patience of women in the past. Significantly, these offerings, which feminist anthropologists have supplemented, include proof of the vast differences among women that their specific places in history and society inexorably breed.

To a degree that we might have forgotten, the most influential feminist theoreticians after World War II wrote histories. Simone de Beauvoir in 1949, Betty Friedan in 1963, Juliet Mitchell in 1966, Toni Cade's anthology *The Black Woman* in 1970, Kate Millett in 1970—all pictured women in the past. In part, their purpose was to show some differences among women. Cade focuses on those between black women and white; Millett mentions the interdependence of the differentiating, fractionating structures of race, class, and gender.[3] Except for Cade, however, the greater purpose of history was to legitimate theory, to demonstrate its seriousness and validity. History showed that the collective effort to imagine Life Without Father was neither hysterical nor hallucinatory but an act of theoretical, political, and individual necessity. Imagining Life Without Father was inseparable from figuring out why Life With Father had gone so wrong. Feminist theory was, then, a search for historical and psychological causality, for explanations of the structures of gender and the conditions of women. Because these imaginary and analytical acts were *in writing*, because they were texts, they showed the power and danger of literate women. They justified all those blood-curdling warnings about the threat to the established order of educated women, critical women, who could get themselves into print and then even go off to war in print.[4]

Because the horrors of history were an impetus to theory, early theoretical statements were organizing principles for a movement that would affirmatively alter history as well. These statements all built on the perception of the pervasiveness of sex and gender difference. They were:

1. We must distinguish sex from sexuality, a biological classification from a way in which the body behaves.

2. Similarly, we must distinguish sex from gender, a biological classification from the social role assigned to any body, a role that scripts sexual behavior.

3. Our gender structures are patriarchal power structures in which men dominate women. If women are cattle, men hold the prod. In less than rigorous talk, "patriarchy" becomes more than the name of a particular form of the family. "Patriarchy" was a pejorative label for any institutionalized form of male dominance.

4. Our representations of gender—be they in psychoanalysis, the media, advertising, or other fictions—help to create and maintain gender. Like the family, they are socializing tools.

5. Women must struggle against patriarchy at home and away from home. For some, the struggle will be for equality, for civil rights and opportunities within a better system. For others, the struggle will be for liberation from "the system" and for the redemptive creation of a radically different future. Millett called for "a second wave of the sexual revolution . . . [to] at last accomplish its aim of freeing half the race from its immemorial subordination—and in the process bring us all a great deal closer to humanity. It may be that we shall even be able to retire sex from the harsh realities of politics, but not until we have created a world we can bear out of the desert we inhabit" (p. 507).[5] Later, Sheila Radford-Hill, an African-American teacher and organizer, was to state, "Mine is a lifetime commitment to empowerment . . . The central task of any movement for social change is empowerment . . . Empowerment endures, i.e., people continue to feel empowered when their collective struggles result in fundamental alterations in social hierarchies that are experienced on a day-to-day basis as an improvement in the quality of life" (p. 159).

Understandably, the "second wave" of feminist theory had its totalizing moments, days, weeks, years.[6] It went more for the wave than for the particles, for the master narrative that would undo the master. This was due in part to the generic rules of theory, which demand comprehensiveness and closure, and in part to the sense of *newness* of feminist theory, despite the historical explorations that accompanied its writing. Being new, it was unrevised, uncorrected. The preference for a grand wave over particles was also partly due to the close connections between feminist theory and feminism, between ideas and an excited movement that was to translate them into a mass agenda. In part, it was due as well to another set of close connections, those between feminist theory and students. Whether these students were in a formal classroom, in a consciousness-raising group, or simply "out there," they responded to passionate clarities. In part, such gestures were more examples of theoretical narcissism, the assumption that "I" can speak for the world because the world is, when all is said and done, the same as me. In part, too, these totalizing gestures unconsciously mimicked traditional theories about women and gender, which have often sought one cause, usually natural or divine, for one effect, immutable gender identities.

Like Super Bowls, such single-minded traditions of theory building continue. On January 2, 1990, the *New York Times* reported a case of scientific error. In 1988, a group of scientists concluded that they had discovered the fountain of perpetual gender identity, a "maleness" gene, which they named ZFY. Ah, crowed one of them, even as he was later eating crow, "Sex determination represents a sort of paragon . . . The organism has to choose between two fates: male or female" (Kolata). Exemplifying the ability of normal science to correct itself, in 1989, another group found some men who did not have the maleness gene. Goodbye, Mr. ZFY.

Three grand feminist theories fed off one another. First, women shared a universal identity, which the metaphor "sister" familiarized. As Nancy Cott has shown, the effort to elaborate the female "we" has bedeviled feminism as a mass movement. Not only is the "we" socially unstable. If feminism seeks equal rights and opportunities for women who lack them, its success will ironically abolish the "we" that deprivation has inflected. Second, being a victim was constitutive of women's identity, de Beauvoir's "Other," Friedan's housewife with a problem without a name, Millett's "immemorial" subordinate. Third and finally, an abuse of "the victim theory" has let some women avoid acting and accepting responsibility. Nonetheless, feminist theory encouraged heroic action. Feminists could immaculately, overwhelmingly "transform" culture and society. such promises were self-consciously, proudly utopian. Feminist speculative fiction and poetry imagined what a feminist utopia might be like, what form its kitchens and altars and beds might take. Even when feminist theory recognized differences among women, it often froze a single set of differences (most often that iron triangle, race-class-gender) into a static picture that promised to render all historical and social processes. Gayatri Spivak had to caution Americans about their misreadings of racism: "In the matter of race-sensitive analyses, the chief problem of American feminist criticism is its identification of racism as such with the constitution of racism in America" (Spivak, p. 81).

Fortunately, feminist theory was both self-correcting and correctable, both self-revising and revisable. The pressures of reality bore down upon it, especially the realities of women of color in the United States; of working-class and rural women in the United States; of women outside the United States;[7] and of lesbians. Younger generations also spoke of their differences from "the mothers." Obviously, women were, and are, everywhere. No matter how much formal systems might cancel them out, women keep on checking in everywhere. The United States invasion of Panama at Christmas, 1989, provides a metaphor for women's *everywhereness*. Though forbidden to be combat troops, women were in combat, either as members of the military or as civilian victims. Moreover, the rhetoric of the invasion incorporated women. Among their many overkill efforts in the discrediting of Noriega, Army propagandists reported that he had the gall to call his mistress before his wife when the United States forces descended upon him. Because "everywhere" is differentiated and complex, not undifferentiated and simple, women necessarily differed among themselves in complex and often painful ways. Helen Reddy might sing, "I am woman," but many, many a woman knew that she was not Helen Reddy, no matter how catchy the melody. Admit, feminist theoreticians insisted, to these complex and often painful ways. However, the wisest of voices called for a celebration of difference as well. In 1978, for example, Audre Lorde located the root of racism, sexism, heterosexism, and homophobia in "an inability to recognize the notion of difference as a dynamic human force, one which is enriching rather than threatening . . ." (p. 45).

Other social and cultural forces pushed theory toward diversity. First, the politics of the 1960s had the potential power to stimulate the recognition of differences among women. On the one hand, the experiences of activist women in the 1960s taught them that sexual differences could be glued to gender hierarchies as a whip handle to a whip. In brief, various post–World War II movements were sexist. On the other hand, black movements revealed racial differences among women; antipoverty work, class differences. Next, the comparative cultural pluralism of the United States inevitably destabilized certainties.[8] It provided feminist theoreticians with a variety of male masters whom they might call into service. The choice of a particular male master as an ally of feminist theory would help to write its pages. If the theories of the 1950s and 1960s excoriated Freud and psychoanalysis, women in the 1970s rubbed salve on their wounds and rejuvenated them in order to construct a theory of subjectivity, a rejuvenation that explorers of "feminism and psychoanalysis" are still enhancing and that feminist theory as a whole has not yet accepted. The twentieth-century schools of linguistics and literary theory that studied the production of meaning from the play of differences within language were also, if adapted, compatible with feminism's passionate inquiries into the relationship of language and a world of differences. In the 1980s, for example, Barbara Johnson sought "to transfer the analysis of difference . . . out of the realm of linguistic universality or deconstructive allegory and into contexts in which difference is very much at issue in the 'real world' " (p. 2).

In the 1970s, male theoreticians gazed more respectfully on feminism, a decorum that Herbert Marcuse helped to initiate in 1974 in a lecture, "Marxism and Feminism," sponsored by the Center for Research on Women (CROW) at Stanford University. Citing a debt to Angela Davis, Marcuse called women's liberation "perhaps the most important and potentially the most radical political movement that we have" (p. 279), for the movement could "transcend the framework within which it now operates" and construct a different "Reality Principle" for society: new norms, values, institutions, and relationships (p. 281). Powerful enough to compel the respect of a Marcuse, feminist theory was also powerful enough to split and divide and then to provide a number of feminist theoreticians from which to draw. A sophomore in the United States, especially if she knew French, might joyfully roam through Cixous, Clément, Irigaray, Kristeva, and Wittig. In brief, as early as the 1970s, feminist theory was established enough to multiply.

To add to the sense of form being multiform, feminist thought preferred not to privilege any single genre or format over another. Theoreticians could be painters, poets, witches, doctors, journal-keepers, and journalists. Theory could appear on the streets, in the alternative press, or even in an academic seminar. In any or all of these genres, women were to speak for themselves. The phrase "the personal is the political" did not mean collapsing the political into the personal, structures into subjectivity. Rather, it called for an analysis of the ways in which the political had shaped the personal, structure had shaped subjectivity. Through reading and writing and talking, the individual subject could understand this process. Through understanding, at once cognitive and therapeutic, the individual subject could then reshape, reform, "transform" the self-in-the-world and the self-and-the-world. Alix Kates Shulman, an early radical feminist, recalls, "our purpose was not simply to improve our sex lives or to find some personal solution to our problems. We wanted nothing less than to understand the social basis for our discontents, including the sexual, and then to do something to change it—for everyone" (p. 593). Through all this, feminism would inductively and pragmatically rebuild theories. A statement of Raymond Williams applies here: "It is the special function of theory, in exploring and defining the nature and variation of practice, to develop a general consciousness within what is repeatedly experienced as a special and often relatively isolated consciousness. For creativity and social self-creation are both known and unknown events, and it is still from grasping the known that the unknown—the next step, the next work—is conceived" (p. 212).

Despite its social and political sweep, the commitment to "the personal is the political" joined with the analysis of women's sphere as a domestic sphere to commit feminist theory to a special responsibility: the articulation of everyday life. Here women might dissimulate (all those naughty fake orgasms), but their everyday life is no simulation. The bed and the sheets that would have to be washed were there. In the 1980s, Teresa de Lauretis was to write:

Feminism differs from other contemporary modes of radical, critical or creative thinking, such as post-modernism and philosophical anti-humanism: feminism defines itself as a political instance, not merely a sexual politics but a politics of experience, of everyday life, which later then in turn enters the public sphere of expression and creative practice, displacing aesthetic hierarchies and generic categories, and which thus establishes the semiotic ground for a different production of reference and meaning.   (p. 10)

Necessarily, as women spoke about their dailiness, they vigorously revealed the differences among themselves. During the 1970s, these differences were codified, organized, and, if marginally, institutionalized. As Charlotte Bunch recalls, "a more diverse range of women were now defining feminism and seeking changes in their own lives as well as in society. There were more working women's groups—blue- and pink-collar as well as professional; there were increasing numbers of women of color—black, Hispanic, Asian, and Native American women—and there was a movement of women emerging globally" (p. 16). Significantly, as new roots were planted amid the grasses, as feminist theory and practice became rhizomatic, as diversity became a feminist ideal, the mass media wrote a somber master narrative: the death of feminism. Baby had gone a long way—to the grave. The stony truth seems to be that the TV camera, in ordinary times, best captures monoliths, two-sided conflicts (football, mud wrestling, presidential horse races), and celebrities. Feminism was beyond its frame.

. Among the emerging institutions that defied the media's obituaries was women's studies. I love and celebrate women's studies. It has respected and explored diversity.[9] Nevertheless, I feel some ambivalence about its consequence for feminist theory. Women's studies has given theory a home and a site in which to nurture the next generations of theorists. However, colleges and universities have subjected theory to their discipline. Theory now tends to adhere to a specific academic discipline, especially literature, history, and philosophy. Moreover, each discipline imposes its own regulatory pattern of rewards and punishments, its own criteria of "good" and "bad" work. As a result, feminist theory has matured quickly, but its connections with artists, "crazies," spiritualists, and "nonacademic" feminist writers are far more tenuous than they were in the 1960s. Only a few nonacademic feminist writers—for example, Margaret Atwood, Audre Lorde, Barbara Ehrenreich, Carol Gilligan, Adrienne Rich, Alice Walker—commonly travel among several domains of discourse. Yet, nonacademic writers—Marilyn French, Elizabeth Janeway, Robin Morgan, Letty Cottin Pogrebin, Gloria Steinem, Wendy Wasserstein—articulate feminist theory for a general reading public. Unfortunately, except for Steinem, they do little with TV—or more accurately, TV refuses to have much do with them. As a result, they may not extravagantly help feminist ideas "find a louder, stronger voice in popular culture and consciousness," a voice crucial if they are to "have a lasting impact on state power" (Petchesky, p. 319).

In the 1970s, thinking about diversity met at least two sources of tension. First, many women wished to redeem the female, a sexually different "woman." Such a desire inexorably veers toward a universal and essentialist theory of gender. As Diana Fuss has pointed out, the concept of essentialism itself then becomes essentialized. The motives for redeeming the female varied. In some part, as Elizabeth Gross suggests, the internal logic of feminist theory demanded such a move. Having asked to be included in men's theoretical domains, women discovered that they were nonincludable. These domains, like an all-male club, were designed to exclude women. In order to do theory at all, women had to conceptualize their autonomy (Gross). In some part, feminism saw moral purpose and value in aspects of women's traditional role. Women might not be lesser men. On the contrary, men might be lesser women whose salvation would lie in becoming more feminine. Finally, in some part, certain public policy issues—pay equity, for example—had to continue to present women as a class if they were to propose remedies for the disabilities of this class.

The second source of tension was the inadequacy of simply admitting to the diversity among women. Much of the energy of the 1970s and 1980s went into repairing a horrendous weakness. Theoreticians both of the materiality of culture and of postmodernism rushed to this work because each had, in its way, an analysis of power. The weakness was to forget that diversity is not synonymous with equality. The equivalences of the bloc/ks in a pluralist landscape were spurious. Relations among women were power relations. Sisters were mistresses and slaves, professional women and baby-sitters, doctors and nurses, diners and waitresses, butches and femmes. Women were also mothers, who had power over both daughters and sons, especially when the sons were babies and little boys. Moreover, women in the United States wore garments that Third World women had stitched together in sweatshops in "developing countries," that minority and poor women had stitched together in tenements in the United States. Keenly aware of global structures, Chandra Mohanty, a postcolonial critic, extended Adrienne Rich's vision of a "politics of location." She asks us to locate ourselves scrupulously in the body, geography, language, sociopolitical space, and even in theory. If we do so, we will see how entangled our differences are in hierarchies, in relations of domination and dependency (Mohanty).

Each woman then internalizes the diversity of her public and historical space. The psychic consequence, a decentered subject, is less a heap of fragments than a network of forces, often in conflict with one another. As de Lauretis writes, "What is emerging in feminist writings is, instead, the concept of a multiple, shifting, and often self-contradictory identity, a subject that is not divided in, but rather at odds with, language; an identity made up of heterogeneous and heteronomous representations of gender, race, and class, and often indeed across languages and cultures; an identity that one has to reclaim from a history of multiple assimilations" (p. 9). More autobiographically, María Lugones begins an essay in feminist philosophy: "This paper weaves two aspects of my life together. My coming in consciousness as a daughter and my coming to consciousness as a woman of color have made this weaving possible. This weaving reveals the possibility and complexity of a pluralistic feminism, a feminism that affirms the plurality in each of us and among us as richness and as central to feminist ontology and epistemology" (p. 275).

In the late 1980s, under postmodernism's increasing influence, feminist theory foregrounded an appealing set of propositions. Theory would question a single, universal concept of truth; the immateriality of language; and the possibility of a single, objective, neutral gaze, those old blue eyes of a universal knowing subject. So doing, theory would deconstruct all binary oppositions, including a master binary opposition—that between knower and known, the epistemological version of "me Tarzan, you Jane." Avowing its own perspectivism, theory would analyze the interplay of subject and object. Reveling in the materiality of language, theory would seek new forms of writing and new kinds of discourse.

A consensus now exists about feminist theory: it is a contested zone, or, more accurately, a cluster of contested zones. One zone is within feminist theory: the now-familiar arguments about truth, representation, and the subject that postmodernism stimulates. The controversy over Joan Scott's linkage of poststructuralist theory and women's history provides a portfolio of these arguments.[10] A second zone questions the value of theory itself. Some of these zone-dwellers are old-timers who have long glowered at theory as a "male" trap. Mary Daly does not list theory in the "word-webs" of her dictionary for feminist hags and

crones. "Methodolatry," however is a "common form of academic idol-
atry: glorification of the god Method; boxing of knowledge into prefab-
ricated fields, thereby hiding threads of connectedness, hindering New
discoveries, preventing the raising of New Questions, erasing ideas that
do not fit into Respectable Categories of Questions and Answers"
(p. 82). In the 1980s, less recalcitrant feminist critics began to ask if
theory were not a destructive force. Nina Baym tartly accused feminist
critics of doing theory in order to please their masters and in order to
bully pluralists into conformity (Baym). Barbara Christian pointedly
wondered why postmodern theory became influential when new, previously despised subjects were claiming public status as knowing subjects. "I see . . . the language it [theory] creates," she writes, "as one
which mystifies rather than clarifies our condition, making it possible
for a few people who know that particular language to control the critical scene—that language surfaced, interestingly enough, just when the
literature of peoples of color, of black women, of Latin Americans, of
Africans, began to move to 'the center' "[11] (p. 229). In minds less sophisticated and tested than those of Baym and Christian, "theory" col-
lapsed into "French theory." "French" into a metaphor for fin de siècle
intellectual decadence, drunk on the wine of the signifier, stumbling
after the cancan girls of the semiotic female, indifferent to the folks back
home in plain-speaking, truth-telling America.

A third zone, neoconservative thinking about women, has one feature in common with the second: the suspicion of postmodern theory,
abbreviated to "theory." Otherwise, this zone opposes nearly all feminist
theory and scholarship. Allegedly, feminists are a part of the barbaric
cultural decadence of the 1960s. They kick out at objectivity, rational
inquiry, and aesthetic judgments. Not surprisingly, then, feminist
theory and scholarship are partial, biased, and polemical. Knees jerk-
ing, feminists cannot grasp the market or women's choices about entering a market economy. They are sloppily, even lasciviously, attracted to
moral deviancy. Finally, they have a bad attitude. Like arrogant head-
waiters, they snippily dismiss the people they pretend to serve.

Neoconservative thinkers have become more aggressive in their ob-
jections to feminist thinking, especially through an organization
founded in the 1980s, the National Association of Scholars. So doing,
neoconservatism is moving from a theoretical response, no matter how
superficially and angrily made, to action. The body of late-1980s feminist theory I described earlier, if in a threadbare way, also endorses a

constant movement between theory and practice. Obviously, what acting will mean to various people in their various locations will itself vary. Elizabeth Gross suggests that feminist theory could lead to "a local, specific, concrete intervention with definite political, even if provisional aims and goals" (p. 196). This is similar to the post-Marxism of Ernesto Laclau and Chantal Mouffe that places "socialism in the wider field of the democratic revolution . . . founded on the plurality of social agents and of their struggles . . . This also means that the extension and radicalization of democratic struggles does not have a final point of arrival in the achievement of a fully liberated society" (Laclau and Mouffe, p. 106).

Presumably, women in their own specific situation would plot the transitions from theory to strategy, strategy to tactics. Indebted though I am to Gross, such a statement provokes certain political questions. Like Wendy Brown, I ask if feminist theory can construct a "we" strong enough to create a program, a radical political critique that would be "supple *and* militant, porous *and* potent" (Brown, p. 64). Are we in the presence not simply of utopian but of magical thinking? Is this a romanticism of the small, a sublime of the finite? Is this not a pastoral poetics of powerlessness? Without subscribing to a grandiose vision of the ends of history, might I ask if all these local, specific, and concrete interventions can add up to anything? Or are we simply to assume this will happen, as corporate chiefs planning a merger of companies vow that "synergy" will flow from their manipulations? Or is the local enough? Will telecommunications be able to rescue the local from parochialism and ennui? Even if the local is enough, how are women to resolve their differences if differences become divisions? By a due process not yet invented? By a vote not yet tallied? By a judge not yet roped in and robed? By an arbitrator not yet appointed? By the blood that no one wants to shed?

Though I ask these questions, I believe these late-1980s ideas have shimmering political promise. Questioning the very term "human nature," such feminist theory cannot provide the foundation for an authoritarian regime that justifies its power through a defense of a clenched vision of man's being and needs. On the contrary, such feminist ideas are consistent with the reciprocities and exchanges of coalition politics. Next, during a conservative period, such as mine in the United States, authority cannot find a fixed target, a single body to repress. Rather, multiple camps of resistance are in constant, frustrating motion. Similarly, during a period of concentrated media that emit too few representations of women, these localities send out lots of alternative signs and signals. Among them can be women's statements—on the page, in videotext, in performance—of their precise wants, needs, and desires.

Next, in a world of global economic practices, women can adapt this theory to any place, at any place, without succumbing to a single ascribed status that global economic practices encourage. We might have a globalization of feminist theory that avoids the totalization of a female political identity. Next, internationally and nationally, we live with a well-known paradox: consolidations of political, cultural, and economic power co-exist with, indeed provoke, a number of groups that seek a separate national, ethnic, or religious identity. These groups then claim for their identity a metaphysical and ontological status. These claims intensify group conflict. Opposed to the centripetal urge toward massive consolidations, feminist theory seems to have internalized the centrifugal urge toward splits, fragmentations, separations. Yet, it seeks peaceful cohabitation, differences that are more play than power plays.

Finally, such a feminist politics, with its countless small theaters and arenas, is partially compatible with more conventional United States practices. Here groups and individuals have their demands and desires. They elect candidates from competing parties who promise to take care of these demands and desires in councils and legislatures, executive offices and courts. To win, a candidate must usually speak a politically acceptable language. In the past two decades, since Kate Millett was on the August 31, 1970, cover of *Time* magazine and described as the "Mao Tse-tung of Women's Liberation," feminism has inserted some of its demands and desires into a politically acceptable language. To be sure, women had stated these demands and desires well before the publication of *Sexual Politics*. Nevertheless, since 1970, "mainstream" feminism has translated many statements into party platforms, policies, and laws. So doing, it has had to operate within a self-divided culture in which "majority opinion" supports feminist goals but chokes on the word "feminist," in which being a feminist seems distinct from claiming the name. Like "woman" herself, feminism in the United States is both visible and invisible.

The feminist issues now before the United States Congress reveal the semantic field of a currently acceptable political language.[12] Resting with comparative ease in this field are questions about the family and childcare; employment and welfare; education; civil rights, despite the conservative attack on civil rights legislation; the elderly poor; domestic violence; the concerns of women veterans; housing and the homeless. Together, they represent some commitment to families during a period of change, to female victims, and to equitable economic opportunities within capitalism. In turn, these commitments are responses to genuine social needs. The "stalled revolution" that Arlie Hochschild describes in *The Second Shift* is not a dummy parachutist in free fall (Hochschild). The number of women and children in poverty, more than 75 percent of the nation's thirty-two million poor, is not the figment of an arithmetical imagination on a frolic. In 1990, it was not a flight of theoretical fancy about marginality and invisibility to say that only fifty of the seven thousand programs in the United States treating drug and alcohol abuse provided female patients with child care and obstetrical services (Diesenhouse). However, a notorious gap exists between the power necessary to fulfill legislative commitments and the extent of women's needs. Harmful in itself, the gap is also a metonymy for the chasm between the grandeur of feminist aspirations, at every degree of theoretical aplomb, and the unevenness of feminist political strength.

With wearying predictability, the semantic field I have noted breaks apart over reproductive rights. As Rosalind Petchesky has shown so formidably, reproductive rights and abortion are the "battering ram . . . in a much broader (conservative) offensive" against challenges to male authority and to a sexuality that may overtly express itself only within the nuclear family (pp. 241–325). In 1970, while feminists were buying *Sexual Politics* and marching past St. Patrick's Cathedral in New York City, the Catholic Church was organizing right-to-life committees.

Since Stonewall, the homosexual body, largely construed as male outside of feminist and pornographic discourse, has joined the pregnant body, always female, as the site of the fight for moral control. They supplement each other with terrifying efficiency. Both bodies refuse to reproduce heterosexuality: the male homosexual because he sleeps with men and refuses to be a father; the woman who needs an abortion because she has slept with men and then refused to be a mother. If conventional discourse noticed the lesbian, it would doubly damn her. Refusing to sleep with men, she cannot even be a dam. For demographic, cultural, and psychological reasons, the homosexual is an especially fabled scapegoat. Gay men, now ravaged by AIDS, and lesbian women are a numerical minority. Of the 91 million households in the United

States, only 2.6 million consist of unmarried couples of the opposite sex, 1.6 million of unmarried couples of the same sex. Of these, perhaps 40 percent are homosexual. The homophobic stigma is also deeply rooted in religious tradition and virulently rooted in heterosexual defenses against polymorphous desires. If The Homosexual did not exist, Jesse Helms would have had to invent him.

Located both within and beyond this discursive field, most feminist theoreticians of differences support reproductive rights. So, of course, do a majority of Americans. More explosively, feminist theoreticians speak affirmatively of gay men and lesbian women in an extensive vocabulary of love, sexuality, work, and identity. In these tongues, "whiteness" is no longer a mark of privilege. "Redness" is a mark of a text we have put down or of the title of a Rita Mae Brown novel, not the mark of a ghastly, demonic Other. Pressing in against a conventional, more liturgical political language, like a demonstrator against a police barricade, this feminist speech might be the raw material of the conventional political language of my old age.

Notes from the Jacket

I appear in *The Company We Keep*—twice. First, I wrote a blurb for the hardcover edition (1988). It is printed on the left flap of the jacket. Next, I am part of a footnote that praises feminist criticism as "the most original and important movement on the current scene" (p. 188n. b). These appearances are a synecdoche for my relationship to Wayne Booth's magisterial book. Because I admire both Booth and his book, I am glad to be noted. He has the splendid virtues of critical pluralism, virtues we would miss if we did not have them: learning, sensitivity, generosity, flexibility. The Wayne Booth who inhabits this book is a character with character. As such, he respects the need, which teachers and readers are now expressing, to bind ethics and poetics more tightly together.[13] So doing, he is willing to make distinctions, to separate nourishing narratives from poisonous ones. Yet, like a jacket, I can be pulled away from the book's cover and pages and, I fear, possibly torn up. I am both adherent and detachable. In this sticky situation, let me speak of Booth as a feminist critic. Although I am aware of the arguments about "men in feminism," I will simply assume that men can be feminist critics without being mimics, parodists, colonizers, or voyeuristic creeps.[14]

The figure of Booth as feminist critic appears in *The Company We Keep* in at least four scenes. The first is the preface, the book's brief account of its own history and hopes. Graciously, lovingly, Booth thanks his wife, Phyllis Booth, for her ethical criticism of his pervasively "over-confident judgments." He also acknowledges a debt to his wife and two daughters for "whatever validity" there might be in his efforts to correct his "male bias." Apologetically, modestly, Booth has adapted two principles of feminist criticism: masculinity breeds moral and cognitive error in men, in part because masculinity diabolically assures men of their moral and cognitive powers; next, women can push men toward greater accuracy, in part because men in power exempt women from masculinity. He also establishes the *family* as exemplary practitioners of "coduction," his neologistic term for our collective, lifelong, comparative efforts to gain a sense of what values narratives embody. His use of "family," plus his metaphor of friendship to depict the relationship between a book and its reader, de-eroticizes reading. He thus pulls away from and covers up the eroticized hints of his title that whisper that close, even intimate relationships nurture ethical critics. "Keeping company" can mean "dating," at least it did when and where I grew up.

The second scene reinforces the image of Booth as a correctable husband and the family as a site of conversation about narrative values. Such a husband inverts patriarchal convention. That inversion, in turn, helps the family to perform as ethical critics together. Booth imagines that he and Phyllis have been to the movie version of *The Color Purple*. Acting out a stereotypically feminine, sentimental role, he weeps "at several points" (p. 74). Acting out a stereotypically masculine, rational role, Phyllis is dry-eyed. She clearly sees the film's manipulative rhetorical devices. These actions, however, are not an end but the beginning of discussions about the film that will alter both the work and their first convictions. Immediately after this fantasy, Booth moves into an autobiographical account of his changing responses to *One Flew Over The Cuckoo's Nest*. In 1962, it bowls him over. His critical practice, however, pins him down. He must reread the novel. He must talk about it, especially with women. This *"prolonged conduction"* (p. 76) leads him to find the novel not an epic of heroism but "a sentimentalized dream of male freedom from and revenge against 'Big Nurse'" (p. 75). It is racist as well.

The third scene is Booth's most extended engagement with feminist criticism. He uses Bakhtin to reread Rabelais and finds both sexist, for they both erase the speaking female subject. In more detail, Booth applies a formal syllogism to Rabelais, a raucous, adored canonical author. If a work is sexist, it is flawed. Rabelais, to such and such a degree, is sexist. Therefore, "we must—to some degree—lower our esteem for the work, and perhaps even for the author" (p. 389). Even if Booth must lower his esteem for Rabelais, he shows his respect for him by articulating the doctrinal differences that divide them. He also signifies his respect for others, and his ability to listen to them, by paraphrasing his critics succinctly and answering them courteously. In the fourth scene, Booth uses feminist criticism to reread canonical Jane Austen, a speaking female subject, as a possible alternative to and corrective of Rabelais. If Rabelais shrinks, Austen looks "perhaps even greater than she did before" (p. 435).

The readings of Rabelais and Austen are brilliant exercises. As Booth traces his own maturing as a reader, he is teaching a master class in ethico-formalist criticism for a variety of students. The reading of Rabelais, however, has provoked far more howls, yowls, and yips than the reading of Austen. In a note of *The Company We Keep*, Booth allows that an "early version of this chapter . . . raised more cries of outrage than almost anything else I've published" (p. 389). He isolates two kinds of unkind, mutually contradictory attacks, which unite in their perception of his unkindness to Rabelais. He has failed to read Rabelais according to the standards of sixteenth-century Europe, but neither has he recognized that Rabelais was a great feminist in comparison to the really standardized louts of his time.

Charitably turning the other cheek, Booth has perhaps been unwilling to glimpse other attackers. They began to emerge during Booth's first presentation of his revisionary reading of Rabelais, a paper called "Freedom of Interpretation: Bakhtin and the Challenge of Feminist Criticism," in fall 1981, at a symposium, "The Politics of Interpretation," which *Critical Inquiry* sponsored at the University of Chicago. *Critical Inquiry* published the papers in September 1982. The edition of the journal then became a book. At the conference, he delivered a famous paragraph, published in *The Company We Keep* as:

> When I read, as a young man, the account of how Panurge got his revenge on the Lady of Paris, I was transported with laughter and rushed to tell my [male] friends about it. When I later read Rabelais aloud to my young wife, as she did the ironing (!), she could easily tell that I expected her to be equally delighted. Of course, she did find a lot of it funny; a

great deal of it *is* very funny. But now, reading passages like that, even
though everything I know about the work as a whole suggests that my
earlier response was closer to the spirit of "the work itself," I draw back
and start thinking rather than laughing, taking a different kind of pleasure with a *somewhat* diminished text. And it is my feminist criticism
that has done the dirty work.   (p. 411)

I primarily remember two responses to this passage and its endorse-
ment of feminist criticism. A group of men openly mourned Booth's
inability to laugh so heartily at Rabelais. They spoke as if he had not
acted freely; as if ferocious, unstoppable feminist critics were castrators
who had cut off his joy. Intensifying their alarm was the fact that
"Wayne Booth" had spoken. In a self-contradictory move, they feared
that the most prestigious of United States critics had freely chosen feminist criticism. If Booth had gone, who next? What defense was left
against the castrators? He had, moreover, used feminist criticism to
smoke out a well-guarded and regarded figure, a major writer, a biggie.

Feminists, however, laughed. In part, they enjoyed an intertextual
detail: the relationship between Phyllis Booth's implicit ethical criticism
at her ironing board and Tillie Olsen's feminist story "I Stand Here Ironing." This detail was also a reminder of the premise of feminist criticism
that the personal is the political; that the experience of everyday life tests
the very discourse that mediates it and the theory that explains it.
Booth's anecdote fits into the sociology of Dorothy E. Smith, the cultural studies of Teresa de Lauretis. In part, feminists laughed because
they felt freer at the conference now, in a more comfortable space.
Their laughter, of course, masked two discomforts. They worried that
Booth's strength, rather than their own, had purchased that comfort.
Moreover, had Booth put them at ease by borrowing and appropriating
their tools? He had acknowledged feminist critics warmly, but had the
surprise and wonder of his acknowledgments obscured the nature of the
debt he was acknowledging?

These two groups—the angry and grieving men and the politely
cheerful and laughing feminists—were in the same room, at the same
conference, but not in the same company. Their antagonism—the
feminists' desire for change, the men's desire for the status quo—soured
whatever creamy conversations about criticism the conference might
have poured out. Indeed, the quickness with which conversations could
curdle is a warning against our infatuation with the concept of "conversation." Moreover, outside of the conference and other arenas of con-

versation, that antagonism has appeared again and again in politically charged decisions that only one group can win: a tenure decision, a proposal for curricular reform, a federal policy about culture. Another example: I am willing to read all sorts of narratives about a proven sexual harasser, to encounter his "otherness," and to speak about those narratives with as much subtlety and flexibility as I can muster. I am not willing to have him in my department or institution.

Booth is aware of the horrors of the "real world." He is serious about their need of remedy. Yet, *The Company We Keep* may minimize the antagonisms that feminist criticism has provoked and the passions (both love and hate) it has aroused.[15] It will then understate how much resistance to feminist criticism hinders the readings he advocates and the equity he seeks. These underwritings may occur because "the personal" of Booth is too benign to feed the "political" a rich enough diet. Moreover, no matter how strong his commitments, feminist criticism seems less a primary intellectual and moral endeavor for him than a primary intellectual and moral endeavor for others that helps him clarify what his own primary intellectual and moral endeavors might be. Booth believes (rightly) that he is supporting feminist criticism. His mode of support is to have feminist criticism *represent* a central, all-encompassing problem.[16] This drift toward the universal (upward, outward, and downward simultaneously) also reveals itself in the rhetorical specific "I" who reads and teaches and wonders and makes mistakes and talks to his wife, and the more diffuse "we," who reads and teaches and wonders and makes mistakes. The easiness of this "we" masks a difficulty that feminist criticism has, after false starts, refused to evade: the impossibility in the late twentieth century of an easily uniform "we," let alone an easily homogeneous "I."

As a Boothian metonymy for complex literary and critical issues, feminism and feminist criticism stop being self-divided particulars in a world full of divisions, ruptures, and discontinuities.[17] Rather, feminist criticism is a complicated particular that illuminates a general difficulty: the relationship of doctrinal purity and narrative impurities. In brief, we might like books that are not very likable, that are, for example, anti-Semitic or anti-Arab. "Our coductions," he writes, "are not finally *about messages*: they are *constructions of experience*" (p. 377). Because an ethical criticism must, finally, disrobe itself of neutrality, it confronts the conclusion that what these constructions say about experience does matter. How, then, does one "face squarely the folly, viciousness, and

plain falsity that we meet in too many of our would-be narrative friends"
(p. 377)?

Folly, viciousness, and plain falsity about women are awash among
the classics, in the canon, and in our social discourse. Booth urges feminist criticism, as it sniffs out and seeks to drain this cesspool, to serve as
a model discourse. It must not abandon the ideology/politics that demands opposition to such a cultural stink. Equally, it cannot make its
discourse "indistinguishable from politics" (p. 388). It must value form
and aestheticized patterns. This mixed and mingled discourse will feed
on and serve interpretive freedoms. It will avoid two imprisoning errors
of thought, which the poststructuralism Booth treats with severe polite-
ness also abhors: first, setting up unbridgable binary oppositions—here
between literary and political criticism—and next, reducing poly-
chromes to monochromes—here the conviction that all criticism ultimately services power.

Address to the Future

I hope this section will not prove to be a straitjacket on "conversations."
I do not subscribe to a constrictive pragmatism that insists that each
theory be tested *right now* for its palpable, programmatic, testable util-
ity. Gerda Lerner has long distinguished between a "woman's right
movement," concerned with winning equality between men and
women, and "woman's emancipation." Emancipation signifies "freedom from oppressive restrictions imposed by sex; self-determination;
and autonomy" (Lerner, p. 221). Emancipation's precondition is consciousness, "a stance, an attitude" (p. 237). Within these terms, the task
of theory is emancipatory, the interrogation of the construction of discourse and consciousness, the measurement of a stance. Nevertheless,
as an experiment, theoreticians might ask themselves two simple questions about each of their interrogations and measurements: First, how
would a "nontheoretician," which I admit is a dreadful naming of identity through negation, hear this? How might it touch his or her perspective? His or her sense of location? And second, how much does my idea
matter for human survival? And what does that grizzly, elemental cliché
mean? Does my feminist literary criticism, for example, have anything
to do with literacy?

Let me offer two examples of feminist theory that explicitly or implicitly ask such questions. The first, from moral theory, swerves back toward the proposal of a moral idea with broad applicability and deontological force. In "Beyond Gender Difference to a Theory of Care," Joan Tronto argues for an ethic of care. Such an ethic would matter for both patterns of moral thought and "concrete daily experience" (p. 663). She asks not whether caring is intrinsically female but if it is sufficiently adequate as a moral theory to ground action and policy. The second is a brilliant demonstration of the rhetorical analysis of a political text. In "Sex and Death in the Rational World of Defense Intellectuals," Carol Cohn presents herself as a participant/observer in the learning of the language of defense intellectuals, "technostrategic" speech. She expresses her debt to poststructuralist literary theory for showing her how to deconstruct texts and "narrative authority" within them (p. 715). Although she declines the easy temptations of demonizing these men, she toughly analyzes the strategies—the phallic imagery, for example—through which highly intelligent theoreticians hide what they are doing from themselves. For they are planning how to kill other people. Despite their designs on our bodies, their language is strangely without a bodily referent. Lurking behind are a set of concepts, programs, computer models—the "hyperreal," I presume. Then Cohn explains the "why" of her enterprise. She is interested in policy questions. Why, for example, does the state obsessively modernize weapons systems? Beyond that, she cares about the discourse of policy, which she and her colleagues must first dismantle before they can create "compelling alternative visions of possible futures, a task of recognizing and developing alternative conceptions of rationality, a task of creating rich and imaginative alternative voices—diverse voices whose conversations with each other will invent those futures" (pp. 717–18).

This passage exults in the possibilities of herterogeneous theory making. Cohn's alternatives would risk turbulence and confidently jostle against the present and against one another. Cohn prefers the plural to the singular form of nouns: futures, not future; conceptions, not conception; voices, not voice; conversations, not conversation. This is the grammar of herterogeneity. She asks us to see, to have a perspective on the world, to speak, to vocalize a part of a world, and to listen, to hear from and about other parts of a world. Seeing, hearing, talking—Gertrude Stein said these were the marks of genius. As seers, auditors, and speakers, we will not hide away from irregularities, puzzles, discontinuities, or monstrosities. Confronting the monstrous, we will ask if it is sublime (galactic space), new (a space suit), merely unusual (a plastic wrap suit), or morally monstrous (a suit of prison clothes for Vaclav Havel or for a battered woman). Vitally, as we key in and print out our narratives, we will exercise our capacities for analysis, generalization, and hope.

I share this spirit. Yet, I must add a final picture. The other day, I, a white, professional woman in the late twentieth century in the United States, was eating breakfast: orange juice, vitamin pills, grapefruit, All-Bran, and Twinings Ceylon breakfast tea. A theme of Gayatri Spivak's work is "the micro-politics of the academy and its relation to the macro-narrative of imperialism" (MacCabe, p. x). I wish I could say that I was thinking about the connections among my breakfast, the supermarket in which I bought my food, and the reasons why Twinings Ceylon tea was on my table in Staten Island.

However, I was not. I was awake, but my consciousness was flicking in and out of the trivia of everyday—the damage the cats had done to the furniture, the bullet hole in the dining room wall, the telephone call I had to make, who might buy the house for sale next door. Then, an ad for General Electric came on the television. Capital was surging through morning in America. Though General Electric owns NBC, I was watching a CBS network station. In the ad, a nocturnal cat steps through the equipment on a bench in a laboratory. Despite its caution, it knocks a beaker to the floor. In the morning, Dr. Fox, a white, male scientist, enters the lab and rummages through the debris. But—eureka!—the translucent material in the broken beaker has hardened into a miracle substance, a nearly unbreakable clear plastic, "Lexan," which General Electric will give to a needy world. The ad's voice-over reminds us, in warm tones, "You never know where the next great idea will come from or how far it will take you."

The utopianism of herterogeneous feminist theory has one distressing resemblance to the General Electric punch line: have an idea, have some ideas, and swing into the future. However, herterogeneous feminist theory has one, more reassuring distinction from the General Electric punch line. Feminist theory wants to know where the idea comes from. Such interrogations are a part of its program. My fear is that we will only say that we want our conversations to translate theories into policies; the politics of location into locatable activities that both conflict and connect with each other. We will not surge beyond speaking our desires. In Gertrude Stein's last play, *The Mother of Us All*, Susan

B. Anthony is on a platform at a meeting. She is to debate pompous, corrupt old Daniel Webster. Before she calls him up on the stage, she warns her audience, "Ladies there is no neutral position for us to assume. If we say we love the cause and then sit down at our ease, surely does our action speak the lie" (act 2, scene 4). Feminist theory has analyzed the illusion of the neutral position. It has said it loves the cause. What actions now will theory speak? Where will it lie?

Notes

This paper builds on some of my previous work, particularly "Nancy Reagan Wears a Hat," in *Where the Meanings Are* (New York: Methuen, 1988), pp. 179–96. I am grateful to the Harland Lectureship at Duke University, to the Critical Theory Institute of the University of California–Irvine, and to the Diane Weiss Memorial Lectureship at Wesleyan University for inviting me to give versions of this paper on January 15, 1990; January 18, 1990; and October 23, 1990 respectively.

1. *Herterogeneity* is a neologism of my own, which names the effort to theorize and experience the differences among people through theorizing and experiencing the differences among women. Lugones and Spelman are an especially influential call for the recognition of these differences. Snitow provides a lovely overview of the diversity within feminist theory. West offers a compelling general picture of global diversity in the postcolonial period.

2. This paper will touch on the several meanings of theory that Kramarae and Treichler outline in A *Feminist Dictionary*: a way of looking, of seeing, feminist theory seeks to give a sense of the whole through connecting itself to everyday experience, to the material. Unfortunately, it can be a "form of policing" and a "master's tool" (pp. 447–48).

3. Millett's career indicates how flexible and self-inventive feminist theoreticians of the 1960s in the United States could be. A brilliant scholar who earned a first at Oxford, she was a graduate student at Columbia when she wrote *Sexual Politics*,which was her doctoral dissertation. Though she had taught very successfully at Barnard College, the English Department had terminated her before its publication. She was also a serious sculptor and, to a lesser extent, a filmmaker. After *Sexual Politics*, she was to write a series of autobiographies and meditations. Before joining the New York chapter of the National Organization for Women and chairing its Education Committee, she had participated in the civil rights movement. Bisexual, she was married when *Sexual Politics* was published.

4. In *Passionate Politics* Charlotte Bunch discusses the importance of the printed word, especially that distributed through alternate media, to the development of feminist theory (pp. 217–39). Like Millett, Bunch shows the capacity of feminist theoreticians who began in the 1960s to cross borders. An intelligent, conscientious, and trusted builder of bridges between theory and practice and among activist groups, Bunch marks 1963 as a key year. Then an undergraduate at Duke, she became involved in civil rights, antipoverty projects, and the Student Christian Movement. She also read *The Feminine Mystique*. During the 1960s and 1970s she expanded her efforts to include the antiwar and anti-imperialist movements, the gay and lesbian movement, and international feminism.

5. Millett's language is revealing. Her metaphor "the second wave" compresses her theory that the nineteenth century generated a sexual revolution, which then provoked a repressive reaction from 1930 to 1960. In turn, repression produced the revolt of contemporary feminism. Her word "humanity" shows her explicit allegiance to a humanism that postmodern feminist theoreticians were later to deconstruct; and "bear," an implicit allegiance to women as bearers, as maternal figures, which feminist theoreticians were very soon to valorize.

6. For an assault on a totalization of today, see Wendy Brown's 1990 review of Catharine MacKinnon.

7. Narayen's "The Project of Feminist Epistemology" is a lucid recent survey of the misfittings between the epistemological and political theories of "Western feminism" and "nonwestern" life, a term she uses with tactful irony.

8. Ellen Rooney asks if feminist theory itself is another manifestation/infestation manifestation/infestation of pluralism. She argues that it both can and cannot be, depending on its self-consciousness about its place, its location, and on its commitment to the possibility of general persuasion. "Anti-pluralisms are inflections or versions of discourses that can also be spoken—in fact, often are spoken—in nonsubversive forms, that is, in pluralist forms" (p. 249).

9. Two textbooks show how diversity might be structured for the classroom. In one, Jagger and Struhl outline the "oppression" of women; then give examples of conservative, liberal, traditional Marxist, radical feminist, and socialist feminist theories about women; and finally show how each theory can operate in practice; e.g., as an illustration of liberalism, Maureen Reagan supports the Equal Rights Amendment. In the second textbook, Kauffman organizes a dialogue about specific problems.

10. Koonz, reviewing Scott's *Gender and the Politics of History* in *Women's Review of Books*, believes Scott has given too much power to discourse: "by discounting the role of material circumstances in shaping reality, she implies that a change in 'discourse' about women and men can transform the position of real women" (p. 19). Scott responds to a letter to the editor with a brief

adjoining reply from Koonz, in *Women's Review of Books* 6, no. 6 (March 1989): 4, which Russ later finds too polite.

11. The Kauffman volume mentioned in note 9 includes the version of Christian's essay I cite and a Michael Awkward response, "Appropriative Gestures: Theory and Afro-American Literary Criticism," pp. 238–46.

12. My source is the 1989 issues of *Update*, the newsletter of the bipartisan, bigendered, bicameral Congressional Caucus for Women's Issues. Although only twenty-six women are in the House and two in the Senate, the Caucus has about eighty members. In 1963, the year of *The Feminine Mystique*, a presidential commission on the status of women issued an important report, *American Women*. The report minimizes differences among women. It also romanticizes the "family" and promises that gender change, if administered wisely and fairly, will do nothing but strengthen that "core" institution. Nevertheless, the issues it addresses—employment, education and literacy, social insurance and tax policy, civil and political rights, such home and community services as child care, the need for governmental monitoring of change—are remarkably similar to those of Congress over a quarter of a century later. This shows the prescience of the report, the continuity of liberal feminist discourse, and the stamina supporting a feminist agenda demands.

13. Obviously, these expressions vary according to a speaker's ideological position and intention. Explicitly conservative commentators berate "the left" both for lacking values and for having rotten ones. Statements of need also arise from a teacher's belief that a literature classroom, which deals with culture, should offer an image of civilized life, a knowledge of virtue and vice, as well. As obviously, ideological positions and intentions help to dictate what such knowledge might be. Anne Barbeau Gardiner, for example, writes of using Dante as a moral guide to contemporary behavior (1989). So doing, she will convince her students that Milton is right, that "the lifeblood of master spirits lives on in their books." Such master spirits offer students "wise friendship and discerning guides" (p. 26). The language of friendship makes Gardiner compatible with Booth; her refusal to analyze the "master" in master spirits does not.

14. Jardine and Smith, *Men in Feminism*, is a most subtle collection of investigations into the problem its title names.

15. Perkins (p. 51) suggests that the most powerful criticism may come not from comparison and coduction but from "love and hate."

16. Scholes (pp. 89–155) also uses feminist criticism as a central issue in an argument about the relationships of literary criticism to ethical-political issues. For Scholes, the inability of deconstruction to engage fully with feminism, e.g., its theories of a gendered reader and of a class of readers with a vision of justice, reveals the weakness of deconstruction.

17. Rooney discusses Booth's pluralism from a perspective that both femi-

nism and poststructuralism have informed. Nussbaum, who shares the former perspective but not the latter, reviews Booth with fine intelligence.

Works Cited

Baym, Nina. "The Madwoman and Her Languages: Why I Don't Do Feminist Literary Theory." In *Feminist Issues in Literary Scholarship*, ed. Shari Benstock, pp. 45–61. Bloomington: Indiana University Press, 1987.

Booth, Wayne C. *The Company We Keep*. Berkeley and Los Angeles: University of California Press, 1988.

Brown, Wendy. "Consciousness Razing." Review of *Toward a Feminist Theory of the State*, by Catharine MacKinnon. In *The Nation* 250, no. 2 (January 8/15, 1990): 61–64.

Bunch, Charlotte. *Passionate Politics: Essays 1968–1986*. New York: St. Martin's Press, 1987.

Christian, Barbara. "The Race for Theory." In *Gender and Theory: Dialogues on Feminist Criticism*, ed. Linda Kauffman, pp. 225–37. Oxford: Basil Blackwell, 1989.

Cohn, Carol. "Sex and Death in the Rational World of Defense Intellectuals." In *Signs: Journal of Women in Culture and Society* 12, no. 4 (Summer 1987): 687–718.

Cott, Nancy F. *The Grounding of Modern Feminism*. New Haven: Yale University Press, 1987.

Daly, Mary. *Webster's First New Intergalactic Wickedary of the English Language*. "In cahoots," with Jane Caputi. Boston: Beacon Press, 1987.

de Lauretis, Teresa. "Feminist Studies/Critical Studies: Issues, Terms, and Contexts." In *Feminist Studies/Critical Studies*, ed. Teresa de Lauretis, pp. 1–19. Bloomington: Indiana University Press, 1986.

Diesenhouse, Susan. "Drug Treatment Is Scarcer Than Ever for Women." In *New York Times* (January 7, 1990), section E, p. 26.

French, Marilyn. *Beyond Power: On Women, Men, and Morals*. New York: Summit Books, 1985.

Friedan, Betty. *The Feminine Mystique*. Reprint. New York: Dell, 1967. Originally published in 1963.

Fuss, Diana. *Essentially Speaking: Feminism, Nature, and Difference*. New York: Routledge, 1989.

Gardiner, Anne Barbeau. "The Teaching of Ethics through Literature and Dante's *Inferno*." In *ADE Bulletin* 93 (Fall 1989): 22–26.

Gleick, James. *Chaos: Making a New Science*. New York: Viking Penguin, 1987.

Gross, Elizabeth. "Conclusion: What Is Feminist Theory" In *Feminist Chal-*

lenges: Social and Political Theory, ed. Carole Pateman and Elizabeth Gross, pp. 190–204. Reprint. Boston: Northeastern University Press, 1987. Published in Australia in 1986.

Hochschild, Arlie R. *The Second Shift*. New York: Viking, 1989.

Jagger, Alison M. *Feminist Politics and Human Nature*. Totowa, N.J.: Rowman and Allanheld, 1983.

Jagger, Alison M. and Paula Rothenberg Struhl. *Feminist Frame-Works: Alternative Theoretical Accounts of the Relations between Women and Men*. New York: McGraw-Hill, 1978.

Janeway, Elizabeth. *Powers of the Weak*. New York: Knopf, 1980.

Jardine, Alice, and Paul Smith, eds. *Men in Feminism*. New York: Methuen, 1987.

Johnson, Barbara. *A World of Difference*. Baltimore: Johns Hopkins University Press, 1987.

Kauffman, Linda, ed. *Gender and Theory: Dialogues on Feminist Criticism*. Oxford: Basil Blackwell, 1989.

Kolata, Gina. "Scientists Dismiss Finding of 'Maleness' Gene." In *New York Times* (January 2, 1990), section C, p. 3.

Koonz, Claudia. "Postscripts." In *Women's Review of Books* 6, no. 4 (January 1989): 19–20.

Kramarae, Cheris and Paula A. Treichler. *A Feminist Dictionary*. With assistance from Ann Russo. Boston: Pandora Press, 1985.

Laclau, Ernesto and Chantal Mouffe. "Post-Marxism without Apologies." In *New Left Review* 166 (November–December 1987): 79–106.

Lerner, Gerda. *The Creation of Patriarchy*, vol. 1. New York: Oxford University Press, 1986.

Lorde, Audre. *Sister Outsider: Essays and Speeches*. Freedom, Calif., Crossing Press, 1984.

Lugones, María. "Playfulness, 'World Traveling,' and Loving Perception." In *Women, Knowledge, and Reality: Explorations in Feminist Philosophy*, ed. Ann Garry and Marilyn Pearsall, pp. 275–90. Reprint. Boston: Unwin Hyman, 1989. Originally published in 1987.

Lugones, María C. and Elizabeth V. Spelman. "Have We Got a Theory for You!" In *Women's Studies International Forum* 6, no. 6 (1983): 573–81.

MacCabe, Colin. Foreword to *In Other Worlds: Essays in Cultural Politics*, by Gayatri Chakravorty Spivak., pp. ix–xix. New York: Routledge, 1988.

Marcuse, Herbert. "Marxism and Feminism." In *Women's Studies* 2, no. 3 (1974), 279–88.

Millett, Kate. *Sexual Politics*. New York: Ballantine Books, 1978. Reprint, 1983. Originally published in 1970.

Mohanty, Chandra Talpade. "Feminist Encounters: Locating the Politics of Experience." In *Copyright* 1 (Fall 1987): 30–44.

Narayen, Uma. "The Project of Feminist Epistemology: Perspectives from a

Nonwestern Feminist." In *Gender/Body/Knowledge: Feminist Reconstructions of Knowledge*, ed. Alison M. Jagger and Susan R. Bordo, pp. 256–69. New Brunswick: Rutgers University Press, 1988.

Nussbaum, Martha C. "Reading for Life." In *Yale Journal of Law and the Humanities* 1, no. 1 (December 1988): 165–80.

Perkins, David. Review of *The Company We Keep*, by Wayne C. Booth. In *ADE Bulletin* 94 (Winter 1989): 49–52.

Petchesky, Rosalind Pollack. *Abortion and Woman's Choice: The State, Sexuality, and Reproductive Freedom*. New York: Longman, 1984.

President's Commission on the Status of Women. *American Women*. Washington, D.C.: U.S. Government Printing Office, 1963.

Radford-Hill, Sheila. "Considering Feminism as a Model for Social Change." In *Feminist Studies/Critical Studies*, pp. 157–72. Bloomington: Indiana University Press, 1986.

Rooney, Ellen. *Seductive Reasoning: Pluralism as the Problematic of Contemporary Literary Theory*. Ithaca: Cornell University Press, 1989.

Russ, Joanna. Letter to the Editor. In *Women's Review of Books* 6, no. 7 (April 1989): 4.

Scholes, Robert. *Protocols of Reading*. New Haven: Yale University Press, 1989.

Scott, Joan Wallach. *Gender and the Politics of History*. New York: Columbia University Press, 1988.

Shulman, Alix Kates. "Sex and Power: Sexual Bases of Radical Feminism." In *Signs: Journal of Women in Culture and Society* 5, no. 4 (Summer 1980): 590–604.

Snitow, Ann. "A Gender Diary." In *Rocking the Ship of State: Toward a Feminist Peace Politics*, ed. Adrienne Harris and Ynestra King, pp. 35–73. Boulder, Colo.: Westview Press, 1989.

Spivak, Gayatri Chakravorty. *In Other Worlds: Essays in Cultural Politics*. New York: Routledge, 1988.

Tronto, Joan C. "Beyond Gender Difference to a Theory of Care." In *Signs: Journal of Women in Culture and Society* 12, no. 4 (Summer 1987): 644–63.

West, Cornel. "The New Cultural Politics of Difference." In *October* 53 (October 1990): 93–109.

"Who's Come a Long Way, Baby?" *Time* (August 31, 1970), cover story.

Williams, Raymond. *Marxism and Literature*. London: Oxford University Press, 1977.

JOHN CARLOS ROWE

The Writing Class

A schoolteacher posed the following question: Why
don't workers write? He showed in a profound way how
this is due to their total situation in society and also to
the nature of the so-called education dispensed by
schools in capitalist society. He also mentioned that
workers often think their experience "isn't interesting."
—Cornelius Castoriadis, "What Really Matters"

The concept of class seems almost an embarrassment to critical theorists
today. Even the familiar triad for the conceptualization of social relations—race, class, and gender—is beginning to assume the dyadic features of "race and gender." In a recent collection of essays, *Critical
Terms for Literary Study*, notable for its attempt to take seriously the
influence of essential terms of critical theory for literary and humanistic
study in the twentieth century, race and gender, along with ideology,
culture, canon, discourse, and representation, are subjects of excellent
individual essays. There is no essay on class, although James Kavanagh's
essay on ideology devotes six pages to the integral role Marxist theories
of ideology ascribe to class relations. For many critical theorists, class
consciousness and class struggle have become quaint reminders of
nineteenth-century industrialism, relevant for historical studies but not
of much use in addressing the contemporary political practice of the
critical theorist. This is surprising in light of the extensive work among
social theorists roughly since the end of World War II on the precise
ways that class divisions have changed along with transformations of

41

society and economics in specific twentieth-century cultures. In fact, differences in the relative treatment of class as a significant category for theoretical work strike me as effective ways of understanding the implicit distinction we make today when we use the terms *critical theory* and *social theory*. It goes without saying that critical theory *is* (*ought to be?*) social theory, but popular usage within the academy suggests that the two terms have come to represent "disciplines" with increasingly distinct methods and aims.

For post-Marxian "critical theorists," there is the implication of a certain naïveté to the class distinctions developed in Marx and Engels and those interpreters who followed a strict construction of their writings. In his essay "Ideology" Kavanagh is typical of post-Marxians in this regard:

> When Marx and Engels first developed a critique of ideology, the Anglo-European popular classes were largely illiterate agricultural or first-generation urban workers, there was no universal public education or political suffrage, no technology of mass entertainment, and one social institution—religion—that influenced every practice and offered everyone—in discourses, rituals, and images—an explanation and justification of the world and society. Thus, the first Marxist attempt to understand ideology was inevitably limited by a relatively simple psychology of the social subject and was dominated by closely intertwined philosophical and political criticisms of European religious ideology.[1]

Kavanagh is quick to point out that the relatively coherent social institution of religion includes philosophical idealism, and he thus suggests that the nineteenth-century "critique of ideology" follows the relatively straightforward model of Marx and Engels in *The German Ideology*. Much as we may admire Marx and Engels' analyses of idealist philosophy's role in "refunctioning" religious ideology and thereby legitimating the bourgeois subject, their arguments that such an ideology ought to be taken at face value as central to the development of a political ideology governing social reality and individual behavior appear to critical theorists today as reminders of bygone social orders in which class distinctions were clearer because the defining terms of ideology were more coherent.

Kavanagh argues that the influence of psychoanalysis on our theories of the subject has had much to do with complicating our understanding of ideology. Although he does not explicitly say so, Kavanagh implies that traditional class divisions are only crude approximations of the complex and manifold modes of subject formation operative in any concrete historical situation. From Gramsci and Lukacs to Althusser and, more recently, Laclau and Mouffe, the focus of ideological analysis has shifted from the broadly defined hierarchies of Marx's class analysis to the more intricate modes of hegemonic determination. "In this framework," Kavanagh writes, "ideology designates a rich 'system of representations,' worked up in specific material practices, which helps form individuals into social subjects who 'freely' internalize an appropriate 'picture' of their social world and their place in it" (p. 310). To be sure, such an account of what Althusser termed the *interpellation* of the subject complicates enormously the important task of identifying the social and economic relations defining a particular subject—that is, those affiliations of the subject that we might still identify abstractly as "class."[2] It also complicates the distinction between "class affiliation" and "class interests," the former determined traditionally by systems of ideological domination and the latter as a consequence of a "class consciousness" formed in response to such domination. Some of the embarrassment of critical theorists regarding the concept of class may well have to do with their recognition that class consciousness may well be as ideologically constructed as class affiliation, or at least that their political differences are no longer so strictly defined as once imagined.

Althusser's critique of the strict dependence of superstructure on the economic base in traditional Marxist theories relies upon his claim that the relation between social and economic practices is heterogeneous, often discordant, and certainly not historically sequential.[3] Class interests defined primarily in and through the conditions of labor could thus not hope to comprehend those social practices and everyday behaviors that often precede and inform changes in the so-called material conditions of human production. The deliberate *confusion* of economic forces and social life is one of the hallmarks of post-Marxian theories, but it has often resulted in a certain uneasiness about the very category of class.

My claim that contemporary critical theorists are abandoning class as an essential concept may seem extreme. Continental feminism, deconstructive criticism, and a broadly defined set of "poststructuralist" and "postmodern" methods have been criticized vigorously and often quite effectively for totalizing theories of gender, race, language, the psyche, culture, and even history that fail to take into account the effects of class in concrete historical circumstances. Valid as such criticism often is, the appeal for class analysis is often conventional and the radical demand for the "specificity of class" little more than a ritual invocation of those ghosts of the industrial age: the revolutionary proletariat. Such appeals tend to be taken for mere gestures made halfheartedly in the direction of the "proper" spirit of Marxism. In academic discussion, they are the equivalents to the old political slogan, itself an embarrassment if overhead on our Western streets: "Workers of the world, unite!" In practice, cultural criticism has turned our attention more fully to residual and emergent social groups, the culture and everyday practices of the working class, the subtleties of bourgeois domination in the economy and social life, and the common political interests of colonized peoples and the proletariat. Even so, the fundamental assumptions of the Marxist theory of class formation remain rooted in a narrowly defined economic model that seems incompatible with the complex systems of hegemonic domination at work in social and political spheres.

This *formation* of class solidarity is still presumed to derive from the perception of an economic relationship established primarily through shared or coordinated labor. That perception ought to produce a class consciousness capable of defining class interests that include social, political, and cultural organization.[4] Since such class consciousness is constituted in and through the recognition of an adversary to such consciousness itself, in Marx and Engels' famous reworking of the Hegelian dialectic of master and servant, then the formation of class consciousness and the necessity of class conflict are dialectically constituted. Just what constitutes "shared or coordinated labor" is, of course, an old issue for Marxism that leads to some familiar intellectual impasses. In some sense, the only shared or coordinated labor actually exercised by the proletariat under the exploitative conditions of capitalism is that of *class formation* itself. Marx and Engels are careful in *Capital* to insist upon that *labor power*, rather than labor itself, that belongs to the worker— the potential of the body to perform work. Once that labor power is contracted by capitalism, it achieves material reality only in and through practices of exploitation designed to alienate that labor power from the worker. I need not rehearse the Marxist analysis of capitalism's strategies of alienation, commodity fetishism, and such later elaborations as Lukacsian *reification* to make my point that shared or coordinated labor under capitalism can be perceived as such only in the formation of class consciousness.

It is interesting how commonly the term *formation* is used in the place of what would seem the more appropriate term, *production* of class consciousness. After all, the perception of an economic relationship established by domination and exploitation is not to be confused with class consciousness. Class consciousness must be *produced* by *working* on that negativity. In keeping with Marx and Engels' troublesome enthusiasm for the virtues of human *techne*, the work of such class consciousness is the transformation of the negative conditions of labor under capitalism into the forces of a new social order defined by the revolutionary politics of the proletariat.

To speak in this way of the production of class consciousness, class conflict, and the eventual utopian aim of a society governed by those who have produced it is only metaphoric if we accept distinctions between *economy* and *politics*, between *work* and *social life, commerce* and *culture*. These are just some of the divisions of lived reality that are fundamental to capitalist strategies of domination and control. In this view, the disciplinary divisions of knowledge follow a similar logic, which merely works out the initial distinction between *thought* and *matter, ideas* and *things*. Marx and Engels' materialist critique of idealism in *The German Ideology* is not an anti-intellectual trivialization of the social value of intellectual inquiry. Quite the contrary, they are concerned precisely with the alienation of thought from the material world, and it is just this division between idea and thing that is the focus of their critique. The ultimate purpose of *The German Ideology* is to develop a social theory that would integrate intellectual work into the general economy of social activity.

In their discussion of the relation of "forms of intercourse" to the means of production in *The German Ideology,* Marx and Engels still maintain the priority of material production, even though utopian historical development suggests the progressive incorporation of the forms of intercourse into the means of production. Thus even when Marx and Engels remind the reader that "the fundamental form" of human self-activity is "material, on which depend all other forms—mental, political, religious," and so on, there is a suggestion of uncertainty, a defensiveness regarding material production at odds with the utopian aims of their argument.[5] After all, the "contradiction between the productive forces and the form of intercourse" remains for Marx and Engels one of the historical bases for revolution, and thus one of the surest indications of social crisis: "Thus all collisions in history have their origin, according to our view, in the contradiction between the productive forces and the form of intercourse" (p. 89). In a classless society, the successful coordination of productive forces and their forms of intercourse could no longer be understood in hierarchical terms; human self-activity would be defined by dialectically complex productivity in both material and discursive realms: "The transformation of labour into self-activity corresponds to the transformation of the earlier limited intercourse into the intercourse of individuals as such. With the appropriation of the total productive forces through united individuals, private property comes to an end" (p. 93).

One of the obvious ways in which intellectual activity can be understood to be *productive* is in the class interests and class consciousness it helps form. To be sure, "philosophy" alone cannot construct class consciousness, even if we were able to imagine a philosophical discipline far more attentive to historical circumstances and human diversity than we have yet had. But Marx and Engels' point in *The German Ideology* is that no single discipline of either thought or material labor governs the production of class consciousness. Too often understood only in terms of its material examples, coordinated labor does not just describe the experience of people working together to produce a material object. In its largest sense, coordinated labor is the multidisciplinary production of society itself, and it depends upon an interpretation of how those disciplines ought to be coordinated. There is thus nothing at all metaphoric—if by *metaphor* we mean something deriving from a more literal or concrete proposition or realm of objects—about the coordinated social production that is the utopian aim of classical Marxism. In the wildest, perhaps most poetical, imaginings of such of such utopian thinking, commodities as such disappear to be replaced by that heterogeneous "object," whose conditions of production deny any such vulgar materialism: a classless society is the ideal commodity that dissolves the very notion of commodification and the implicit division between matter and spirit, industrial production and social behavior.

Very metaphysical, decidedly romantic, to be sure, but hardly the economically determined model for class that so often passes for the "Marxist theory of class." Marx and Engels give sufficient hints in *The German Ideology* and other writings that the *production* of society in this very utopian sense would have to be conceptualized in hermeneutic terms, since that thing we call *society*, instead of being understandable as a commodity or manufactured object, would have to be comprehended as a *language*. In *The German Ideology* there is a peculiar relation between the authors' nostalgia for a more direct connection between material activity and its forms of intercourse, and their utopian aims. In their effort to illustrate how the capitalist distribution of labor drives human beings to specialization, they write: "He is a hunter, a fisherman, a shepherd, or a critical critic, and must remain so if he does not want to lose his means of livelihood." Lumping the "critical critic" with the preagrarian activities of hunting, gathering, and tending is, of course, meant to be ironic, but the serious side of this nostalgia is evident when they conclude: "In communist society, where nobody has one exclusive sphere of activity but each can become accomplished in any branch he wishes, society regulates the general production and thus makes it possible for me to do one thing today and another tomorrow, to hunt in the morning, fish in the afternoon, rear cattle in the evening, criticise after dinner, just as I have a mind, without ever becoming hunter, fisherman, shepherd or critic" (p. 53). A few pages earlier, they write: "The production of ideas, of conceptions, of consciousness, is at first directly interwoven with the material activity and the material intercourse of men, the language of real life," as if to suggest that only *later* historically, under capitalism, were these mutual activities alienated from each other (p. 47).

Anticipating Nietzsche's arguments in *The Genealogy of Morals* that modern history describes the alienation of word from thing, of sign and referent, Marx and Engels are imagining less a return to some primal bonding of material activity and its representation than a higher mode of social integration of action and thought, objectification and representation. For Nietzsche, this means extramoral interpretation, beyond good and evil; for Marx and Engels, it means the realization of the phrase "real sensuous activity" in and through social organization. Marx and Engels did not develop a systematic theory of language in this regard, and this may well explain why the modern elaboration of Marxian social theory has stressed its materialist dimensions, often at the expense of the proposed integration of material and ideal. The genealogy of the Marxist theory of class has thus achieved a certain sedimentation of meaning that subordinates the production of class consciousness to the economic facts of class interests. One result of this condensation of meaning, which involves a certain historical *repression*, has been the specter of economic determinism that continues to haunt Marxist theories of class. And it is just this economic determinism, understood in its narrowest sense, that has caused our contemporary embarrassment regarding class as a category for understanding and a means of analysis.

It is little wonder, then, that the binary analysis of proletariat and bourgeoisie, however much those categories may be complicated and subdivided, should appear archaic today. Developed primarily in relation to the economic conditions governing European industrialism, such class definitions are primarily descriptive and lack their own means of historical transformation. As I have argued, the *revolutionary* purposes of the Marxist proletariat involve a fundamental transformation of the *means of production*, not just a reshuffling of those in charge of production. So long as this basic economic transformation is not incorporated into the theory of class, such a theory remains perfectly descriptive and subject to the historical circumstances so described. The "formation of class consciousness" is in fact merely a *representation* rather than a *production*, and what is represented too often follows what was *produced* under industrial capitalism. We might conclude from this, as Baudrillard has in *The Mirror of Production*, that the Marxist critique of capitalism ended up merely *representing* ("mirroring") the essential terms of capitalist production in a manner that unwittingly legitimated those founding principles.[6] More relevant to my current topic, however, is the notion that class, lacking an adequate means of transforming itself according to new historical conditions, has remained a merely descriptive category for conditions specific to one phase of capitalist development. And the means of such transformation must be understood as that language through which class consciousness articulates itself and thus may be said to be a mode of *production* rather than merely an effect of political organization.

There have been, of course, diverse and sustained efforts by a number of social theorists to reformulate the theory of class in terms more appropriate to late or advanced capitalism. Work by Ralf Dahrendorf, Pierre Bourdieu, Jean-Claude Passeron, and Erik Wright is specifically concerned with the ways that new modes of production and new habits of social life affect the classical Marxian theory of class.[7] William Reddy has argued that this "new thinking about class among social historians" has been one of the motives for "the rediscovery of Gramsci" and is characterized by its criticism of both "the means of production as an unambiguous marker of class identity" and the traditional equation of political interests with specific class interests.[8] I shall not attempt to review the theories of class worked out by these important contemporary social theorists, except to claim that most of them are predicated on revisions in the theory of class that still preserve the distinctions in traditional Marxism between production and representation, between economics and social life, between class interests and political action.

Bourdieu's notion of how "cultural capital" functions to legitimate the power of the ruling class has immediate relevance to my argument in this essay, since cultural capital is for Bourdieu clearly produced and transmitted by way of educational institutions and practices ranging from the university and schools to the museum and mass media. Even so, Bourdieu's cultural capital, as the term itself suggests, remains a metaphor developed out of the more fundamental economic practices still governing the distribution of labor and conventionally established class affiliations. The manipulation of cultural capital may result in forms of power and the extraction of "surpluses" very different from those we associate with traditional Marxism, but the ruling class has basically the same characteristics, just more sophisticated *methods*. In one sense, Bourdieu simply elaborates the logic of Veblen's *Theory of the Leisure Class* by demonstrating how social and cultural practices contribute to masking the arbitrariness of the capitalist distinction between bourgeoisie and proletariat.

Erik Wright's effort to explain the complexity of contemporary class divisions in the industrially advanced nations by adding "skill-based and organization-based" exploitation to the customary repertoire concentrates more concretely on changes in actual production.[9] His aim is to broaden working-class interests to include those assigned in traditional Marxism to the petit-bourgeoisie. As I shall argue later in this essay, this strikes me as an important way to redefine class interests in postindustrial capitalism, in which the illusion of "managerial authority" is far more widespread than in industrial economies. Yet, like Bourdieu, Wright merely adds dimensions to the traditional Marxist categories of class without taking into account the fundamental changes in the actual modes of production, reproduction, distribution, and consumption.

The fact is that we have hardly begun to theorize the ways postindustrial economies have transformed the elementary terms of class, production, consumption, and the commodity, among many other crucial categories for any social theory. In these postmodern economies, the means of production are no longer primarily *material* but discursive. In a simple system, exchange value might be judged in terms of quantitative equivalences, but we know that the complex processes of economic circulation in a global economy generate their own "relative motivations" and "conventions" (to borrow terms from the linguists) that have semiotic values. Capital itself is no longer accumulated wealth, tangible assets, but credit. Credit itself is not understandable as a quantitative category, measurable in the exchangeable currencies of money and time. To be sure, we still live in a transitional world, and enormous government deficits still provoke calls for a "balanced budget," "savings incentives" for the average citizen, moral cries against the "debtor" nations and their social "irresponsibility." Yet, there is little likelihood that the credit economies of the West will balance their books. The metaphor of the accounting "book" is interesting, because credit economies are open systems shaped by future productivity and expectations; they are narratives, rather than books, which must produce new debts.

I myself am not competent to articulate precisely the narratological dimensions of a new global credit economy, but such would have to be one feature of a comprehensive theorization of the representational logics of postmodern economies. In "Consumer Society," Baudrillard notes the significance of credit in the general semiotic functions of the circulation of commodities when those commodities are reconceived as "signs," as he insists they are in our advanced (or late) capitalist societies. Yet, Baudrillard treats credit merely as another means of fueling consumer desire and thus as one more strategy in dealing with the problem of overproduction. He treats credit merely at the level of the individual consumer, mystified by the growing repertoire of marketing devices at the command of those whose secret power still seems to be simply possession of sufficient capital.[10] By the end of this century, there can be little doubt that capital as we once understood it will have been replaced by other means of commanding both the processes of production and distribution. What the financier terms *leverage* has far less to do with accumulated wealth than it has to do with a wide variety of means of negotiating credit. The credit cards sold to consumers are not the best metaphors for this process; we need the help of economists to explain the increasingly complex suite of representations through which major projects are financed. What sort of promise of future production is involved in such financing, and to what extent is it dependent upon reinterpretations of the traditional relation between time and labor? And at what point does refinancing become an integral part of the credit narrative?

At the macroeconomic level, spiraling debt, often bemoaned as "excess" and viewed as a sign of economic irresponsibility, actually justifies more credit, including wider and more complex social and political responsibilities. That is the favorable interpretation; a more skeptical reading would substitute "powers" for "responsibilities." The credit economy is so entangled with the national debt and government spending that its system depends upon the expansion of political influence as well as the growing confusion of economic and political domains. Of course, even the lay person understands that national debt is intricately related to the international markets and the balance of payments, which are determined by a wide range of factors beyond the more traditional measures of *productivity* (as in the measures included in the determination of the gross national product). Is it possible, then, to speak of credit in rhetorical terms—in the simplest sense, that is, as a system of figuration constituted by complex relations within a discrete field of signs? In his early writings, Baudrillard referred to the *semiotic* functions of the circulation of commodities as a *system*, rather than a *language*, arguing that the rapid proliferation of exchange values lacked the "grammar" of what we ordinarily recognize as a language.[11] This was his way of preserving a certain utopian hope for a more participatory language through which social individuals might discover the sorts of reciprocity (and thus "community") merely simulated in late capitalist societies. It may be that in the last quarter of the twentieth century, the apparently banal but nonetheless powerful system of exchange valuation has assumed its own figural qualities as well as its own narrative regularities (its conventions, even *genres*). If so, then the circulation of commodities as signs will have to be theorized in relation to the kinds of complementary processes sustained by credit. It is less likely that the intersection of these two processes (perhaps impossible to keep discrete any longer) will be in the "desire" of the consuming subject. More likely, we will discover that such systems of signification have transformed utterly the very concept of what we once recognized as subjective *agency*, in terms of both what the subject *makes* (production) and what it *uses* (consumption). Something like a new production and reception model will be needed to articulate such subjectivity (if such a term could still be used under these circumstances) to translate what we once understood as "author" and "reader/audience" into the economic terms of production and consumption.

I am suggesting that postmodern economies transgress the customary boundaries between production and consumption, the "factory" and the "market," economic and social spheres. When was it historically that the representation of a commodity—that is, the representation of a representation—became an essential part of the commodity's *production?* In one sense, of course, such representation may be considered an essential component of any commodity's production. The boundaries separating production, marketing, and consumption are always fragile and thus dependent on specific historical circumstances. Historical dating will hardly help us here; Baudrillard is certainly right to argue generally that social organization begins with symbolic exchanges that initiate those cultural narratives in which hierarchies of use value and exchange value are constituted.[12]

Yet there are obvious disadvantages to the conclusion that since some system of exchange constitutes any social order, then every society's production is always already a complex semiotic system of exchange values that simulates its needs, its various natures, and its empirical world. Such may be the logical conclusion to be drawn from the assumption that the human being is defined in and through his or her use of language—that is, the capacity to *produce* a world that is the referent for human representations. But there is a crucial difference between this *given* for "being human" (however we may debate this ontology of the sign) and the willful production of signs that realize their materiality in and through their semiotic system. I use the term *materiality* here for want of a better term, although *embodiment* might well be a substitute. For what distinguishes postmodern, technologically advanced societies is their capacity to give the appearance of both animation and physical substantiality to the products of technical invention. In this regard, the commodity in its usual garb—an object of specious usefulness tricked out to seduce us with the disguised lure of our own condensed labor— will have to be reinterpreted according to a far more complex model. The postmodern commodity par excellence is no longer the inanimate object filled with our stolen labor and animated by our mystified desire; instead, it is the *invisibility* of the technological transformation of nature made *visible* in a form (an *eidos*) whose incarnation depends crucially on our willingness to give such unnatural magic a habitation and a name. What was once simulated as a mysterious second nature animating the glittering objects in the department store display window is now more adequately figured in the recognizably human forms that technology assumes on the screen of social reality. What we now desire is the life that technology acts out in those narrative forms made so explicit in film and television's scenes and episodes. The commodity is no longer an object; it is an *actor*.[13]

Jean-François Lyotard understands the specific features of postindustrial economies in terms of systems of exchange that are themselves *genres of discourse*. His reflections on the "economic genre" in *Le Différend* are extraordinary and exceed considerably the mere rhetoric of "economics" in Foucault and Derrida in order to theorize a genuinely *rhetorical economy*. Even so, Lyotard views the "economic genre of capital" as concerned primarily with the "suppression of . . . heterogeneity," which is the effect of those social discourses for which there can be no standard of equal exchange.[14] Crudely put, the economic genre must be intent upon the suppression of the incommensurability of the multiple language-games at work in the everyday use of language. Aware that mythic narratives exercise their own forms of discursive domination in societies that depend centrally on storytelling to establish social consensus, he nonetheless recognizes that such "narrative pragmatics" are more capable of accommodating social differences. In the interest of performative efficiency, the economic genre works to destroy narrative as a formal means of establishing the terms of social community. "In an exchange, the debt must be canceled, and quickly. In a narrative, it must be recognized, honored, and deferred. (And the differend, accordingly comes to light in deliberation, and even in narrative, or around it.) Communities woven through narration must be destroyed by capital: 'backward mentality' " (*Differend*, p. 178).

But this conclusion—tempting as it is to humanists concerned with preserving and even celebrating "narratives" of various sorts (literary, historical, visual, political, and social) as bases for "higher" (that is, more ethically just) communities than those offered by capitalism's cynical, ceaseless production—misses the point. Capitalism in its postindustrial formulation is not intent on the "debt" being "canceled . . . quickly." The maintenance, expansion, and complication of the mere monetary debt is crucial to this credit economy. And what follows from such expansive debt is not simply massive deficit spending—whether morally justified on the part of the first world nations or morally condemned in the cases of third world nations (here already appears the incommensurability of debt in geopolitical terms)—but a complex narrative that links credit and its apparently obvious relation of temporality and production to the confusion of political, economic, psychological, and ethical discourses, among others.

Credit establishes "obligations," which conventionally involve simply future production but have become *ethical* obligations linking subjects (consumer credit), merchants (revolving credit), corporations (investment credit), and nations (national debt). These ethical obligations constitute semiotic links that are by no means simple measures of time owed by way of the conventional Marxist equation of time and money. Such equations no longer function, and probably never did, but instead are replaced by distributions of class and measured by rhetorical authority. *Credit, debt, obligation, responsibility, promise,* and *productivity,* to mention only a few of the terms that begin to assume a certain syntax, are *narrativized* in ways that generally establish functional policies, attitudes, behaviors, and understanding. Such terms follow a rhetorical temporality essential to any narrative that is itself by no means simple or unitary. A wide range of temporalities are at work in the economic discourse, of which the time of labor is only the most elementary. "Speculative time," which finds no measure in labor (quite the reverse; speculation depends upon maximizing profits and minimizing labor), and "political time" or "timing" (e.g., economic production initiated in a time politically determined as favorable) are only two examples. Good timing in business is a functional temporality, which is by no means commensurable with the time expended in production; it relies on a time measured qualitatively.

In his afterword to *Just Gaming,* Sam Weber has astutely observed that Lyotard's "notion of incommensurability is reminiscent of a certain Marxist critique, which represents commodity production as the quantitative leveling of use values—which are supposed to be qualitatively incommensurable—by exchange values (see, for example, the use of the concept of the incommensurable in the writings of Lukacs)."[15] Weber goes on to suggest that Lyotard, "during his 'American' phase," responds to such criticism by "pushing the notion of exchange, or of circulation, to the point that is is no longer conceivable within the horizon of the identical or commensurable" (Weber, p. 104). This conclusion suggests that Lyotard has already turned his argument in the direction of the narratives produced in and through the economic discourse. Even so, Lyotard still clings to the notion that the economic genre in

capitalism is destructive to narrative, especially those narratives fundamental to ethical communities.

Lyotard makes frequent recourse to the epistemological functions
of popular narratives, often using anthropological accounts of story
telling's central role in the society of the Cashinahua Indians.[16] For
Lyotard, the narrative tradition relies on a "threefold competence—
'know-how,' 'knowing how to speak,' and 'knowing how to hear' . . . —
through which the community's relationship to itself and its environment is played out. What is transmitted through these narratives is the
set of pragmatic rules that constitutes the social bond" (*Postmodern
Condition*, p. 21). If Lyotard sentimentalizes the "mythic knowledge"
of such societies, he does so primarily to stress the narrowness of the
language games played under capitalism, especially in its postindustrial
phases. It is the special temporality of telling and reciting (retelling) that
is one of the crucial features of such narrative knowledge for Lyotard,
because the past is "always contemporaneous with the act of recitation"
(p. 22). Such narrative pragmatics keep the issue of collectivity ever
present in the act of social discourse, and repetition in this context differs fundamentally from the supposedly ceaseless reproduction of commodities under capitalism. Narrative surpluses are functional elements
of the system, so that any given repetition (or recitation), even while
nominally commanded by a single teller, works to keep the narrative's
communal function operative. Lyotard is not arguing for a return or
revival of such narrative pragmatics in the same sense that such mythic
telling functions among the Cashinahua Indians; he realizes well
enough that there is not likely to be a return of this sort in urban, technological societies. Yet as a paradigm or even an analogy—paralogy?—
such "pragmatic narrative" knowledge identifies the essential poverty in
terms of collectivity and social ethics that governs those capitalist language games whose primary criterion is performative efficiency.

There is much in Lyotard that provides the foundation for a retheo-
rization of class in terms of discursive authority (or its lack), since all
social theory for Lyotard ought to be conceived in terms of "phrases in
dispute" or the degree to which discursive conflicts are permitted or
suppressed. Nevertheless, both Lyotard's pragmatic narratives and his
postmodern equivalent, "the quest for paralogy" or "paralogous activity," assume that the efficiency of capitalist production works to subordinate the incommensurable qualities of language to the contrived

equivalences of exchange values. The quest for literal equivalents between incommensurable representations may well be what gives rise to a market economy in which *mathematical* representation (the *quantity of currency*) governs otherwise qualitative values representable properly only through a language. Nevertheless, there persists in such arguments the old Marxist assumption that capitalism is destructive to community and, remote as this notion often is in Lyotard's writings, that such destruction assumes the more general mode of capitalism's internal decay. Thus late capitalism or the appearance of capitalism's contradictions still becomes the historical narrative of postindustrial societies.

Without dismissing the importance of Lyotard's effort to retheorize both society and the economy in rhetorical terms, I would argue that capitalism has succeeded in its postindustrial phase precisely by having constructed a complex social narrative in which performative incommensurability is essential. It is a narrative that by no means measures its success in terms of performative efficiency but employs every possible rhetorical strategy to encompass ever-greater regions of discursive control. That this narrative of postmodern capitalism produces a community that is *unethical* and founded on the most elaborate injustice is by no means ruled out by this conception of capitalism's rhetorical legerdemain. Quite the contrary, such injustice is precisely the aim of such story telling, and it legitimates itself by hierarchizing different rhetorical competencies according to their economic productivity.

The success of capitalism depends fundamentally on its production of mass media as the means of shaping consensus and simulating community. Mass media are not simply instruments of maintaining that "reality principle" through which the arbitrariness of the division of labor and thus of elementary class distinctions are maintained. Media for communication are still part of the system of marketing, distribution, and the reproduction and proliferation of desires in consumers that allow capitalist economies to function in terms of the most extraordinary contradictions. Yet, to speak of the production of mass media seems contrary to the customary understanding of their social and political functions. *Production* is precisely the term I want to use in order to suggest how such media emerge from the logic of capitalist development. In a traditional Marxian analysis, the accelerated production of industrialism required far more comprehensive and rapid means of marketing those products. Mass media opened new markets and helped standardize "consumer expectations" in ways homologous with mass production. Beyond this, such media made available the *language* through which such productivity would be translated into accessible and conventional signs in everyday social reality. We need to think of such signifying practices as complementary to the productive process itself, especially when the infrastructure of such production is increasingly entangled with technological innovation—for what mass media accomplish is precisely the voicing of such technology. The ceaselessly told story of the various media has little to do with their actual contents or even with the different and often class-specific subgenres (of newspapers, films, advertisements, magazines, et al.) that can be identified. The story is the power of technology to speak and thus assume the material substance that every mass-produced page and every repeatable film announces without embarrassment, even with a certain perverse pride. This is the "ghost in the machine" that renders all the subordinate speech acts (of editors, authors, copiests, actors, readers) mere parts in its script. Without such technology, without what Benjamin termed this power of reproduction on an ever-vaster scale and with increasingly accelerated speed, our social communication would be reduced to that of country provincials. This technology that speaks through mass media, in which it finds its proper voice in our own echoes, achieves its legitimation—its voicing and ultimate embodiment—in order to instantiate a new relation of labor and value. For what technology offers is what is only more crudely figured in a speculative economy: the inverse ratio of value to labor. The *telos* of technology is the displacement of human labor by that of the invention (no longer merely a "machine" in our electronic age).

Amid the rhetoric that stretches back to the industrial age regarding the virtues of labor-saving devices and the liberation of human beings from the drudgery of repetitive tasks, there is the new and unbridgeable class division between those who command technology and those who merely produce and consume it. Today, the once-venerable myth of scientific genius merely covers the corporate character of technological research and development. Backyard Edisons (myths though they are) have been replaced by international research teams, whose assignments are determined by market projections and by the logic of current modes of production. Scientific competency is no longer a consequence of formal education and the luck of the inspired tinkerer; such competency follows well-regulated procedures too complex to be commanded by the individual inventor.

The grammar of postmodern societies must be sought first in the discursive laws governing technological research and development. Ordinary language, whatever exceptions or irregularities may still be possible, is now subject to a technology whose realization in and through human production and consumption is one of the principal economic purposes in postindustrial, postmodern societies. What Francis Fukuyama cheerfully views as an emerging global consensus established by consumer desires and habits is the tacit acceptance of a system whose values are founded solidly on the technological sublime: the reorganization of natural forces into recombinant forms whose mutations can be represented in the discourse of science.[17]

The technological substrate of a postmodern economy is a rhetoric, or a system of figuration by which new meanings are made possible by what classical rhetoricians would term *catachreses*. The economics of this rhetorical power depends upon a system of exchange through which commodities ultimately embodying such technological innovation find their market value according to the extent of their circulation, rather than their consumption. As signs, such commodities achieve their value in the supplementary production they provoke in their reception and thus their value is a measure of the rhetorical credit they are capable of commanding.

The relative value of individual labor in such an economy could thus be measured by the standard formula for informational entropy. Traditional information theory values the relative economy of an informational model according to the useful information it can generate. The value of a word-processing program depends upon the number of functions it can perform in proportion to the ease of using it. Behind the cliché of "user-friendly" software, however, is the relative simplicity of its program design. And the most sophisticated programs are not valued exclusively for the quantity of information they allow users to access and store but for the different kinds of information. Programs that map from one informational register to another, involving thereby certain narrative designs that allow the user to translate from spreadsheet to document, from visual to verbal to musical data, have the greatest value.

In an analogous sense, the value of labor in our information-intensive economies depends upon the ratio of time invested in the production of a particular commodity and the time of its circulation. Such temporality is that of speculation, rather than production, in which an equivalence between labor time and value might be established. Yet before we rush to condemn the rhetoric of speculation as a mere corruption or mystification of what ought to establish economic value (equivalence of labor time to value), we should ourselves speculate a bit about the significance of such speculative production for class divisions and the distribution of labor. In *Le Différend*, Lyotard writes:

> In a communication theory, a unit countable in Boolean algebra has been determined for phrases in general, the bit of information. Under this condition, phrases can be commodities. The heterogeneity of their regimens as well as the heterogeneity of genres and discourses (stakes) finds a universal idiom in the economic genre, with a universal criterion, success, in having gained time; and a universal judge in the strongest money, in other words, the most creditable one, the one most susceptible of giving and therefore receiving time.   (*Différend*, p. 177)

The quantification of that commodity's circulation is only in part determined by its mass-marketability but also by its capacity to produce demands for yet other commodities. In this regard, the commodity is at once both credit and rhetoric rather than primarily a consumable object.

The "spin-off" effect of the postmodern commodity is understandably best illustrated by the most immaterial products, such as the entertainment industry offers. Mass-market films regularly produce markets for children's toys, tapes and CDs of their sound tracks, books based on the film scripts, film studio tours, advertising endorsements for other products, videotape royalties, VCR and television monitor sales, and so forth. Even so, the time of circulation for most mass-market films is extraordinarily short when measured simply in the time such films are shown in theaters, and even the after-market circulation of such films is relatively brief. The successful design of a mass-market film in this context is the work of producers and marketeers, and the value of their work depends upon their abilities to produce a film capable of rhetorical translation from the screen into the widest range of other modes of representation.

But such examples are merely crude approximations of the spin-off effects so crucial to technological innovation. The value of laser technology is precisely its adaptability to a wide range of applications that cross the boundaries of specific industries and include everyday social life. What enables the "smart bomb" to find its target also accelerates and improves telecommunications and surgical procedures. It is not a question of weighing the moral advantages of such technology against its possible immoral applications, since the development of such technology is predicated on its transgression of ethical categories. The most sophisticated procedures for regulating the proper use of such technology can never police successfully its proliferation, in that figure so commonly employed by national security experts intent on nonproliferation treaties and the like. Such proliferation is built into the system of technological *production*, which depends equally upon the industrial processes through which its hardware is made, the mass media through which its uses are clarified and conventionalized, and the markets by which such technology lives out its "half-life."

This new productivity has, of course, immensely complicated the fields of patent and entertainment law, both of which revolve around the determination of authority for a product that is not simply the work of the many people involved in making the film but also of the many other industries in which such work may be said to circulate. George Lucas and Steven Spielberg sued successfully to keep a toy manufacturer from selling unauthorized *Star Wars* figures, primarily because the manufacturer was competing with similar products sold at theaters and manufactured under an agreement with their production company. Media coverage of this relatively trivial chapter in the history of capitalism arguably contributed to the profits from the *Star Wars* series of films and the after-market products they generated. By such logic, the author of the story in the *Los Angeles Times* could claim points in the films, but Lucas and Spielberg could technically claim some share in the profits of the *Los Angeles Times*, insofar as such profits might be measured in terms of that journalist's story on the legal fight surrounding *Star Wars* toys. Although most corporations and research universities control the patents for new technologies developed by their employees, there are frequent accounts in the news of legal disputes over enormous sums regarding the rights to such technological developments as the microchip, other information industry hardware, and software programs.

The legal discussions of what constitutes a "creative" or "scientific" property are remarkably old-fashioned, citing as they do the creative talents of the artists or scientists involved and sifting through "data" concerning "original inspiration," "first drafts," laboratory experiments, even tapes of "concept discussions" or scientific "brainstorming" over beer.[18] Not only does the corporate nature of film production and technological research flatly deny the possibility of original authority for any given product but the technical competencies involved in both mass media and scientific development suggest that the real authority for products in both fields belongs to the educational processes through which such technical innovation becomes possible. In all of this, it is quite clear that the relation of work to product has changed dramatically either from what we understand to be the Marxian theory of labor or the actual conditions of labor in the nineteenth century. To be sure, Spielberg still profits by stealing the labor power of others, but that labor power must now be understood to include the traditional networks of consumption through which the product continues to be produced and reproduced. The transgression of the categories of production and consumption includes, of course, the penetration of the individual subject by systems of control intended to create new desires and markets. Telling friends the story of a film, quoting R2D2, using "Star Wars" as a popular name for a quixotic national space defense system, even cursing the tiny, gold plastic figure you step on as you make your sleepy way toward the bathroom contribute to the circulation of the elaborate sign system we understand under the title *Star Wars*.

Such rhetorical power only incidentally involves money or the accumulation of capital traditionally figured as both the goal and the secret despair of the capitalist as judged by Marxism. For Marx and Engels, the capitalist desperately substitutes the quantification of his or her profits for the satisfactions of honest labor and the technological sublime of experiencing the transformation of the world in and through the energy of the body itself. Gold is a fetish in the most obvious sense, a substitute for the productive potency of labor, that in the end will only betray its own illusory status. As a defense against our profound dread of mortality, such accumulated wealth offers little real protection and only the illusion of its apparent materiality. However much the capitalist seeks to transform its sameness into a rich and variegated life-style or narrative of power and authority, such wealth never expresses more than the capitalist's *lack of being,* his or her own status as a metonymy for all the labor power the capitalist has stolen.[19]

But signs achieve their value not in their sheer accumulation, not in their repetition of the same hollow truth, but in their manifold deployment in and through the usages of others. Lucas' and Spielberg's wealth is quite literally their command of our rhetorical attention, their circulation in conversation, their capacity to organize the labor of others to represent *them* as always beyond any mere body or mortal horizon. In this regard, the cult of celebrity is not just an incidental development of a corrupt system of speculation—that is, the translation of speculation into the simulated body of the publicly circulated figure—but essential to the operation of this rhetorical economy. "Celebrity" is the sublime of capitalist technology, in which the self-activity of human transformation now takes just this transforming power as the object of corporeal production. The body of the celebrity is indistinguishable from its *roles*, its capacity to enter into future exchange relations, and this applies not only to the film or television star but to corporate celebrities—the new technology—as well. The rhetorical power of postmodern capitalism is its capacity to translate its products into different discursive registers and achieve even a limited proliferation that opens markets for yet other acts of representation. In this context, the traditionally defined proletariat is defined less by the theft of its *physical* power—labor power per se— than by its exclusion from the diverse media through which the economy produces its effects. The primary basis for formulating class interests and articulating class consciousness would thus have to begin with redefining what we mean by *rights to the mass media* and the technologies they embody. Such rights or competencies would have to be understood today as the political and economic refunctioning of the narrowly educational rights to cultural literacy.

The contemporary debates regarding literacy revolve almost exclusively around educational or sociological issues. Literacy touches economic questions only when the issue of educational opportunity is raised. But the traditional Marxist aim of workers controlling their own means of production today involves literacy as a fundamental economic category. Well-intentioned studies like Shoshana Zuboff's *In the Age of the Smart Machine* attempt to assess how the traditionally defined working class is adjusting to technology. The interviews she conducted with American workers do provide valuable insights into the ways traditional modes of industrial labor are changing as a consequence of industrial computerization. Zuboff still relies on the ideas of industrial labor and productivity as measured by finished goods to be consumed. It is, however, the growth in professional, service, and information sectors that are transforming the economy and social life in the postindustrial nations. In these fields, technology is integral to the work itself, not just an innovation, whether that technology is as elementary as a fountain pen or word-processor or as sophisticated as the computer models used to target specific socioeconomic communities with different advertising campaigns for the same product. In these contexts, the function of cultural literacy in determining the individual's everyday labor and his or her potential class interests cannot be underestimated. In these fields, the worker's relative command of and access to rhetorical power determines that worker's class interests and enables us to retheorize the class conflicts operative behind the chatter about "classless consumerism."

As Zuboff's interviews with paper-mill workers indicate, the "computerized industry" means the technical use of computers to improve the efficiency, the quality, and the speed of industrial production. The product is still finished paper, and its market uses remain much the same as they have for centuries. Yet the new generation of mill workers, together with many managers, understand how introduction of new technologies requires the development of different analytical skills as part of the production process. In Zuboff's view, adapting to these new working conditions requires the development of theoretical knowledge, in order to learn how to respond to "an electronically presented symbolic medium" rather than to base understanding on "knowhow derived from sentient experience."[20] Theoretical knowledge is especially crucial for Zuboff in order for workers to comprehend "the total process" of production and overcome the inherently alienating effects of the symbolic medium of computer representation (Zuboff, p. 96).

All this seems to suit well the model of gradual transformation in the workplace without taking into account corresponding changes in the economy. As a consequence, Zuboff can earnestly recommend training in what she terms *intellective skills* and the development of theoretical knowledge that resembles the traditional aims of liberal education. Thus we need only adapt the existing practices of educational institutions, in which theoretical knowledge and intellective skills are normally taught, in order to develop certain cognitive methods suited to social reality for workers to gain more competency in computerized industry and thus a greater measure of control over their productive processes. I do not want to trivialize what strikes me as an important dimension of Zuboff's work: that education must involve technological literacy, and then not simply for those planning scientific careers. The ability to read and write, certainly one of the several class markers in industrial societies, needs to be supplemented by very practical training in the comprehension and interpretation of technological processes.

But for the worker to "comprehend the whole process" of even paper production in our postindustrial societies, he or she would have to comprehend the politics of timber harvesting (ecopolitics domestically and in conjunction with foreign policies regarding the harvesting of timber in the rain forests of the Amazon or Southeast Asia), the marketing and consumption of paper products, the financial purpose of the paper division in the larger agenda of the diversified corporation that owns it, the economics and politics of the publishing ventures supplied by that mill, and a host of other interactive social systems of signification sustained in large part by the daily production of paper. And to address those semiotic consequences in some manner competitive with those of the diversified corporation's management and public relations' divisions, as well as commercial advertisers and distributors, the mill worker (a synecdoche for any organization of his or her labor) would require *access* to the various media, especially mass media, through which such production is accomplished.

Certainly even the wealthiest, most powerful union organizations can hardly claim such educational or political powers to resist the political and economic transformation of the simplest industrial act of labor into the narrative purposes of economic production. This complex representation of the product is, of course, vastly compounded when that product is itself already a self-evident representation, such as we class crudely under the heading of "information" and by which we mean all the symbolic systems that govern the material production of their hardware. The disparity between worker and manager is thus fundamentally determined by a certain cultural literacy that need have nothing to do with differences in education, levels of intellective skills, or verbal competencies. For corporate managers, any differences in what I have termed *cultural literacy* at the productive level of the economy are trivial when measured by the primary criteria of access to the media of communication and competency in the technologies they employ.

Thus access to the media should be the primary foundation not only for retheorizing class interests but also for the work of producing class consciousness. The first step would be to theorize the extent to which workers are defined in and through their alienation from the primary means of mass communication and thus any genuine control of their labor power, in terms both of the *representation* of that labor power in the mass media and of the status of such labor power as *itself* a mode of representation. Put in these very general terms, the proletariat as traditionally conceived would change drastically to include a wide range of workers in professional and service sectors as well as in so-called middle-management positions. The classic distinction between hourly and salaried workers would have far less significance than the common incapacity of such workers to control the narrativization of what they produce. A corollary of competency in such narrative strategies would, of course, be technological competency, not simply in the ways such communication is achieved but also in the manner its technology prefigures subsequent communicative forms.

Zuboff contends that the distinction between "white-collar" and "blue-collar" labor begins to disappear as "the work of the sentient body is displaced by the newer demands of intellective effort" (Zuboff, p. 97). Her interpretation of postindustrial economies is guardedly optimistic, insofar as the new technologies require the development of intellectual and theoretical abilities at all levels of work. In this regard, Zuboff's is typical of a critical view of capitalism—its class hierarchies and methods of exploitation and domination—that looks hopefully to the newer technologies not just to liberate us from the drudgery of manual labor but to inspire our imaginations and enrich our intellectual lives. Today there is particular currency to this view among intellectuals otherwise prone to be morosely skeptical about social and economic reform. The new technologies of personal computing, computer networks, inexpensive videocameras and recorders, and a host of other communication devices now widely accessible for private use promise some access to those media that I have argued play such a central role in postmodern economic production.

Reports of the important roles played by privately circulated video and audiotapes in the recent revolution in Czechoslovakia and the much-publicized computer networks that provided news access for the students and workers protesting political and economic oppression in China have given some warrant for such optimism. The alternative media, often relying on very modest production and distribution budgets, now amount to a substantial communications network, albeit not an organized one, in the United States and Western Europe. And the promise that such alternative modes of communication might develop into the popular media once dreamed of by Brecht, Enzensberger, and other theorists of the Frankfurt School in the simpler communications environment of their age, will remain only another fond illusion, an elusive, Sisyphean lure, so long as what I would term "critical media" are understood to function primarily in the social and political spheres.

Such optimism for popular media must be qualified by the speed and apparent efficiency with which both the media of communication and the new technologies can be employed by the few whose access to these means of social production is without reserve. The events of the recent Persian Gulf War indicate the staggering imbalance of power that exists in the division of labor relevant to the media and technology's production of social reality. No historical crisis in recent memory demonstrates more clearly how access to mass media and the command of technology are complexly interrelated in the U.S. political economy. Design of the media show that accompanied our rapid acceleration of the Middle Eastern political crisis to full-scale war was clearly an integral part of military strategy. The success of the entire campaign in both its speed and its public acceptance (the highest popularity ratings of any modern war) should remind us that the political promise of critical media can be realized only by addressing realistically the existing disparity between the few who design and employ media power and the vast majority receiving its messages.

New class formations must be produced on the bases of careful analyses of how various kinds of labor in postindustrial societies are distributed according to hermeneutical categories pertinent to the rhetorical powers governing social production. It goes without saying that "subject positions" are consequences of the individual's relation to the means of socioeconomic production, a suite of activities that includes at its horizon social reality as it is lived. Considerations regarding a priori subjectivity may still focus, as they have since Kant, on those human potentialities realized in specific historical and cultural circumstances. Yet the basic Kantian paradigm will have to be modified to take into account the existence of those other faculties historically made available by technology and living outside the biological body. For Kant, the a priori forms of time and space are the preconditions for the categories themselves, and the special interdependence of the forms of time and space constitute what is essentially human in subjectivity.

Even the most elementary technologies of our postmodernity, such as photography and film, suggest supplements to our cognitive faculties of duration and extension. As Roland Barthes points out in "The Rhetoric of the Image," the photograph makes possible a "presence" of the "past" in the image that differs significantly from the forms of memory available through imagination and verbal representation. A literal "here-now" is given to perception in an image explicitly presenting a "there-then," involving what Barthes considers the introduction of a conceptuality that exceeds the capabilities of cognition unassisted by technology: "Hence the photograph is not the last (improved) term of the great family of images; it corresponds to a decisive mutation of informational economies."[21]

Technology's transformation not only of *what* we see but of *how* we see has often been the central concern of film theory. In "The Work of Art in the Age of Mechanical Reproduction," Benjamin observes that film technology makes available camera angles that exceed the limitations of ordinary subjective vision: "With the close-up, space expands; with slow motion, movement is extended. The enlargement of the snapshot does not simply render more precise what in any case was visible, though unclear: it reveals entirely new structural formations of the subject."[22] The technology of film is not simply an addition to or extension of human understanding but a transformation of perception and thus cognition: "The shooting of a film, especially of a sound film, affords a spectacle unimaginable anywhere at any time before this. It presents a process in which it is impossible to assign to a spectator a viewpoint which would exclude from the actual scene such extraneous accessories as camera equipment, lighting machinery, staff assistants, etc.—unless his eye were on a line parallel with the lens" (Benjamin, pp. 232–33). However we understand these new relations of technology and the human subject, we will have to take account of how such relations inform our conceptions of collectivity and consensus. Both social communities and economic classes cannot be imagined apart from their relations to technological modes of knowing.

In this postmodern context, "cultural literacy" would require some understanding of the relative distribution of rhetorical authority (often determined to a large extent by technical competencies in the various genres of the economy) as well as a complementary understanding of the implicit models for reception (the spectatorial position) within the hierarchy of such rhetorical power. In this latter regard, consumption would no longer be understandable as the passive and ideologically overdetermined process in the distribution of social production. Different kinds of rhetorical production would entail different reception models, ranging from the crudest model of consumption to more sophisticated modes of reproduction and transformation as forces in the overall productive process.

The old categories, terms, and assumptions regarding class boundaries and the general distribution of labor will have to be abandoned before new coalitions can be imagined. Zuboff's hope that the boundaries between blue- and white-collar jobs are vanishing is not confirmed by any developing relations between the working class and middle-level management professionals to define the terms of conflict with those who effectively control the means of communication and interpretation. Any effort to "theorize" a new working-class consciousness by merely grafting a model of rhetorical competency to the existing economic divisions of labor is doomed to failure. We must begin by reinterpreting the commodity in terms of its condensation of representational practices and thus the subordination of materialization to the decisively immaterial processes of the economic system.

We might begin this theoretical work by developing a taxonomy of the ways in which working subjects theorize their own productive processes. Given the intertextual, multidisciplinary productivity of a postmodern economy, economic exploitation and domination could be understood in relation to the relative competency of the worker to comprehend his or her contribution to this narrative of production. From this standpoint, the theorization of production in terms of the material object produced would constitute the most profound mystification of the rhetoric of production. In this regard, the instrumentality of technical, managerial, and marketing discourses with respect to the production and distribution of the nominal commodity would be assumed and the division between material labor and the discursive practices of management reinforced.

By the same token, the fetishism of the body would have to be considered a part of any general theory of the rhetorical strategies employed to produce the commodity. The specular, voyeuristic commodification of women's bodies would have to be interpreted in relation to the rhetorical constraints effecting the production of marketable commodities, and such a process restricted not merely to advertising and mass-media modes of distribution and marketing but to the modes of everyday psychic and social behavior as well. Thus the work of poststructuralist feminists like Luce Irigaray should be considered essential to this theoretical work, since the body of woman as commodified by patriarchal capitalism would provide some clue to the diverse rhetorical means through which economic and social commodities are allowed to appear as such—that is, with the appearance of a certain stubborn materiality. [23] In an analogous sense, the rhetorical production of the racially, ethnically, or nationally figured "other" would also provide clues to the rhetoric of a new materiality beyond the binaries of material and ideal, objective and subjective, cultural and natural.

The reduction of the complex representational economy into the apparent literality of the commodity would constitute only the most elementary level of mystification and exploitation. Theorizing the object of production as the condensation of (the synecdoche for) a suite of interrelated practices specific to the discipline or industry presumed to define the boundaries of such production would appear to give the worker greater authority over his or her labor by virtue of comprehending the coordinated process in which he or she performs a function. At this level of theorizing production, the subject's labor could be understood only in terms of specifically related acts by others, and the community so constituted would appear to reduce alienation and provide a model for relating work and social life. But insofar as this theorization of the subject's relation to the productive process remains specific to the formal boundaries of the industry or discipline in which such production occurs, then more sophisticated modes of exploitation, domination, and alienation of labor may be said to operate. The specialization of language apparently necessary for such production together with daily acts of communication and exchange restricted primarily to those within the formal boundaries of such a microeconomy—the auto industry, or steel, or paper, for example—encourages an economic formalism whose coherence and totality appear to be understandable to workers competent in the systemic functions of that industry or discipline.

Those capable of theorizing the production of commodities in intertextual, antiformal terms of production as translation would be in positions to command and exploit the labor of those at lower levels of rhetorical competency. Such knowledge would be available not merely to the corporate director but also to those in less powerful positions with respect to the traditional command of capital. These would include workers involved in labor at the margins of the industry's formal, disciplinary boundaries, where productivity must be mapped from one rhetorical system to another. Such workers would include market analysts, advertisers, communications professionals, and a wide range of elected and appointed government officials charged with the adjudication of the boundaries between the economy and the civic domain, between production and social life in the most general sense. Political lobbyists and political campaign fund-raisers would also claim some competency in such intertextual, multidisciplinary production. To be sure, the levels of competency would be quite various, but this general theorization of the productive process would still govern analyses of the various discursive practices that might help us redefine that class whose adversarial relation to other workers in the system might give new urgency and impetus to the old names of "working class consciousness" and "class conflict."

In that context, the degree of competency any worker has with respect to that rhetorical system of production may give us the initial parameters for class differences as they are constituted by the distribution of labor and help determine the terms by which a new writing class might be articulated—which is to say, produced. Traditional analyses of the processes of reification through which labor power is alienated in and through the commodity's production would touch only the most elementary and transparent modes of mystifying the worker's rights to his or her production. The transformation of the mysterious commodity form into those narratives of mass media communication through which our very beings are told to us and our social consensus determined would describe approximately the far more complicated processes through which our production of social reality is alienated from us and yet made to appear "just like home." Cultural literacy (rights of access to mass media) would thus not be simply an educational or sociological issue but the basis for political organization motivated by the recognition of a certain economic dispossession. Access to the mass media would be one means of controlling our social production. Adjudication regarding ownership of television, film, and computer representations, rights to airtime, education in the pertinent technologies, and communicative access to elected officials could no longer be left to the free marketplace, since that market has already shown itself to have produced the most elaborate and exclusive hierarchies. In fact, all these issues, each of which could be transformed into a cause for legal or social activism likely to be ultimately powerless in political terms, revolve around the same general concern: who should *use* the means of mass communication in a just society? The ethical judgment of that issue involves, of course, a host of related issues, not least of which are issues of temporality: not just *how much* time but also the *quality* of time (as in "prime time").

The networks of communication would have to be socialized, and access to the power of representing economic and political issues would have to become central to the activities of representative government at all levels. A first step toward this utopian goal, of course, would be political action designed to reform the current systems of communication whereby representative government claims to represent its citizens. I need not detail for this audience how profoundly corrupted those means of political communication have become. We are inclined to believe that such corruption is merely a consequence of the inequitable distribution of wealth, that those with money can be heard politically— thus the scandals surrounding bribes, kickbacks, and payoffs from lobbyists and corporate interests to politicians fill the news.[24] But it is the rhetorical power of corporate and mass-media interests that constitutes the inequitable access to government in a more profound way than mere financial corruption. Such power derives after all from the productive capabilities of those workers at many different levels of the economy who are divided in a host of ways from each other and who find their communities either in the powerless margins of private social life or in the underpowered machinery of labor organization and its inclination to industry-specific conduct.

I have attempted to sketch the terms by which class might be retheorized according to postmodern societies' fundamental concern with the textual qualities of their own productive processes in both the economic and social spheres. A new working-class consciousness and the definition of working-class interests would have to begin with the technological and philosophical issues involved in an economy of representation. I give the name *writing class* to such an new working-class formation both to mark the limitations of our current theoretical terms regarding representation and to call for a more adequate terminology that would express effectively the representational productivity of workers active in a postprint socioeconomic situation. The name itself is nostalgic for a more writerly mode of communication, now translated to productive relations in which the command of the technology and its circulation are crucial to our rights to our own labor power.

Seizing the means of representation does not, of course, begin with occupying the television station (although such acts may well be part of a larger repertoire of necessary political action) or fighting within the courts for the reinstatement of public access cable. Mass means of communication define the intersection of the modes of distribution, production, and social life. They are the crucial determinants of anything we might in the future call "social consensus" or functional "community." The exploitation of the postmodern working class begins with our exclusion from these media and the transformation of our coordinated labor into the simulated lives that are produced in and through such media. To control the means of our production in this age means some measure of control over how *we* are represented to each other. And since such self-representation has always been one of the motives for human labor, however disguised or perverted, then controlling the reflections in the mirror of technology must be the prolegomena to getting full measure for what we produce.

What roles are educational institutions and the professoriat to play in this new system of production? It would be tempting to follow the leads of Habermas, Rorty, and even Stanley Fish and develop the professoriat as a model for the sort of writing class I have attempted to theorize. After all, we self-consciously produce representations, and we value our labor in terms of the communication it makes possible, often just in proportion that such communication exceeds existing epistemological and disciplinary boundaries. The interpretive communities we sustain even in our most critical and adversarial gestures seem microcosms of that utopian synthesis of material and immaterial production I presume to have understood in the furthest imaginings of Marx and Engels: the social language that is the ultimate aim of human production. And however ruthlessly our institutions commodify what we produce, we think we know in our more optimistic moments that the value of such communication exits only in its circulation—in the heterogeneous reception of knowledge that is its interpretation and application by students and fellow scholars. The communication theory developed by Habermas as a model for social life and the rational adjudication of conflicting interests in complex societies would thus appear to be merely an expanded version of the seminar room or the scholarly conference. Teaching and research might then become the occasions for a certain role playing, exercises in the ways we might perform in the "life world" as well as practices designed to increase knowledge.

Before we entertain such utopian possibilities, however, we will have to understand better how educational institutions and the professoriat are used for economic purposes both more banal and more complex than the restricted economies of communication we presume to control in our teaching and our interpretive (scholarly) communities. In short, we will have to investigate the degree to which "professing" is simply another mode of production and for all that as subject to the mystifications of the labor process as other sectors of the economy. We will also have to understand the corporate functions of the university in ways that seem ever closer to the purposes of more traditionally defined corporations.

Now twenty years old, Pierre Bourdieu and Jean-Claude Passeron's *La reproduction: éléments pour un théorie du système d'enseignement* is still a remarkably contemporary analysis of the ideological functions of educational institutions and practices as well as of the class interests of the professoriat. Yet it is primarily "cultural capital" that is transmitted by the professorial petit-bourgeoisie, and the homology between laissez-faire pedagogy and free-enterprise capitalism is merely a general figuration of the coordination of superstructural practices with the dominant mode of production.[25] Entrusted to the educational institutions and the cultural capital they transmit are the customary practices of *embourgeoisement*, including subject formation and disciplinary distinctions, together with the more general discrimination of intellectual from material discourses (*La reproduction*, p. 234).

Yet, cultural capital can no longer be nominally distinguished from the accumulation and transmission of postmodern capital, especially when such capital is redefined as credit. The extent to which postmodern universities have been able to accommodate the traditional aims of liberal education to the economic purposes of defense contracts, technological research and development, real estate development, stock-market investment and speculation, political lobbies, and international trade might provide us with a model for understanding many of the newer modes of mystification that have emerged along with postindustrial economies. The degree to which the professoriat disguises, legitimates, or contributes directly to these economic interests is a subject of immediate political concern as well as a topic worthy of historical study and theoretical analysis.

The aesthetic ideology continues to be produced and communicated by the professoriat, especially in the so-called human sciences, but it is today far more complexly bound up with basic economic processes than we had previously imagined. Studies in the liberal arts can no longer be criticized simply as the cultivation of leisure activities that contribute materially to the signs by which the bourgeoisie claims its privilege. The liberal arts involve strategies of representation that have direct applicability to the economic purposes of mass media and a wide range of industries concerned with the production and control of information. Yet,

the curriculum of any department of English at a major university in
the United States seems to argue against this relevance of hermeneutical
abilities to our participation in the productive mechanisms of the mass
media. We appear to have forgotten that the motive for literary studies
in the first place had much to do with the recognition that literature
itself constituted one significant force in the development of social consensus in print-oriented societies. The bourgeois fetishization of the
novel generally depended upon the novel's incorporation of technical
and formal features of myth, epic, romance, and religious interpretation: earlier media for the production of social consensus. Implicit in
this very recent invention of the novel was the assumption that the
novel played a central role in social communication, however priva-
tized such communication may have come to appear under industrial
capitalism. I need hardly point out, however, that the novel only serves
a peripheral role in the production of a social consensus that is achieved
today primarily through the electronic media. Of course, the history of
the novel provides many instances of powerful social criticism that
understandably employ the communicative conventions of this popular
form. We can learn from just such novelists (and other writers in other
literary genres) how to use socially powerful genres to cut across the
grain, to transvalue the conventions for reception for which there is
already tacit acceptance. In our electronically mediated postmodernity,
film and television and computer technologies ought to be the sites for
what was once considered the subversions of the literary avant-garde.
And as "residual" forms, literary modes of production might find new
purposes in contesting the rhetorical and technological powers (and
thus class divisions) of our new socioeconomic configurations.

In this regard, then, the professoriat may take up the challenge of
reconceptualizing classes—workers' relations to what they produce—
only to discover greater solidarity than they had expected with the political and economic situations of workers in more demonstrably material
jobs. The production of a new writing class that would depend upon
the interests intellectuals share with industrial and professional workers
might enable more effective reforms of a university system that claims
to educate a classless student body but that in practice largely serves the
interests of the bourgeoisie. Like other middle-management professionals, we might discover the contradiction between our working-class situation in relation to the ultimate production of the university and our
bourgeois self-image. For us, as for other workers under these new eco-

nomic conditions, access to the primary means of social communication—that is, the mass media—would have to become a primary issue if not a political right. And all the screen discourses of our formally closed interpretive communities would have to be understood as inadequate compensations for the ways we continue to be silenced, even as our work can be made to tell another story.

Notes

1. James Kavanagh, "Ideology," in *Critical Terms for Literary Study*, ed. Frank Lentricchia and Thomas McLaughlin (Chicago: University of Chicago Press, 1990), pp. 309–10.

2. Louis Althusser, "Ideology and Ideological State Apparatuses," in *"Lenin and Philosophy" and Other Essays* (London: New Left Books, 1971). Althusser's notion of the ideological interpellation of the subject has often been cited as a key concept for those attempting to adapt psychoanalysis to Marxist cultural criticism. Althusser develops the term from its usage in politics as a "form of political challenge to governmental officials," the formal "calling to account" of a minister, for example, by a legislative body. What he has in mind is a legal or political language game in which debate is ruled by a set of prescribed rules and conventions that must be obeyed in order for one to speak. Generalizing this language game for ideology, Althusser wants to suggest how subject formation occurs by way of ideologically determined discursive rules. One of the crucial rules or limits on the kinds of speech available to the subject would be class affiliation. Psychoanalysis may enable us to understand better the complex ways by which a "subject" is "spoken" through the available rhetoric of a particular sociohistorical moment, but it must take into account the often explicit and obvious differences among subjects constituted by class affiliations. Freudian psychoanalysis has virtually no theory of social class, although assumptions about class differences often shape Freud's case studies. If post-Freudian psychoanalytical theory seeks to overcome the limitations of Freudian theory, then it will have to include class as well as gender among the significant repressions in Freud. Just what role does class affiliation (conventional) or class consciousness (revolutionary) play in the structuring of the unconscious? If such a question can now be asked, then it must be followed by its corollary: Is the general theory of repression amenable to class analysis?

3. Raymond Williams in "Base and Superstructure in Marxist Cultural Theory" (1973) insists that this disparity between production and social relationships is fundamental to Marx: "For while a particular stage of the development of production can be discovered and made precise by analysis, it is never

in practice either uniform or static. It is indeed one of the central propositions of Marx's sense of history that there are deep contradictions in the relationships of production and in the consequent social relationships. There is therefore the continual possibility of the dynamic variation of these forces." "Base and Superstructure in Marxist Cultural Theory," in *Contemporary Literary Criticism*, ed. Robert Con Davis and Ronald Schleifer (New York: Longman, 1989), p. 380. What is interesting about Williams's formulation of the problem is that "cultural analysis" is largely responsible for the "verbal habit" that has turned "productive forces" into "the [economic] base" understood "in essentially uniform and usually static ways" (p. 379). Williams is writing these lines in what I would term his "structuralist" phase, so there is a subtextual commentary on the contemporary debates between "scientific" structuralists and those understanding the structural model as a dynamic system of relations. The point to keep in mind is that there are intellectual motives for distinguishing sharply between base and superstructure that may not so easily fit the customary arguments concerning capitalism's familiar modes of ideological mystification. The commodification of the base serves often enough to contain and control economic forces even while insisting upon their essentiality. Lip service could be paid to the base, but serious attention paid only to so-called superstructural forces. The complicity of such intellectual methods of analysis with the development of bureaucratic communism is worth considering.

4. I use "organization" rather than "organizations" here because I want to suggest that class consciousness involves a coordination of these nominally separate spheres of experience, rather than organizations specific to different social activities (e.g., political party, aesthetic values, educational institutions).

5. Karl Marx and Friedrich Engels, *The German Ideology*, pp. 92–93.

6. Jean Baudrillard, *The Mirror of Production*, p. 152: "Marxism is incapable of theorizing *total* social practice (including the most radical form of Marxism) except to reflect it in the mirror of the mode of production. It cannot lead to the dimensions of a revolutionary 'politics.' From our current position, Marxist analysis, in its revolutionary rationality, no longer illuminates either modern societies or primitive societies." Mark Poster's analysis of Baudrillard's "effort to call into question the nature of the theoretical model of historical materialism, not simply its contents," is particularly relevant here: "The first error derives from Marx's Hegelianism which asserts an overly absolute truth value to historical materialism because capitalism creates the conditions for universal, scientific knowledge. Ironically, this is the Althusserian position that attributes to Marxist knowledge the quality of finality. All of history can be objectively read by Marxism because of a favored historical position. With this claim Marxism gives up its own self-relativization: it is dependent upon a certain historical conjuncture, but at the same time, this conjuncture affords it an absolute priority over all previous ages. Marxism becomes ideological not

where Althusser thinks, in its relation to practice, but in its truth claims, its scientificity" (translator's introduction, ibid., pp. 13–14). In *The Mirror of Production*, Baudrillard calls for a more radical theorization of class, more pertinent to the historical changing relations of production to social life, but that project seems to have been abandoned in *For a Critique of the Political Economy of the Sign*. It is not just that Baudrillard mocks the plodding work of sociologists intent upon reading the signs of social class distinctions in furnishings, fashion, neighborhoods, and other material markers, but that he argues more sweepingly for a postindustrial system of exchange production that subordinates all cultural reception to bourgeois values and standards. The classless society is ironically, perversely realized in this new mode of semiotic production, and it seems to render the old notions of class consciousness and class struggle powerless. Baudrillard's subsequent writings only reinforce this sense of resignation from the project of retheorizing class distinctions and class relations. What is initially Baudrillard's recognition of an important limitation in Marx's theory of class (and its interpretation) becomes eventually an unwillingness to consider class as a useful social or economic sign. It is just this blockage in Baudrillard's writings that motivates my own work in this essay.

7. I am thinking of Ralf Dahrendorf's *Class and Class Conflict in Industrial Society* (1959), Pierre Bourdieu and Jean-Claude Passeron's *La reproduction: éléments pour une thèory du système d'enseignement* (1970), Nicos Poulantzas' *Political Power and Social Classes* (1973), Bourdieu's *Distinction: The Social Critique of Judgment*, and Erik Wright's *Classes*.

8. William M. Reddy, *Money and Liberty in Modern Europe*, p. 30.

9. Erik Wright, *Classes*.

10. Baudrillard, "Consumer Society," *Selected Writings*, p. 49: "Credit [in consumer society] plays a determining role, even though it only has a marginal impact on the spending budget. . . . Presented under the guise of gratification, of a facilitated access to affluence, of a hedonistic mentality, and of 'freedom from the old taboos of thrift, etc.,' credit is in fact the systematic socioeconomic indoctrination of forced economizing and an economic calculus for generations of consumers who, in a life of subsistence, would have otherwise escaped the manipulation of demands and would have been unexploitable as a force of consumption. Credit is a disciplinary process which extorts savings and regulates demand—just as wage labor was a rational process in the extortion of labor power and in the increase of productivity." Baudrillard's final sentence suggests a more comprehensive theory of credit's role in the transformation of productive relations and thus of the entire social system, but he never develops this theory. Instead, he reverts to the cruder model of credit as simply a means of exploiting workers in their roles as consumers. Insofar as credit is crucial to the different valuation of temporality in postmodern economies—i.e., the relation of time to value can no longer be understood in terms of the ratio of time to

labor—then we will have to reconsider credit as a much more influential predicate of the general thesis of postmodernity.

11. Bandrillard, "The System of Objects," in *Selected Writings*, p. 16.

12. Baudrillard's argument that symbolic exchange is fundamental to social
organization is derived from the anthropological writings of Marcel Mauss,
especially *The Gift* trans. Ian Cunnison (New York: Norton, 1967). The universal claims Baudrillard makes for the social function of symbolic exchange
have often been criticized, notably by Poster in his translator's introduction to
The Mirror of Production. Baudrillard also displays a certain nostalgia for the
reciprocity of communicative acts in symbolic exchanges—in which the sign
is established by the mutual acts of giving and receiving. This same nostalgia
shapes his distinction between the more fundamental (and often recognizably
existentialist) desire he identifies at the root of symbolic exchanges (a desire he
defines as an elementary desire for socialization) and the simulated desires of
consumers. The entire category of desire under the conditions of postmodernity will have to be reconsidered, especially as such desire is philosophically
linked with memory and imagination. Quite clearly, the desire that might be
generalized from the workings of a postmodern economy is not a simple simulation of consumer demand.

13. Benjamin anticipates this conclusion in "The Work of Art in the Age of
Mechanical Reproduction," in *Illuminations*, p. 231: "The film responds to
the shriveling of the aura with an artificial build-up of the 'personality' outside
the studio. The cult of the movie star, fostered by the money of the film industry, preserves not the unique aura of the person but the 'spell of personality,' the
phony spell of the commodity." Benjamin understands that the public personality of the movie star is itself a defensive act against the recognition that the
actor has no agency beyond what is given by the technology of film (which
must be said to include directors, producers, editors, scriptwriters, etc., as well
as the putative apparatuses of camera, lighting, sets, etc.). Yet, the compensa-
tory mechanisms of celebrity merely repeat and affirm that authority the actor
seeks vainly to overcome in a desperate bid for his or her own identity with the
public. For the movie star is simply one aspect of the film industry's elaborate
devices for advertising its product, as the celebrated publicity stunts of 1940s
and 1950s Hollywood stars make so clear. What the fan seeks desperately in the
movie star is precisely the authority that is situated elsewhere: the command of
the technology of film that assumes the borrowed body of the star.

14. Jean-François Lyotard, *The Differend*, p. 178.

15. Sam Weber, "Afterword: Literature—Just Making It," in Jean-François
Lyotard and Jean-Loup Thebaud, *Just Gaming*, p. 104.

16. Lyotard, *The Postmodern Condition*, pp. 20ff.

17. Francis Fukuyama, "The End of History?" in *The National Interest*, 16
(Summer 1989): 3–18.

18. The Buchwald suit against Paramount Pictures and Eddie Murphy regarding the rights to the film, *Coming to America*, has some interesting political consequences for my argument in this essay. Buchwald has relied on a political rhetoric in the media that insists upon the rights of authors to their material that parallels the rights of workers to their production. The suit is thus symbolic of a class-action suit and in the interests of writers exploited by studios and celebrities. Yet the question of who "owns" any kind of mass communication is beside the point, since even the mass marketeers justify their products by way of demographic studies that *prove* these are the products that the people want. These needs may be viewed skeptically, of course, as simply simulated and stimulated by advertisers, but there is some truth to the notion that representational products (films, newspaper reports and columns, fiction and non-fiction books, etc.) rely upon the linguistic conventions, social behaviors, and other semiotic elements of the popular habitus. However ideologically saturated or controlled, the popular basis for representation at any given historical moment argues that only the people using such representations may be said to have any rights of ownership over them. This is the theoretical basis, supported by the work of structural linguistics from Saussure to the present, for my insistence that the mass media must be socialized. Who "owns" language? It belongs only to those who *use* it. On the interesting issue of entertainment law and its reflection of changing attitudes toward the subject, author, authority, and discursive property in general, see Jane Gaines, *Contested Culture: The Image, the Voice, and the Law* (1991).

19. Karl Marx and Friedrich Engels, *Capital*, trans. Ben Fowkes (New York: Random House, 1976), vol. 1, pp. 164–67.

20. Shoshana Zuboff, *In the Age of the Smart Machine: The Future of Work and Power*, p. 95.

21. Roland Barthes, "Rhetoric of the Image," in *Image-Music-Text*, p. 45.

22. Benjamin, "The Work of Art in the Age of Mechanical Reproduction," in *Illuminations*, p. 236. Throughout this essay, Benjamin suggests that both the emancipatory and totalitarian purposes of film technology are potentially served by the ability of the camera (synecdoche for the entire apparatus) to allow us to "see" what the eye alone cannot see. In terms of class affiliation, for example, the camera can allow us to visualize what is otherwise the sheer abstraction of "class consciousness." But the same tracking shot, for example, that might allow us to see the coherence of workers striking in a way that would be impossible for any subject involved in such a strike could also be employed to construct those images of the "mass" so familiar from the shots of political rallies in Nazi propaganda films. Nazi propaganda was certainly served by the use of film technology to add to our ordinary perceptions, not simply expanding but transforming those perceptions. Leni Riefenstahl's *Olympia*—that advertisement for Nazism made about the 1932 Berlin Olympiad—was considered

innovative in its time, because Riefenstahl went to such lengths (and such costs, subvented by Hitler) to represent aspects of the athletic body unavailable to ordinary sight. In one often-cited example, cameras were placed in trenches covered with thick glass beneath high-jump and pole-vault pits to reveal the movement of the athlete's body from a perspective utterly unavailable to the spectator. The camera thus offers a nature putatively "there" but nonetheless never before seen. Needless to say, Riefenstahl's more infamous Nazi propaganda film, *Triumph of the Will* (1935), incorporates even more sophisticated instances of the camera as a supplement to sight.

23. Luce Irigaray, "Women on the Market," in *This Sex Which is Not One*, pp. 17–73: "Marx's analysis of commodities as the elementary form of capitalist wealth can thus be understood as an interpretation of the status of woman in so-called patriarchal societies. The organization of such societies, and the operation of the symbolic system on which this organization is based . . . contain in a nuclear form the developments that Marx defines as characteristic of a capitalist regime: the submission of 'nature' to a 'labor' on the part of men who thus constitute 'nature' as use value and exchange value; the division of labor among private producer-owners who exchange their women-commodities among themselves, but also among producers and exploiters or exploitees of the social order; the standardization of women according to proper names that determine their equivalences; a tendency to accumulate wealth, that is, a tendency for the representatives of the most 'proper' names—the leaders—to capitalize more women than the others: a progression of the social work of the symbolic toward greater and greater abstraction." Insofar as Baudrillard is an important theorist for my argument, I would add that Baudrillard's general theory of the exchange system of signs in postmodern economies must be reinterpreted in light of the special consequences of this economy for gender and race as well as for class. Baudrillard has often been criticized justifiably for his neglect, if not trivialization, of the issue of gender.

24. Criticism of the political lobbying system and the access of special-interest groups to elected officials has by now reached such a pitch that President Bush addressed the problem in his State of the Union Address in January of 1991. To be sure, the president spoke in an emphatic tone about ending the privilege of special-interest groups and political lobbies, but there were few particulars. It is unlikely that the systems of political patronage, corporate and other special-interest lobbies, and the like can be significantly reformed from within the current practices of state and federal governments. Reform can only be carried out by those effectively dispossessed of significant and equitable access to their elected officials, and then only by means of political activism, including initiatives and referenda.

25. Pierre Bourdieu and Jean-Claude Passeron, *La reproduction: éléments pour une thèorie du système d'enseignement*, p. 247.

Works Cited

Althusser, Louis. *"Lenin and Philosophy" and Other Essays*. London: New Left Books, 1971.

Barthes, Roland. *Image-Music-Text*. Trans. Stephen Heath. New York: Hill and Wang, 1977.

Baudrillard, Jean. *For a Critique of the Political Economy of the Sign*. Trans. Charles Levin. St. Louis: Telos Press, 1981.

—— *The Mirror of Production*. Trans. Mark Poster. St. Louis: Telos Press, 1975.

—— *Selected Writings*. Ed. Mark Poster. Trans. Mark Poster and Jacques Mourrain. Palo Alto: Stanford University Press, 1988.

Benjamin, Walter. *Illuminations*. Ed. Hannah Arendt. Trans. Harry Zohn. New York: Schocken Books, 1969.

Bourdieu, Pierre. *Distinction: The Social Critique of Judgment*. Trans. Richard Nice. Cambridge: Harvard University Press, 1984.

Bourdieu, Pierre and Jean-Claude Passeron. *La reproduction: éléments pour une thèorie du système d'enseignement*. Paris: Editions de minuit, 1970.

Dahrendorf, Ralf. *Class and Class Conflict in Industrial Society*. Palo Alto: Stanford University Press, 1959.

Fukuyama, Francis. "The End of History?" *The National Interest*, 16 (Summer 1989): 3–18.

Gaines, Jane. *Contested Culture: The Image, the Voice, and the Law*. Chapel Hill: University of North Carolina Press, 1991.

Irigaray, Luce. *This Sex Which Is Not One*. Trans. Catherine Porter and Carolyn Burke. Ithaca: Cornell University Press, 1977.

Lentricchia, Frank and Thomas McLaughlin, eds. *Critical Terms for Literary Study*. Chicago: University of Chicago Press, 1990.

Lyotard, Jean-François. *The Differend: Phrases in Dispute*. Trans. Georges Van Den Abbeele. Theory and History of Literature, vol. 46. Minneapolis: University of Minnesota Press, 1988.

—— *The Postmodern Condition*. Trans. Geoff Bennington and Brian Massumi. Theory and History of Literature, vol. 10. Minneapolis: University of Minnesota Press, 1984.

Lyotard, Jean-François and Jean-Loup Thebaud. *Just Gaming*. Trans. Wlad Godzich. Theory and History of Literature, vol. 20. Minneapolis: University of Minnesota Press, 1985.

Marx, Karl and Friedrich Engels. *Capital: A Critique of Political Economy*. 2 vols. Trans. Ben Fowkes. New York: Random House, 1976.

—— *The German Ideology*. Ed. C. J. Arthur. New York: International Publishers, 1970.

Poulantzas, Nicos. *Political Power and Social Classes*. London: New Left Books, 1973.

Reddy, William M. *Money and Liberty in Modern Europe: A Critique of Historical Understanding*. Cambridge: Cambridge University Press, 1987.

Rowe, John Carlos. "Modern Art and the Invention of Postmodern Capital." In *American Quarterly* 30 (Spring 1987): 79–90.

—— "Surplus Economies: Deconstruction, Ideology, and the Humanities." In *The Aims of Representation*, ed. Murray Krieger. New York: Columbia University Press, 1987.

Williams, Raymond. "Base and Superstructure in Marxist Cultural Theory." In *Problems in Materialism and Culture*. London: Verso, 1980, pp. 31–49. Reprinted in *Contemporary Literary Criticism*, ed. Robert Con Davis and Ronald Schleifer. New York: Longman, 1989.

Wright, Erik Olin. *Classes*. London: New Left Books, 1985.

Zuboff, Shoshana. *In the Age of the Smart Machine: The Future of Work and Power*. New York: Basic Books, 1988.

GABRIELE SCHWAB

The Subject of the
Political Unconscious

My reading of Fredric Jameson's *The Political Unconscious*[1] is an attempt to come to terms with a text that has kept a grip on me since I first read it nearly ten years ago. To this day, I am captivated by Jameson's book and the project it promises to outline in its suggestive title. Jameson has offered a most intriguing and complex conceptual design of the political unconscious that continues to invite further inquiry and a wider critical debate—especially since it gains a new momentum in the wake of cultural criticism.

The crucial driving force behind the following critical reading of Jameson is a sense that the implications of Jameson's project—which, in fact, extend beyond his own realization—have not yet been fully grasped. It is symptomatic of the suggestive but simultaneously elusive character of Jameson's concept of the political unconscious that—even though the very term is invoked in the most diverse theoretical contexts—the model as such has never received the same critical attention as his much more debated theory of postmodernism. Likewise, we have not yet seen a thorough debate about the implications of Jameson's con-

83

cept of the political unconscious for feminism and feminist theory. This seems all the more astonishing considering the intense reception and revision of psychoanalysis within feminist theories in general.

The following reading attempts to prepare some ground for such a discussion by shaping critical arguments and concerns and by outlining those internal ruptures or conflicts in Jameson's text that I perceive as forces that explode the boundaries of the proposed conceptual model(s) of the political unconscious. Ideally this could turn into a dialogue, a confrontation between different ways of pursuing a similar goal— namely to find a theoretical model that allows one to think together the political and the unconscious. Jameson has undertaken what I consider one of the most important current tasks in critical theory: to develop a model of reading and textual production that merges the political and the psychological. Ideally, such a model would be able to account for the political function of the unconscious, as well as for the politics of the unconscious, in specific historical periods and cultures.

My critique of Jameson is also motivated by an attempt to rethink Jameson's notion of both culture and the unconscious in a less deterministic and more interactive framework. Culture would then appear not exclusively under the perspective of its determination by the modes of economic production in late capitalism but rather under the perspective of a systemic interplay of forces and modes of production that can be economic, political, institutional, artistic, or unconscious, to name only some of the most prominent ones. Such a perspective replaces the sense of a priority of the political over the psychological (or the inverse) with the assumption of an inseparable nonhierarchical dynamic between the two in every cultural production.

Jameson focuses his attention on the function of the unconscious in literary texts. Literature, for Jameson, constitutes a "socially symbolic act" in which the political unconscious appears mainly as the site of a repression of social, political, and economic interests. Literature may then be read in a symptomatic way, and the function of the critic is to read the symptoms and make explicit what they expose in displaced or symbolically veiled forms.

I want to argue for a more encompassing model of the political unconscious that assumes a dynamic notion of the unconscious as developed by Freud and expanded by later psychoanalytic theories. The unconscious, as I see it, operates not only as a scene of desire and repression but also as one of the main productive forces in the formation of culture as well as of the "subjects" who create and are created by this culture. Many literary texts use the unconscious and its mode of production, the primary processes, as a means to communicate with their readers in ways that exceed conscious reception. Thus literature is not only under the power of the unconscious; it can also engage and mold the unconscious.

Such a perspective is grounded in a cultural theory where the political and the unconscious are conceived as interactive forces. Culture in this model figures as an open system with variable "environments." The observer's or critic's perspective defines the heuristic boundaries of what is in a concrete case analyzed as a cultural system, and so determines which of the many possible environments are brought into play. A literary critic may, for example, choose to focus on literature as a specific cultural system and consider the social, political, or literary history as environment for the literary system.

To think of culture as an open system already precludes a whole range of conventional perspectives on culture as, for example, a unilinear cultural determinism, a fixed hierarchization of cultural spheres, or a strict separation if not antagonistic polarization of the political and the psychological, or the political and the aesthetic. Once we connect this notion of culture with a dynamic notion of the unconscious we cease to see the unconscious only as an effect of psychology or a "false literary consciousness." Instead it also appears as an effect of materialized linguistic, rhetorical, institutional, or urban structures—to name just a few—structures, in other words, that are affected by the whole dynamic of repression and the return of the repressed.

We can assume that each manifestation of the political is pervaded by unconscious forces, and each manifestation of the unconscious has a political aspect. Within this framework, literary texts may and will still be read symptomatically. But even though literature is seen as symptomatic for our culture and certainly does not altogether escape the dynamic of cultural repression, it is also seen as an agency within our culture that provides a voice for what I would call a "politics of the unconscious." The latter implies that literary texts are conceptually granted the capacity to work against or even undo certain forms of cultural repression and to provide a mode of communication that allows for a meaningful engagement of unconscious experience. This has been, I think, one of the important cultural functions of literature throughout history.

When Paul Ricoeur argues that Sophocles' *Oedipus Rex* does not simply expose the psychological and cultural disposition that Freud came to label as the Oedipus complex but also provides a culturally meaningful way of dealing with this disposition,[2] he emphasizes a crucial function of literature in relation to the unconscious: its capacity to "work through" (in the Freudian sense of *durcharbeiten*) and to mold unconscious material.

A second, perhaps even more important productive function of the unconscious pertains less to the literary enactment and transformation of unconscious fantasies than to the manifestation of the unconscious in the formal structure of literary texts. This "structural unconscious" may appear as an effect of materialized cultural and social structures, however, it may also appear in a refined literary use of the rhetoric of the unconscious, such as primary process, condensation, displacement, verbal and visual overdetermination, slippages, puns, and the like.

The most elaborated model of the structural unconscious in artistic production has been developed by Anton Ehrenzweig,[3] who argues that literature, art, and music can productively bring into play primary processes as the mode of production of the unconscious for purposes of unconscious communication. Among other things, the structural unconscious fulfills an eminent function by sustaining a balance between primary and secondary processes that Ehrenzweig sees as a basic condition for keeping cultural and psychological systems alive and flexible.

This cultural function of literature is widely neglected by literary critics. I see it in close connection to what Jameson calls the "ideology of form." Jameson, however, emphasizes the negative ideological aspects of literary form in contrast to the positive utopian elements of literature. A systemic model such as that of Ehrenzweig would allow one to expand this perspective conceptually and consider aspects of literary form that are ideological as well as others that work against specific ideologies or cultural norms in relation to the unconscious and cultural politics.[4] I even think that such a dynamic concept of the unconscious as a productive force would allow Jameson to ground his arguments about the dialectic between ideology and utopia in literary form.

The unconscious may thus fulfill multiple functions in relation to literature. It can work as an unconscious dimension of language in both its thematic and its formal aspects, and it can subvert as well as support signifying or ideological dimensions. The political status and function of the unconscious in literature depends upon historical conditions.

Numerous critics have convincingly argued that a culture that is too repressive toward unconscious forces and libidinal energies tends to become destructive, authoritarian, or totalitarian.[5] These critics assume that there is a "politics of the unconscious" that directly bears upon the formation of both culture and its subjects and hence upon politics at large.

Since the unconscious operates within what we used to call *subjectivity*, its political dimension is closely tied to the status of the subject in a given culture or, for that matter, a given theory. Among other things, the politics of the unconscious affects issues of gender and sexual politics and thus becomes in itself a burning political issue. One of the most crucial functions of literature and the arts may well consist in the pursuit of a specific politics of the unconscious in the formation of subjects and the cultural shaping of subjectivity.

When Frederic Jameson's *The Political Unconscious* appeared in 1981, it owed its stunning immediate success and widespread reception among literary critics to its taking up a project that emerged in the thirties (with the surrealists in France and Wilhelm Reich in Germany), carried a lot of weight in the sixties, and was taken up again under different premises in the seventies and eighties; that of developing a theoretical framework that links Marx with Freud, politics with psychology, the collective with the individual. The attempt to integrate or synthesize the two most influential theoretical movements (or, as Jameson calls them, "master-narratives")—Marxism and psychoanalysis—envisions a theory of society and culture able to overcome the historically founded antagonism between political and psychological perspectives, a theory able to account for and link together social exploitation and psychic repression.

The seventies and eighties produced highly diverse examples of such a theoretical endeavor. Among those that have most influenced the discussion in literary criticism and critical theory are Deleuze and Guattari's *Anti-Oedipus*[6] (published in French in 1972 and translated into English in 1983), Theweleit's *Male Fantasies*[7] (published in German in 1977 and translated into English in 1987), Jameson's *The Political Unconscious* (1981), and finally Slavoj Zizek's *The Sublime Object of Ideology*[8] (1989). Both Theweleit and Jameson are inspired by *Anti-Oedipus* even though both choose not to subscribe to Deleuze and Guattari's basic theoretical premises. Zizek, by contrast, draws on Marx and Lacan. All five authors share some basic concerns, but they differ substantially in their responses. They all explore the ambivalent status of desire in a "political unconscious" by pursuing questions such as "What is the relationship between political domination, social exploitation, and psychic repression?" "How does desire enter into and shape thought, discourse and action?" "How does desire deploy its force in the political domain?" "What is its ambivalent status with respect to an established order?" "How can we understand the cultural functions of the unconscious in political terms and in relation to politics?"

Jameson grounds his theory of the political unconscious in close readings of fictional texts written by male authors in the nineteenth and twentieth centuries. The political unconscious thus appears as mediated through its expression in very specific cultural objects that pertain to the sphere of literary production. On the other hand, Jameson's theoretical claims exceed this framework of literary production. His theory wants to be cultural criticism in the more general sense of explaining how "desire enters into discourse" and develops its force in the political domain.

Desire and the unconscious in Jameson's theory assume very different qualities and connotations from those we know from psychoanalytic theories. Their status within the political sphere and in relation to the political remains, in fact, very ambiguous. In his introductory chapter, "On Interpretation," Jameson declares that the function of the political unconscious consists in restoring to the surface of the text the repressed and buried reality of the history of class struggle (cf. p. 20). On the other hand, he also links the unconscious with desire. In his dialectic of utopia and ideology, desire is located on the side of utopia as that which resists or works against ideology and the "suppression of archaic mental powers" (p. 228) in late capitalism. As Cornel West points out, Jameson's politicized notion of a desire directly related to class struggle is sustained by a nostalgic utopianism that "promises access to a revolutionary energy lurking beneath the social veil of appearances, an energy capable of negating the reified present order."[9]

This definition recalls certain political reformulations of Freud's concept of Eros as we find them in critics of the Frankfurt School, especially in Herbert Marcuse's *Eros and Civilization*[10] and in Ernst Bloch's *The Principle of Hope*.[11] Desire is conceived as an unconscious force that can be activated against the "increasing fragmentation both of the rationalized external world and of the colonized psyche" (p. 236) in capitalist societies.

On the other hand, Jameson is extremely ambivalent toward the status of desire as a force of the political unconscious. This ambivalence stems from the fact that he links desire not only with the utopian element in class struggle but also with the individual subject and the "vicissitudes of carnal desire" (p. 158). In his chapter on Balzac, Jameson writes: "for us, wishes and desires have become the traits or psychological properties of human nomads" (p. 156). Aware of the historicity of our senses and the susceptibility of desire to historical conditions, Jameson comes to link desire more and more with the fragmentation and commodification of passions in consumer society.

In principle, these two different functions of desire could easily be linked to the fundamental ambivalence in psychoanalytic theories toward desire and the unconscious. But while psychoanalysis reflects the double edge of desire as a structural ambivalence within a dynamic theory of the unconscious that operates through repression and the return of the repressed, Jameson largely ignores the dynamic of repression and thus maintains the double status of desire not as an ambivalence but as an unresolved conflict in his theory.

As a consequence, Jameson's readings engage the unconscious rather as an unarticulated than as a repressed political dimension. Criticizing the poststructuralist refutation of hermeneutics as historically unspecific (cf. pp. 21f.), Jameson pointedly asserts the hermeneutic character of his readings, which aim at spelling out, as culturally meaningful, a political dimension hidden in the explicit narrative of texts. He thus retains the Freudian idea of the readability of the unconscious (hermeneutics) but—following Deleuze and Guattari—he renounces the anthropologically conceived oedipal constellation or, to use his own terms, the whole complex of Freudian individualism and "familialism."

Jameson reasserts "the political content of everyday life and of individual fantasy-experience" against its "reduction to the merely subjective and to the status of psychological projection" (p. 22). According to Jameson, literary texts transform fantasies into "protonarrative structures" that, in turn, are our vehicles for experiencing "the real" (cf. p. 48). Used as a synonym for history, the real is conceived along the lines of Althusser's "history as an absent cause" or else of Lacan's Real, which "resists symbolization absolutely" and "is inaccessible to us except in textual form" (p. 35).

The major achievement of such a model of the political unconscious is its pronounced antiprojectionism. Instead of a Freudian model that assumes a subject (individual) inclined to project oedipal or other fantasies onto a reality outside and who therefore must learn to develop the capacity for distinguishing between inside and outside as the basis for reality testing, Jameson assumes that history (the Real) works itself into (literary) texts or narratives and is retrievable only through texts. He thus deals with a very different object of investigation—namely, an unarticulated historical dimension of texts, in contrast to an unconscious cathexis or shaping of historical and textual representation.

This notion of history and the real also determines Jameson's notion of the subject. In Freud's model the subject is read as an agent of history who has a decidedly intersubjective—if not moral—obligation to represent history without distortions but whose unconscious is nevertheless prone continually to produce such distortions in the form of historical narratives based on unconscious fantasies, desires, or fears. By contrast, the subject in Jameson's model figures as an effect of history. Where it comes into focus at all, the agency of the subject is reduced to the articulation of utopian desire, which remains nonetheless contained within ideological narratives. Accordingly, both models lead to very different theories of literary production and reception. Whereas Freud emphasizes literature's function as mediator between unconscious fantasies or desires on the one hand and the constraints of reality or history on the other, Jameson emphasizes literature in its function as a mediator of history, ideology, and utopia.

For Jameson, the experience of a literary text is a specific experience of history, or the real. Asserting that any approach to the Real must pass through "its narrativization in the political unconscious" (p. 35), he reduces the latter to a collective unconscious that manifests itself in "political or economic fantasies" (Jameson's terms) about history and the Real and forms a persistent yet often unarticulated dimension of literary and cultural texts—that is, a kind of Lévi-Straussian *pensee sauvage* of a whole narrative production (cf. p. 34).

Instead of investigating and mediating the relationship between the political and the unconscious or focusing on the politics of the unconscious, Jameson's theory instead constitutes a new variation of Durkheim's or Lévi-Strauss' collective unconscious. The material of the latter is not a product of repression, censorship, and cultural taboos—at least not in the psychoanalytic sense of a dynamics of repression—but rather of collective political fantasies that appear in literary texts under various disguises without being consciously elaborated. He, in fact, performs a significant inversion of orthodox psychoanalysis. Whereas Freud considered political fantasies as derivative of sexual fantasies and desires, Jameson considers the latter as disguises of economic desires, thus reproducing methodologically the logic of substitution he elsewhere criticizes in Freud.

Once the psychoanalytic dynamic of repression is abandoned, the political unconscious rather resembles Freud's "preconscious" or even Michael Polanyi's "tacit knowledge"—that is, a form of collective knowledge that lacks conscious organization and remains, so to speak, "structurally unconscious." Jameson's tendency to favor a structural over a dynamic unconscious in the psychoanalytic sense leads to major revisions in the models he adopts from Freud on the one hand and from Deleuze and Guattari on the other. No longer the product of dynamic psychic energies, the political unconscious becomes a mere product of concealed social forces. Since the agencies of the political unconscious are no longer individual subjects or texts but transpersonal forces that create history as an effect of discursive formations, this unconscious closely resembles what we commonly call ideology.

According to Jameson's "dialectic of ideology and utopia," this ideological dimension of the political unconscious is, however, counterbalanced by a utopian one. In this context, Jameson endows the political unconscious with a utopian desire that becomes the tacit carrier of social utopias. Yet, Jameson's shift from psychic to social energies has affected the "objects of desire"—that is, the "scenes" (*Schauplatz*) that desire uses to perform its unconscious manifestations or its phantasmatic transformations. Desire now appears as "economic desire," "will to power," or, more surprisingly, as "will to style," manifested in the production of "verbal commodities." [12]

With this recasting of a politicized desire, Jameson, in fact, performs a conceptual move that inverts the Freudian theory of sublimation. Whereas Freud would have seen "economic desires" as a sublimation of displaced sexual or erotic desires, Jameson sees the expression of sexual desires in literature as a displacement of the "more burning" economic desires. [13]

Jameson's shift thus actually suppresses precisely those forces that had been privileged from a psychoanalytic perspective—namely sexuality, the body, and the whole range of archaic emotions. By implication, this shift furthermore also displaces questions of gender. By treating literary representations of gender, sexuality, and the politics of the body as textual disguises for "economic desires," Jameson indirectly declares them as politically irrelevant. In this respect, Jameson shifts away from what is, I think, most urgent not only for a feminist conception of the political unconscious but also for a cultural politics *of* the unconscious in general. Moreover, Jameson reproduces theoretically and methodologically what he himself describes as one of the most devastating effects of capitalism: "the capitalist devaluation of the senses" (p. 220), "the suppression of archaic mental powers" or "archaic functions of the psyche" (pp. 228f.), and the repression and containment of sexuality that, as Foucault has shown, has historically been one of the main strategies of social discipline and punishment.

The effects of the unconscious in the politics of the body, sexuality and gender play only a marginal role in Jameson's theory. Instead of following Althusser's criticism of the primacy of the economic as the determining force in all cultural sectors, Jameson ultimately seems to favor the orthodox Marxian hierarchization of political contradictions in capitalism. Consequently, the "real" area of politics for Jameson is the economic sector and especially the discursive formations, which provide a symbolic organization of "economic desires." Wherever the body, sexuality, or gender appear, they are taken as textual figures, as displaced articulations of repressed economic forces. Even Deleuze and Guattari's notion of an unconscious "desiring machine" that engenders the textual apparatus as a "libidinal apparatus" is recast in terms of a sublimation of libidinal economic desires.

Along with the status of a textual politics of sexuality and the body, Jameson also reevaluates Deleuze and Guattari's linkage between schizophrenia and capitalism. Critical of their anarchy of free-floating polymorphous or anti-oedipal perversities, he takes schizophrenia as the symptomatic expression of the cultural disease of late capitalism. What Jameson calls "postmodern schizophrenia" is thus a sublimated cultural malaise rather than the unbounded anarchy of the schizo who appears as the carrier of the fragmented or organless bodies of the anti-Oedipus. But at the same time this notion of postmodern schizophrenia is equally remote from the conditions of the painful and devastating illness that is clinically labeled as schizophrenia.[14] In its structural alliance with capitalism—the only crucial assumption that Jameson shares with Deleuze and Guattari—schizophrenia appears as a domesticated allegory of postmodern fragmentation. The destructive and self-destructive mechanisms of clinical schizophrenia as well as the untamable subversive powers of resistance that Deleuze and Guattari attribute to the schizo are reduced to mere mirror-reflections of capitalist alienation.

Similar to the ambivalence toward desire, there is, however, also an unresolved ambivalence in the function that postmodern schizophrenia plays in Jameson's theory. This ambivalence stems from schizophrenia's dual set of connotations in Jameson's conceptual framework. On the one hand it figures as a form of capitalist fragmentation that Jameson criticizes, while on the other it signals the end of the bourgeois individual that he celebrates. "Ego loss," far from being seen as a self-destructive or else a healing process that frees desire from the prison house of bounded bodies and selves, appears as a by-product of all those processes that have overthrown or outlived the historical conditions in which bourgeois individuality and autonomy were still viable categories.

Like Deleuze and Guattari, Jameson sees the bourgeois individual replaced by a "postmodern schizo" who, instead of a narrative identity, produces dispersed moments of free-floating intensities and ecstasies. Postmodern "schizophrenic" texts, their free plays or signifiers, their production of difference, flux, dissemination, and heterogeneity are the hallmarks of a new literary production freed from the narrative constraints of "bourgeois subjectivity."[15] On the other hand, Jameson clearly criticizes both—the bourgeois subject and the schizo—as products of different stages of capitalism. This ambivalence between the schizo as a positively conceived alternative to the bourgeois subject on the one hand and as a product of the fragmenting effects of late consumer capitalism remains unresolved.

Jameson's divergence from Deleuze and Guattari's anarchy of unbounded flow becomes most obvious in his own textual production, which retains conceptualization, hierarchization, and totalization as viable modes of theorizing. His shift away from the fluidity of desire and phantasmatic bodies is mirrored in the mode of production that generates his own textual body. While Deleuze and Guattari perform a flowing textual mobility, full of proliferations and disjunctions, Jameson delineates bounded schemata with pyramidal hierarchizations and subdivisions. The only textual feature that undermines this masterful display of what some would call "logocentric" rhetorical strategies is the playfully associative eclecticism, which releases potential readings that exceed the bounds of Jameson's conceptual schemata. This eclecticism creates tensions and fissures that one might be tempted to read as manifestations of the political unconscious of Jameson's own text. Or, more strongly, one could read these as its "ideology of form" according to Jameson's own definition: "symbolic messages transmitted to us by the coexistence of various sign systems which are themselves traces or antic-ipations of modes of production" (p. 76).

It is important to stress here that I do not intend simply to play De-leuze and Guattari off against Jameson. Instead, I want to point out how Jameson's revision of their theoretical apparatus, as well as his reliance on clearly delineated categorical schemata, counteract his *own* notion of "postmodern schizophrenia" in a symptomatic way. I see this tension as reflecting a fundamental and culturally, as well as theoretically signif-icant, ambivalence—if not a clearly conflictive relationship—toward the material and the social processes under investigation. My sense is that if we take the gaps and fault lines created by the collision of theories within Jameson's text as textual symptoms of cultural and political con-flicts, we might further develop our understanding of the relation be-tween the textual, the political, and the unconscious and thus further differentiate the conception of the political unconscious.

Jameson's readings of textual representations of women and gender display similar conceptual tensions. The status he gives female charac-ters or "character-effects" in his readings, and, for that matter, in his theory, is affected by the general displacement of the subject, sexuality and the body, from his analysis of desire. Those women who emerge from literary texts—like Balzac's or Conrad's women—are transformed from objects of desire into allegorical objects for "political fantasies" (Jameson's term). Despite the fact that in his discussion of feminism Jameson exposes "the false problem of the priority of the economic over the sexual, or of sexual oppression over that of social class" (p. 99), he not only asserts the priority of the economic and of social class in all his readings but also substitutes questions of economic oppression for ques-tions of sexual oppression. In this case his theoretical assertions clearly conflict with his methods of reading. This choice of priorities might also explain why the problem of gender is only addressed once as a theoreti-cal issue and then quickly subsumed under that of history in general.

> Sexism and the patriarchal are to be grasped as the sedimentation and the virulent survival of forms of alienation specific to the oldest mode of production of human history, with its division of labor between men and women . . . The analysis of the ideology of form, properly completed, should reveal the formal persistence of such archaic structures of aliena-

tion—and the sign systems specific to them—beneath the overlay of all the more recent and historically original types of alienation—such as political domination and commodity reification—which have become the dominants of that most complex of all cultural revolutions, late capitalism, in which all the earlier modes of production coexist. The affirmation of radical feminism, therefore, that to annul the patriarchal is the most radical political act—insofar as it includes and subsumes more partial demands, such as the liberation from the commodity form—is thus perfectly consistent with an expanded Marxian framework . . . With this final horizon, then, we emerge into a space in which History itself becomes the ultimate ground as well as the untranscendable limit of our understanding in general and our textual interpretations in particular.   (pp. 99f.)

This treatment of women and gender in a theory of the political unconscious not only literally displaces the question of sexual politics onto that of a globalized notion of "History" (which, in fact, allows Jameson then simply to drop the issue) but also eliminates the question of the unconscious as a formative force in gender politics altogether. Literary fantasies or narratives about women are metaphorical substitutes for or displacements of economic and class interests. The problem with prioritizing the economic sphere over desire does not lie in Jameson's assertion that women *are* often taken as displaced objects for "economic desires." Here too, the problem rather lies in a logic of substitution that makes the literary representation of the sexual sphere and of gender politics in general disappear as a central issue of the political unconscious.

This exclusion of questions of gender stems partly from Jameson's tendency to dichotomize the individual and the collective in a project ostensibly attempting to merge psychology and politics. Recent feminist theories have once again challenged the public/private dichotomy that is maintained in Jameson's polarization of the individual and the collective. In his inversion of Freud, Jameson loses precisely that dimension of psychoanalysis that has been most fruitfully adapted and revised by feminist critics: the theory of the psychosexual constitution of the subject as a gendered subject, and, in consequence, the gender subtext of our societies that permeates economic and public life. Sheyla Benhabib and Drucilla Cornell argue in their introduction to *Feminism as Critique* that "whereas communitarians emphasize the situatedness of the disembedded self in a network of relations and narratives, feminists also begin with the situated self but view the *renegotiation* of our psychosexual identities, and their *autonomous reconstitution* by individuals as essential to women's and human liberation."[16] This renegotiation often takes place through what Benhabib and Cornell call "social fantasies."[17] Unlike Jameson's political fantasies, these social fantasies take sexual politics as an outcome of a whole network of energies, including libidinal *and* economic ones. They are not, as Jameson would have it, the product of a translation of the "real" economic energies into a merely metaphorical sexual sphere.

As Nancy Chodorow reminds us in *The Reproduction of Mothering*, feminist critics have argued from different perspectives against a "unilateral model of social determination."[18] In a similar vein, Gayle Rubin stresses the overdetermination of sexual and political economy and concludes that "economic and political analyses are incomplete if they do not consider women, marriage, and sexuality."[19] All these different feminist positions share one assumption—namely that any polarization of the individual and the collective, the psychological and the political, or sexual and political economy tends to operate methodologically according to a logic of substitution, hierarchization, and unilateral determination that simplifies the complex interaction between the spheres and the overdetermination of their respective modes of representation. Furthermore, this logic of substitution analyzes sexual and other forms of politics according to parallel instead of interacting structures, a procedure that, in turn, has to rely on simple analogies and homologies between the two instead of the much more diverse and complex forms of interaction and overdetermination.[20]

Jameson's substitutive methodology appears all the more reductive if one takes into account that a theory concerned with the unconscious deals with an object that can only be mediated through overdetermination. As Jameson himself points out, the unconscious is based on desire and transmitted through fantasies that, in turn, are worked into a literary text. This is why a theory of the political unconscious needs a dynamic concept of how desire finds access to and operates within texts. However, all the different spheres of Jameson's political unconscious analyzed here—the politics of sexuality and the body, of gender as well as of mental illness or "cultural pathology" (schizophrenia)—lack a concept of desire as a dynamic unconscious energy in conflict with social and cultural constraints.

Jameson, in fact, speaks of desire with a certain reticence—if not with a wish to make it simply disappear into something else. Instead of the unbounded archaic desire that, in Freud, is in conflict with the social, Jameson resorts to an already sublimated, displaced, and derivative desire, one based on secondary needs and wishes rather than on unconscious energies. His tamed notion of desire and his persistant uneasiness with the basic psychoanalytic concepts of sexuality, fantasy, and desire—or even with a possible "theory of desire" (his term)—generate another symptomatic blindness in his attempt to conceptualize the unconscious in political terms. Because he is unwilling to engage desire, Jameson cannot grasp the fact that by addressing sexual desire, sexual politics, gender conflicts, family romances, sexual perversions, narcissism, or fetishism—in short, the whole range of phenomena that Jameson classifies as "the thematics of the Freudian hermeneutic" (p. 64)—literary texts deploy a genuinely political concern that pertains to the domain of sexual and gender politics proper and cannot be reduced to a device for concealing economic or state politics.

Throughout literary history, sexuality and desire have always formed the core of literary fantasies and in all its various sublimations—from the epos of antiquity, the tales and satires of the Middle Ages, Renaissance drama and poetry, and throughout the history of the novel and other genres up to the very forms of postmodern pastiche—sexuality and desire have been represented in conjunction with politics. One could argue that throughout history literature has been a field of cultural production in which the interconnectedness of *all* social spheres with the politics of sexuality and the body or desire and interpersonal relations has been enacted.

One of the most crucial cultural functions of psychoanalytic theory is that it has explicitly linked sexuality with the social field by developing a symbolic sign system able to account for significant connections between the two. Such a sign system is necessary to conceive of sexuality and desire as forces that pervade the social field and its systems of representation in a dynamic way.

While Freud's model allows one to conceive of the connections between the sexual and the social in dynamic and systemic terms, Jameson seems to criticize Freud's theory of the drives on the basis of an equation of the drives with the pre- or transsocial. Freud, however, never made such an equation. For Freud, a drive is always already a mental representation of an instinctual force or a need. Or, as Jane Flax argues in *Thinking Fragments*, "A somatic demand must be translated into a psychic one before the organism can recognize and act on it. This process of transformation renders the drives vulnerable to cultural influences."[21] This malleability of the drives informs Freud's model of the two cultural and psychic forces of Eros and Thanatos as outlined in *Civilization and Its Discontents*.[22] Even though Freud posits Eros and Thanatos as drives, he emphasizes how all the concrete forms that drives assume are shaped by social factors. At the same time, he insists on their fundamental ambiguity resulting from the fact that even in their socially formed manifestations the drives, and especially the whole area of desire and unconscious fantasies or wishes, are opposed to prevalent social norms. They are, after all, the energetic forces behind civilization's discontents even though this does not preclude the existence of forms of social control that tend to "colonize" the unconscious and the drives in order to adapt them to cultural norms.

The challenge, then, lies in developing a system of interpreting sexual symbolism in relation to the social and the political that is connective and interactive instead of substitutive. Such a system would have to conceive of the dynamic between desire and ideology in terms different from Jameson's. Ideology would then comprise not only conscious belief systems and collectively shared tacit knowledge but also unconscious ideologies based upon the repression of desires that fall under a cultural taboo. In case such unconscious ideologies are expressed as "political fantasies," an analysis of the political unconscious must investigate the modes of textual operation that transform the unconscious into a literary translation of a political fantasy.

Klaus Theweleit's theory of the political unconscious as outlined in *Male Fantasies*—which is also inspired by Deleuze and Guattari—presents an alternative model for conceiving the relationship between ideology and fantasy. Theweleit shows in the novels read by the German Freicorps soldiers (most of whom later joined the SS) that political, economic, and sexual fantasies are so intricately intertwined that one can understand each aspect only in connection with the others. Starting from Deleuze and Guattari's assumption that "desire orients itself *directly* toward the social arena"[23] and that "the unconscious is a productive force that explodes the framework of authority of every society,"[24] Theweleit develops an analysis of fascism according to which unconscious fantasies pervade and support certain political actions and war operations in significant ways without directly "causing" them in any simplistic sense.

Accordingly, Theweleit analyzes the language of the Freicorps soldiers as a mode of production in which fantasies are developed within a complex and highly overdetermined code. "Woman," for example, can become a code word for a whole chain of connotations associated with the feminine, such as emotions, the unconscious, otherness, or nature. Unlike Jameson, Theweleit, however, does not attempt to translate fantasies about women, sexuality, and desire into something else. He instead analyzes the politics of gender and sexuality in its interchange with other areas of culture and politics, asserting that complex political phenomena like fascism can be more fully understood if one reflects a whole dynamic of the political unconscious in which gender and sexual politics form the core.

As we have seen, Jameson by contrast treats representations of sexuality in literature as if they were a cover-up for repressed economic interests. This substitutive move, however, reproduces conceptually precisely what Jameson criticizes elsewhere as the autonomization of sexuality within the public sphere of bourgeois society and the respective isolation of sexual experience (cf. p. 64). By reading sexual symbolism as a veiled expression of economic desires, he indirectly perpetuates a treatment of sexuality in isolation from the social sphere. Instead of taking up the question of interpretation where it poses itself in regard to the relationship among sexuality, desire, and the social field, Jameson "displaces" it by disconnecting the two fields. The politics of sexuality thus becomes marginalized—if not eclipsed—in a theory of the political unconscious.

I insist so strongly on Jameson's methodological strategies of substitution, disconnection, separation, and isolation because they mark his theory of the political unconscious as a whole. Precisely the strategy of a systemic isolation of fields that Jameson criticizes as an effect of capitalist autonomization and specialization is a structural principle governing his own theorizing. Instead of interconnecting cultural spheres like the private and the public, the sexual and the social, the individual and the collective, or the political and the psychological, Jameson maintains their binary opposition.

This tendency becomes most obvious when he takes up the controversial issue of the subject. Coloring the poststructuralist critiques of the subject with a Marxist disdain for the bourgeois individual, Jameson always refers to the individual subject with a certain contempt. For him, the individual subject belongs to the relics of bourgeois ideology, gone out of fashion in the wake of certain neo-Marxist and poststructuralist theories. Psychoanalytic categories such as "personal identity, ego or self" (p. 60) or even key concepts like "wish fulfillment" are rejected for being "locked in a problematic of the individual subject" (p. 66). For a theory of the political unconscious, however, this undialectic reductionism becomes self-defeating. The "troubled position of the individual subject" becomes even more complicated by a conceptually unmediated oscillation between a Marxian and a Lacanian notion of the subject. In the first case, he opposes what he calls "anarchist categories of the individual subject and individual experience" (p. 286) to a Marxist conception of class; in the second case, he embraces a notion of the subject as a structural or textual effect. Instead of asking *how* textual "subject effects" constitute "meaning as a collective process" (p. 285) within a dynamic of signification that produces the "political unconscious," Jameson opts for Marxism as a foundational master-narrative that explores the unconscious no longer in relation to "subjects" but in relation to class consciousness. Within this framework, the unconscious in question is *always* a collective unconscious purged of any trace of individual textual production.

Jameson's refusal to mediate theoretically between categories of the individual and the collective precludes a dynamic notion of the unconscious and its modes of production. Such a notion would require a theory of the formation of the subject in sociopolitical *and* psychological terms. This lack of a dynamic notion of the unconscious also affects Jameson's politics of interpretation. Rejecting any form of psychological interpretation for being "ethical criticism" and thus bound to "so-called humanism, which is always grounded on a certain conception of 'human nature'" (p. 59), Jameson asserts that "all ethics lives by exclusion and predicates certain types of Otherness or evil" (p. 60). His proposal to transcend the ethical in the direction of the political and the collective (p. 60) makes the tacit assumption that political criticism could do without ethical premises. But as Slavoj Zizek has pointed out in *The Sublime Object of Ideology*, what we call "social reality" itself is in the last resort an ethical construction. According to Zizek, belief systems that are supported by a certain *as if*—"we act *as if* we believe in the almightiness of bureaucracy, *as if* the President incarnates the Will of the People"—are embodied, materialized, in the effective functioning of the social field.[25] Jameson's proposition to transcend ethics in the direction of the collective thus ignores not only the fact that ethics has always been grounded in a politics of transcending the individual toward the collective but also how ethics already operates in a very material way in the social field proper.

As to Jameson's criticism that ethics always rests upon negative predications of Otherness, at least his antagonistic polarizations follow a similar logic when, for example, the psychological and the individual become the negative Other of the political and the collective. Quite apart from the general political importance of cultural formations of Otherness, this all-too-easy polarization of the individual and the collective establishes—as Dominick La Capra incisively notes—an unproductive binary opposition: "When Jameson does try to clarify his grounds, he resorts to the idea that his approach decenters the *individual* while simultaneously centering everything on the *collectivity*. He thereby seeks refuge in the unproblematic logic of binary oppositions."[26]

Jameson's own aim—to develop a cultural theory that avoids simplistic predications of a negative Other—would require a model that allows one to analyze the sociocultural formation of Otherness in psychological and cultural terms. From a psychoanalytic perspective, the very practices of exclusion that predicate Otherness—as well as the cultural modes of dealing with Otherness—are internalized through processes of socialization and acculturation. Supported by unconscious desires, fears, and fantasies, these processes create patterns of relating to Otherness that remain effective throughout life but are also susceptible to being reshaped according to new cultural experiences. (Lacan's theory, for example, which Jameson adopts at times, is to a large extent based on the notion of the symbolic as an internalized Other.) From this perspective, the ethics of psychoanalysis—Freud's "Wo Es war, soll Ich werden"—even shares a central value with Marxist ethics, namely, the reduction of dependency from the other/Other and from repression and reification.[27]

Our cultural patterns of predicating or relating to Otherness also shape our modes and ethics of reading. We could expand Zizek's statement on the relationship between social reality and ethics by arguing that what we call (and how we choose to define) "literature," "text," or, more generally, "cultural object" at a given historical time is equally based on ethical constructions that confer certain reality effects upon our objects of investigation. Our very theories are thus shaped by an implied "ethics of reading."

These observations lead us more directly to Jameson's concrete object of investigation: the political unconscious in literary texts. I see Jame-

son's implied ethics of reading largely determined by his attempt to transcend the individual toward the collective, an effort that shapes his very
perception of the fictional texts under consideration. Jameson uses the
poststructuralist category of the "subject-effect" in order to transcend the
notion of individual characters. "Character-effects" in Jameson's theoretical framework are "transcoded" by the "libidinal apparatus" of the
text, which uses the unconscious political fantasies of an author in order
to produce the "protonarrative structure" of the political unconscious
(cf. p. 48). The protonarrative structure relates to the narrative proper
according to the dynamic of "what the text represses" (p. 48).

Despite his conceptual goal to create a nonrepresentational narrative
theory purged from any representational equivalent of the individual
subject, Jameson's model seems haunted by the insistence of the subject
as an "anthropomorphic figure" in literary texts. The only available
model of a narrative theory unmarred by the conceptual category of the
subject appears to be the structural analysis of Greimas and Propp. And
yet their formalism leaves no room either for the collective subject of
Jameson's political unconscious. In an admittedly "paradoxical reproach" (p. 123), he therefore feels compelled to criticize the formalistic
narrative analysis of Propp and Greimas for "its incapacity to make a
place for the subject" (p. 123).

I am inclined to read Jameson's "paradoxical reproach" as symptomatic of an unresolved conflict in his own model concerning the status
of both the subject and the unconscious. At times, Jameson's goal seems
to be the "deanthropomorphization of the study of narrative." His persistent anti-individualism makes him devalue the structuralist categories
"actant; structural role or character-effect" as "shackled to some ultimately irreducible nucleus of anthropomorphic representation" (p.
123). On the other hand, Jameson criticizes the formalistic limitations
and "scientific" ideals of structuralist narrative theory for their failure to
comprehend the subject: "The anthropomorphic figure, however, necessarily resists and is irreducible to the formalization which was always
the ideal of such analysis" (p. 123).

Lévi-Strauss emerges as a positive exception because he seems to be
able to have it both ways: to retain the "status of storytelling as the supreme function of the human mind" (p. 123) while, at the same time,
avoiding any notion of the individual subject. Jameson's comments on
Lévi-Strauss bring about a symptomatic turn in his arguments:

The key to this paradoxical achievement is, I think, to be found in the
social origins of the narrative material with which Lévi-Strauss deals.
These are evidently preindividualistic narratives: that is, they emerge
from a social world in which the psychological subject has not yet been
constituted as such, and therefore in which later categories of the subject, such as "character," are not relevant.   (p. 124)

While this reading attempts to rescue Jameson from his argumenta-
tive dilemma concerning the "anthropomorphic figure" in literary texts,
it at the same time fails to solve the problem of the subject. Even if it
were true that "storytelling as the supreme function of the human
mind" is unproblematic only in preindividualistic societies and as long
as the psychological subject has not yet been constituted, the question
would still remain of how we are to understand the fact that "psychological subjects" continue to produce stories inhabited by "anthropomorphic figures."

Limiting the time of the individual subject to the historical period of
the rise of the bourgeoisie and the culture of bourgeois individualism,
Jameson argues that the time of the individual subject is past. For him,
our own "postmodern condition" seems therefore more attuned to
preindividualistic cultural formations. The psychic dispersal, fragmentation, fantasy, hallucinogenic sensations, and temporal discontinuities
of the "postindividualistic subject" that Jameson attributes to the "modification of the experience of the subject in consumer or late monopoly
capitalism" (p. 124) display more structural affinities to the experience
of the "preindividualistic subject" of early cultures than to the culture of
bourgeois individualism.

The obvious common experience Jameson refers to here is related to
the fluidity of boundaries between the subject and its cultural environment as well as to the higher impact of primary processes on the organization of subjectivity. Inverting Deleuze and Guattari's positive valorization of these forms of subjectivity, Jameson, however, diagnoses
them as pathologies and opposes them to a Marxian utopia according to
which the loss of the subject is overcome by "a new and original form
of collective social life" (p. 125). The "postindividualistic subject," in
other words, would need the stabilizing boundaries of collective social
bonds similar to those in early cultures in order to ward off the psychic
dispersal and fragmentation imposed by late capitalism. Within such a
collective organization, Jameson argues, "individual consciousness can

be lived—and not merely theorized—as an 'effect of structure' [Lacan]" (p. 125).

This "postmodern" concern with a critique of the subject in conjunction with a utopia of new forms of collective social life inform Jameson's readings of literary realism and modernism. Since both periods, however, pertain to what he calls the culture of bourgeois individualism, he deals with the creation of fictional worlds whose "character-effects" are modeled after an "individual consciousness" of bourgeois subjects that can only be theorized but *not* yet *lived* as an "effect of structure." That their consciousness *is* an effect of structure remains to be shown by a critic able to read the political unconscious.

The latter's function thus appears to be a cultural practice of de-subjectification. If we read (or theorize) properly, we see that the notion of the subject was an illusion all along and that what we need to learn is to perceive literary characters (and by extension, ourselves) as an effect of structure. Our collective political unconscious, then, results less from a repression of individual desires and needs or from unconscious wish-fulfilling fantasies than from a repression of the effects that social structures have on our consciousness and our unconscious. I see this idea as one of the most productive conceptual assumptions in Jameson's theory of the political unconscious but, at the same time, I believe it could gain from inserting it into a more complicated framework than Jameson's overall logic of substitution, which devalues the individual subject as the negative Other of the collective subject. Instead of this negative predication we could conceive of a "subject of the political unconscious"—individual or collective—constituted by a dynamic tension between what *is* an effect of structure and what resists the effects of structure. Such a concept would, in fact, not only be closer to the models Jameson borrows from Lacan and Althusser but also leave more room for theorizing the dialectic between ideology and utopia. It would, moreover, also reintroduce a less mediated notion of desire. In the following, I turn toward Jameson's concrete readings in order to show how, I think, his own theory of the political unconscious—and especially his notion of an "effect of structure"—could be productively expanded if the logic of substitution were abandoned.

Jameson's concrete readings of literary texts bespeak his effort to purge literary characters from their individual subjectivity by translating their emotions and fantasies into mere effects of structure, that is, into the impersonal relations of economic desire and capitalist greed or political and social domination. Heathcliff in Emily Brontë's *Wuthering Heights* may be taken as an exemplary case. Once the romantic hero or tyrannical villain of representational criticism, Jameson has him undergo an "actantial reduction" (pp. 126f.) that dissolves him as a literary character or, for that matter, as a textual subject. Brontë's text is read "not as the story of 'individuals' nor even as the chronicle of generations and their destinies, but rather as an impersonal process, a semic transformation centering on the house, which moves from Lockwood's initial impressions of the Heights, and the archaic story of origins behind it, to that final ecstatic glimpse through the window" (p. 127).

The exorcism of the narratives of individual characters and their lives from critical interest in Jameson's reading of *Wuthering Heights* provides a telling index to his larger notion of the political unconscious. Jameson transposes Heathcliff's function in the narrative from one of love, passion, and power to one of mediating the function of the house as the locus of property, kinship, and filiation. Heathcliff, that is, no longer mediates libidinal or romantic desires—let alone unconscious ones—but socioeconomic values. He thus becomes "the locus of *history* in this romance: his mysterious fortune marks him as a protocapitalist, in some other place, absent from the narrative, which then recodes the new economic energies as sexual passions" (p. 128).

Jameson's reading ingeniously links the new economic energies of the historical period with the metaphorical overdetermination of the house in *Wuthering Heights*—a reading whose extraordinary sensitivity for details releases historical associations that allow one to place Brontë's narrative in a larger cultural context. But instead of revealing how these new economic energies supplement the sexual passions—thus rendering both economy and sexuality more complex—Jameson reduces sexuality to a surface coding that conceals what is supposed to really matter: the use of the new economic energies and the circulation of money, value, and social prestige. Instead of a conception of the political unconscious in which economy and sexuality, or, for that matter, history and fantasy, are understood as interactive forces engendering overdetermined textual representations, Jameson opts for a reading that simply substitutes economics for erotics, sexuality, and desire.

This theoretical sacrifice of desire for political economy, however, replicates structurally the very capitalist alienation that Jameson criticizes. Capitalist economies, too, force their "subjects" to sacrifice or displace their desire. In fact, the literary texts that Jameson reads are so powerful precisely because they use the overdetermination of the sexual/desire and economy/power in the working of the unconscious as a strategy of representation. Therefore they deal with the political unconscious of their own culture in a dynamic sense that is inevitably lost in any reading that proceeds by substitution.

In substituting economics for erotics, sexuality, and desire, Jameson also eclipses the pleasure of the text. He thus ignores precisely that domain in which texts have some of their crucial cultural effects. A reader-response model that Jameson initially names as a necessary basis for his theory of the political unconscious might precisely address the issue of these texts' conscious or unconscious appeal within the context of the new economic energies and structures. Jameson's concrete readings, however, focus nearly exclusively on issues of textual production. One might ask, moreover, if Jameson's substitution of desire does not also, at times, involuntarily reenforce capitalist values of economic rationality or even a puritan devaluation of desire and pleasure.[28]

More importantly, the substitution and displacement of desire reduces Jameson's theory of the political unconscious to a critique of ideology that could ultimately function without any notion of the unconscious. Even when Jameson uses psychoanalytic categories like "wish fulfillment" or "fantasy investment" (p. 169), he transforms them into categories that refer to straightforward wishes and fantasies of Balzac, the author. Fantasies cease to be vehicles for unconscious productions that can create or distort social realities and support ideologies. Jameson reads fantasies rather as allegories of political ideologies. Whatever belongs to the unconscious and its dynamics—repression, libidinal cathexis, displacement of energies, censorship or its circumvention, and so on—becomes relegated to the margins of critical interest.

I have tried to show how Jameson's substitutive readings threaten to undermine his initially stated goal of reconciling his critique of ideology with Freud's theory of aesthetic creation and sublimation (cf. pp. 174f.). I am tempted to see a crucial function of Jameson's logic of substitution in the neutralization of the troubling question of the subject in a theory of the political unconscious. And yet, the question strongly reasserts itself when he addresses the relationship between ideology and desire in Balzac's text. Jameson's Balzac reading indirectly reveals the lack of a model of the political unconscious, which could account for what Zizek in *The Sublime Object of Ideology* calls the structuring of reality by ideological fantasy,[29] or, for that matter, of a textual (narrative) model in which the unconscious is represented as a *political* unconscious by characters who mediate the interaction of desire with economy or of the unconscious with ideology. In lieu of such a model, Jameson resorts to locating desire and the unconscious "outside" the text in the author Balzac. But does his reading of Balzac's novel within the framework of a psychobiography not reassert rather than undermine the authority of the individual subject—in this case the author? Instead of locating the political unconscious in the text, Jameson reconstructs Balzac's life as a phantasmatic subtext of the novels, which, in turn, are seen as impossible resolutions for the original fantasm (cf. pp. 180f.). The political unconscious is thus reduced to the unconscious or, perhaps more precisely, the unacknowledged economic desires of an individual author whose biography is used to support the textual readings.

Like Freud, Jameson works with the assumption that a text conceals some of its motivational forces. But while Freud searches for hidden libidinal fantasies in narratives of power, competition, love, and revenge, Jameson searches for economic energies behind narratives of love and passion. Freud's dynamic theory of the unconscious, however, also differs from Jameson's in that Freud provides an explanation for such a concealment in the dynamic of repression. Jameson's theory lacks such explanatory means since what Jameson calls repression is not really an unconscious dynamic but rather a conscious concealment of economic interests.

I want to end with an important qualification. I have focused my critique mainly on Jameson's conceptual framework and theoretical premises and addressed his readings only insofar as they directly reflect the latter. These readings, however, often exceed the boundaries of Jameson's theoretical schemata in very significant and productive ways. The "surplus value" of Jameson's readings over his theoretical assumptions is often generated by tensions, ambiguities, and contradictions within Jameson's own text. While these might be weaknesses on conceptual grounds, one may also read them as traces of an intellectual vitality that bursts out of the bounds of the theoretical framing. If on one level Jameson's text withholds its promise to outline a theory of the political *unconscious*, on another level it invites further attempts to pursue this project along the lines of those traces that lead beyond Jameson's frame. These traces in fact undercut or counteract what Jameson himself has called the ideology of form and testify to a current of unbound (unconscious?) energies within his own text.

The desire to envision a project that would emphasize those energies has inspired my critique of Jameson's logic of substitution. I see this logic as symptomatic for our continuing tendency to reproduce readings of literature or culture based on practices of antagonistic polarizations, exclusions, and binary oppositions. That Jameson's binary oppositions follow the all-too-familiar gendered polarities—the political versus the psychological, the public versus the private, the collective or universal versus the individual, rationality versus the unconscious—only adds to the urge to reconsider his project from a perspective that moves beyond traditional hierarchizations, polarizations, and substitutions. Such a project can take up the challenge of Jameson's interpretations by reading its own ideology of form against the grain and by using the unbound energies or the political unconscious of Jameson's own text.

Notes

1. Frederic Jameson, *The Political Unconscious: Narrative as a Socially Symbolic Act* (Ithaca: Cornell University Press, 1981). I will refer to this edition throughout my text.

2. Cf. Paul Ricoeur, *Freud and Philosophy: An Essay on Interpretation*, trans. Denis Savage (New Haven: Yale University Press, 1970).

3. Cf. Anton Ehrenzweig, *The Hidden Order of Art: A Study in the Psychology of Literary Imagination* (Berkeley and Los Angeles: University of California Press, 1967).

4. This use of Ehrenzweig would however require one to revise his concrete readings of art from a current perspective. I find Ehrenzweig's conceptual model much stronger than his interpretations of art and his conservative taste in evaluating the experimental forms of modernism. His own readings could in fact be criticized from the perspective of his own theory of the unconscious. See also Gabriele Schwab, *Entgrenzungen und Entgrenzungsmythen. Zur Subjektivitaet im modernen Roman* (Stuttgart: Franz Steiner, 1987), ch. 2, pp. 35–59.

5. Cf. the critics of the Frankfurt School in general, and especially Theodor Adorno and Max Horkheimer, *The Authoritarian Character*. More recent versions of this critique include Klaus Theweleit, *Male Fantasies*, vol. 1: *Women, Floods, Bodies, History* (Minneapolis: University of Minnesota Press, 1987), and Slavoj Zizek, *The Sublime Object of Ideology* (New York: Verso, 1989).

6. Gilles Deleuze and Felix Guattari, *Anti-Oedipus: Capitalism and Schizophrenia* (Minneapolis: University of Minnesota Press, 1983).

7. Ibid.

8. Ibid.

9. Cf. Cornel West, "Ethics and Action in Frederic Jameson's Marxist Hermeneutics," in Jonathan Arac, ed., *Postmodernism and Politics* (Minneapolis: University of Minnesota Press, 1986), p. 127.

10. Herbert Marcuse, *Eros and Civilization: A Philosophical Inquiry into Freud* (Boston: Beacon Press, 1955).

11. Ernst Bloch, *The Principle of Hope*, trans. Neville Plaice, Stephen Plaice, and Paul Knight (Cambridge: MIT Press, 1986).

12. Cf. the chapter on Conrad.

13. Cf. Jameson's reading of Balzac, to which I shall return later.

14. Cf. Fredric Jameson, "Postmodernism and Consumer Society," in Hal Foster, *The Anti-Aesthetic: Essays on Postmodern Culture* (Port Townsend, Wash.: Bay Press, 1983), pp. 111–25. In this article, Jameson in fact defends himself on this ground by arguing that a clinically accurate view of schizophrenia does not matter for his purposes. The perspective on schizophrenia, which Jameson intends to retain from Lacan, "emerges from the failure of the infant to accede fully into the realm of speech and language" (p. 118). This perspective puts Jameson "in the position of grasping schizophrenia as the breakdown of the relationship between signifiers" (p. 119), which gives the schizophrenic over to "an undifferentiated vision of the world in the present" (p. 120). Jameson is interested only in certain structural affinities between the clinical experience of the schizophrenic and the subject in consumer culture. The fact that the concrete experience of similar structures has diametrically opposed experiential qualities for the schizophrenic as it has for the postmodern subject (see p. 120) is not considered relevant by Jameson for his purposes.

15. In this context, Jameson explicitly postulates a link between Deleuze's conception of the schizophrenic text and Derridean deconstruction (see p. 53).

16. "Introduction: Beyond the Politics of Gender," in Sheyla Benhabib and Drucilla Cornell, eds., *Feminism as Critique* (Minneapolis: University of Minnesota Press, 1988), pp. 12–13.

17. Ibid.

18. Nancy Chodorow, *The Reproduction of Mothering: Psychoanalysis and the Sociology of Gender* (Berkeley and Los Angeles: University of California Press, 1978), p. 217.

19. Gayle Rubin, "The Traffic in Women: Notes on the 'Political Economy' of Sex," in Rayna Rapp Reiter, ed., *Toward an Anthropology of Women* (New York: Monthly Review Press, 1975), pp. 209f.

20. See also Cornel West's critique of Jameson's problematic use of analogy and homology in "Ethics and Action in Frederic Jameson's Marxist Hermeneutics," p. 13.

21. Jane Flax, *Thinking Fragments: Psychoanalysis, Feminism, Postmod-*

ernism in the Contemporary West (Berkeley and Los Angeles: University of California Press, 1990), p. 58.

22. Sigmund Freud, *Civilization and Its Discontents* (New York: Norton, 1961).

23. Klaus Theweleit, *Male Fantasies*, p. 213.

24. Ibid., p. 214.

25. Slavoj Zizek, *The Sublime Object of Ideology*, p. 36.

26. Dominick La Capra, "Review Essay," in *History and Theory* (February 1982), 21(1):96.

27. The unconscious overdetermination of money is a classical example that illustrates how both psychoanalysis and Marxism use a certain ethics of reading in order to understand the unconscious value of money. Even though money appears to function socially as a simple embodiment of wealth, both Marxism and psychoanalysis insist that it is also a condensed embodiment of social relations. With respect to this shift in the social value of money, see also David Harvey, *The Condition of Postmodernity. An Inquiry into the Origins of Cultural Change* (Cambridge: Blackwell, 1989), pp. 296–98. As a result money can come to embody commodities and commodity fetishism as well as social power or, on a more individual level, the power of (anal) retention or free dispensation. The ethics of reading in both Marxism and psychoanalysis works against the reification of money in social practice. Slavoj Zizek analyzes the symbolic value of money as a prime example of what he calls "ideological fantasy": "The everyday spontaneous ideology reduces money to a simple sign giving the individual possessing it a right to a certain part of the social product. So, on an everyday level, the individuals know very well that there are relations between people behind the relations between things. The problem is that in their social activity itself, in what they are *doing*, they are *acting* as if money, in its material reality, is the immediate embodiment of wealth as such. They are fetishists in practice, not in theory" (Slavoj Zizek, *The Sublime Object of Ideology*, p. 31). This insight leads Zizek to his crucial redefinition of ideology: "The fundamental level of ideology, however, is not of an illusion masking the real state of things but that of an (unconscious) fantasy structuring our social reality itself" (ibid., p. 33).

28. Even in his own critical discourse, he favors an "impersonal process, a semic transformation" (p. 127) that reminds one of Enlightenment values of scientific objectivity rather than of his own postmodern values of fluidity, openness, and the free play of signifiers.

29. Ibid., p. 44.

Freud, Sexuality, and Perversion

"One must remember that normal sexuality too depends upon a restriction in the choice of object," wrote Freud in one of his lesser-known case histories. "In general, to undertake to convert a fully developed homosexual into a heterosexual does not offer much more prospect of success than the reverse, except that for good practical reasons the latter is never attempted" ("Psychogenesis of a Case of Homosexuality in a Woman," p. 151). The observation that the "practical reasons" of psychoanalysis as a clinical (social) practice were, as they still are, often at odds with its purer theoretical reason is hardly new or, consequently, very interesting. On the other hand, to read Freud's theories as "passionate fictions," as Leo Bersani and Ulysse Dutoit suggest, is a much more interesting and newer project but a more risky and inevitably contested one. This is especially so if such a reading project is carried out in the context of feminist theory and all the more so if in the effort to articulate a theory of lesbian subjectivity.

Freudian psychoanalysis has been marked as the enemy of women more often than not throughout the history of Anglo-American feminism, undoubtedly for very good practical reasons. But, as some feminists have persistently and impressively argued, there are also very good theoretical reasons for reading and rereading Freud. What has not yet been broached is how Freudian theories of sexuality relate to the passionate fictions of lesbian desire today, in the Eurowestern "first world," and it is this gigantic task that I have set for myself in a larger project. The book, still in its early stages, is concerned with what I am tentatively calling sexual structuring. By that I mean the ways in which subjectivity, sexual identity, desire, and the sexual drives are oriented, shaped, formed, and reformed by representation, social images, discourses, and practices that make of each individual, historical being a singular psycho-socio-sexual subject.

The question of what is "normal" sexuality—the term inexorably and almost imperceptibly sliding into "normative"—has been a focal point of feminist criticism since Kate Millett's tendentiously vulgar portrait of "Freud" in *Sexual Politics*. It then quickly spread across the spectrum of feminist critical positions ranging from what may be called the anti-Freudian "right" (e.g., Millett) to the neo-Freudian "left," for whom the value of psychoanalysis is its singular "insistence not upon the regularization or normalization of sexuality but upon the constant failure of sexual identity, its instability or even its impossibility," as Mary Ann Doane says apropos of the work of Jacqueline Rose (p. 76). More accessible than Lacan, Freud has had his supporters as well as his detractors among feminists, although apparently no one can resist an occasional joke on penis envy, his maladroit association of weaving with pubic hair, or the like. By the very fact that I have used the phrase "rereading Freud," I must be counted among the supporters, according to a certain logic. Be that as it must.

My intention, however, is not to praise Freud or to bury him but literally to reread him. Yes, again. The incentive for this project came to me from writing an essay concerned with lesbian representation and (Rose and Doane notwithstanding) lesbian identity in which I was trying to sort out one of the paradoxes that, to my mind, have both constrained and moved along the development of feminist thought in the past two decades. I called it the paradox of sexual (in)difference. Because that first attempt to articulate the discursive double bind in which my thinking was caught is very relevant to what I will be proposing here, I take the liberty of quoting the first four paragraphs of that essay:

> There is a sense in which lesbian identity could be assumed, spoken, and articulated conceptually as political through feminism—and, current debates to wit, *against* feminism; in particular through and against the feminist critique of the Western discourse on love and sexuality, and therefore, to begin with, the rereading of psychoanalysis as a theory of sexuality and sexual difference. If the first feminist emphasis on sexual difference as woman's difference from man has rightly come under attack for obscuring the effects of other differences in women's psychosocial oppression, nevertheless that emphasis on sexual difference did open up a critical space—a conceptual, representational, and erotic space—in which women could address themselves to women. And in the very act of assuming and speaking from the position of subject, a woman could concurrently recognize women as subjects *and* as objects of female desire.
>
> It is in such a space, hard-won and daily threatened by social disapprobation, censure, and denial, a space of contradiction requiring constant reaffirmation and painful renegotiation, that the very notion of sexual difference could then be put into question, and its limitations be assessed, both vis-à-vis the claims of other, not strictly sexual, differences, and with regard to sexuality itself. It thus appears that "sexual difference" is the term of a conceptual paradox corresponding to what is in effect a real contradiction in women's lives: the term, at once, of a sexual *difference* (women are, or want, something different from men) and of a sexual *indifference* (women are, or want, the same as men). And it seems to me that the racist and class-biased practices legitimated in the notion of "separate but equal" reveal a very similar paradox in the liberal ideology of pluralism, where social difference is also, at the same time, social indifference.
>
> The psychoanalytic discourse on female sexuality, wrote Luce Irigaray in 1975, outlining the terms of what here I call *sexual (in)difference*, makes clear "that *the feminine occurs only within models and laws devised by male subjects*. Which implies that there are not really two sexes, but only one. A single practice and representation of the sexual" (Irigaray, *This Sex*, p. 86). Within the conceptual frame of that "sexual indifference," female desire for another female self, cannot be recognized. Irigaray continues: "That a woman might desire a woman 'like' herself, someone of the 'same' sex, that she might also have auto- and homo-sexual appetites, is simply incomprehensible" in the phallic regime of an asserted sexual difference between man and woman that is

predicated on the contrary, on a complete indifference for the "other" sex, woman's. Consequently, Freud was at a loss with his homosexual female patients, and his analyses of them were really about male homosexuality, she observes. "The object choice of the homosexual woman is [understood to be] determined by a *masculine* desire and tropism," Irigaray writes, and, I suggest, that is precisely the turn of so-called sexual difference into "sexual indifference" (the phrase first appeared in *Speculum*, p. 28), a single practice and representation of the sexual. "So there will be no female homosexuality, just a hommo-sexuality in which woman will be involved in the process of specularizing the phallus, begged to maintain the desire for the same that man has, and will ensure at the same time, elsewhere and in complementary and contradictory fashion, the perpetuation in the couple of the pole of 'matter'" (*Speculum*, pp. 101–3).

With the term *hommo-sexuality* [*hommo-sexualité*]—at times also written *hom(m)osexuality* [*hom(m)osexualité*]—Irigaray puns on the French word for man, *homme*, from the Latin *homo* (meaning "man") and the Greek *homo* (meaning "same"). In taking up her distinction between the now common-usage word *homosexuality* and Irigaray's *hommo-sexuality* or *hom(m)osexuality*, I want to remark the conceptual distance between the former term, *homosexuality*, by which I mean lesbian (or gay) sexuality, and the diacritically marked *hommo-sexuality*, which is the term of sexual indifference, the term (in fact) of heterosexuality. I want to remark both the incommensurable distance between them and the conceptual ambiguity that is conveyed by the two almost identical acoustic images.[1]

The point of the terminological distinction, as I saw it at the time, was to suggest, on the basis of my analysis of several kinds of lesbian texts, that there was no simple way of representing or even thinking lesbianism cleanly outside of the discursive-conceptual categories of heterosexuality, with its foundation in a structural difference (masculine-feminine or male-female) that for all intents and purposes sustains a social indifference to women's subjectivities. Therefore, I concluded, our current efforts at lesbian self-representation would continue to be unwittingly caught in the paradox of sexual (in)difference unless we somehow managed to separate out the two drifts of the paradox and then rethink homosexuality and hommo-sexuality at once separately *and* together. I was thus escalating the paradox into an actual logical contradiction.

It seems to me now that my effort to understand one form of sexual (in)difference (heterosexual-homosexual) from the perspective of the other (male-female) as articulated by Irigaray, was not altogether unproductive—all analogical thinking has its usefulness initially—but was inherently limited. By showing that a paradox, or a seeming contradiction, hides what is in effect an actual contradiction, I did not yet displace the terms of the contradiction, although I may have clarified them for myself. Moreover, in borrowing Irigaray's notion of homosexuality, I was dependent on a perspective that did not include the possibility of a difference between heterosexual and gay male sexualities. This further limited the conceptual horizon in which a nonheterosexual, nonhom(m)osexual, but homosexual-lesbian female sexuality might be thought.

I became more sharply aware of these limitations in reading Naomi Schor's "Dreaming Dissymmetry," a critique of what she calls "the *discourse of in-difference* or of *pure difference*" in the work of Barthes and Foucault (p. 48). Schor forcefully argues that this French poststructuralist discourse on sexual difference "shades into sexual indifference" (p. 49) in that, in discursivizing sex, it consistently desexualizes women even as it reclaims the feminine position for male sexuality or proposes a utopia of free-floating desire and sexual or gender indeterminacy (in this regard, see also Braidotti). Though not ostensively referred to Irigaray, Schor's term *in-difference* was very close to my *(in)difference*. I thought, except that she did not address directly the issue of a heterosexual-homosexual difference in her chosen authors. (But could it be a coincidence, I wondered, that she was speaking of Barthes and Foucault?) Although I did share Schor's concern with the returning marginalization of female sexuality in the philosophical, as well as the political, domain, I was struck by the ambiguity of the sexual *in-difference* she pointed to in Barthes and Foucault, an ambiguity that neither she nor they, for that matter, were willing to trace to a heterosexual-homosexual difference—which, however, it seemed to me, loomed large in the background.

Thus Schor's essay helped me to see the limitations of my own concept of *(in)difference*, particularly with regard to the equation I made between it and Irigaray's *hommo-sexuality*. For the latter concept not only underscores the exclusion, the inconceivability of lesbian sexuality (which is the point of her pun) but also forecloses the possibility to think of gay sexuality as another kind of male sexuality, one not homologous or easily assimilable to the "normal." This foreclosure may or may not have been intended on Irigaray's part, but it is not on mine. Although I shall not concern myself with questions of male sexuality, I certainly could not preclude them, nor would I wish to, in my reading of what I call Freud's negative theory of the perversions.

Freud's Negative Theory of the Perversions

If, in works such as mine and many others, today one normally encounters the phrase *"normal" sexuality* with the word "normal" between quotation marks, it is because their authors, whether they have read Freud or not, partake of a cultural and intellectual climate that follows from his work in the first decades of the century and has retained some versions of his "passionate fictions." For it was Freud who first put the quotation marks around "normal" in matters sexual. He did it at a time of general agreement on the natural (i.e., procreative) function of the sexual instinct, which was also interchangeably called "genital instinct" (Davidson, p. 47). And he did it by daring to pursue his exceptional insight—whether genius, vision, or fantasy—into what many see as a revolutionary theory of sexuality; or less romantically, if one attends to Foucault, he did it by making explicit and giving systemic (and highly dramatic) form to certain strategies of power knowledge, certain strategies of social regulation that had long been in operation in dominant European cultures and that comprise the modern "technology of sex"; namely, a "hysterization of women's bodies . . . a pedagogization of children's sex . . . a socialization of procreative behavior . . . [and] a psychiatrization of perverse pleasure" (Foucault, pp. 104–5).

These were indeed the four major themes of Freud's early work: the sexual instinct, revealed by the symptoms of hysteria and the neuroses at the join of the somatic and the mental; infantile sexuality; the Oedipus complex, with its attendant fantasies of parental seduction and the transformations of the sexual instinct at puberty; and the sexual aberrations—in short, the table of contents of the *Three Essays on the Theory of Sexuality* of 1905. While the concern with the normal in sexuality is clearly of paramount importance to Freud at this time (for instance, he closes the third essay with advice for the "Prevention of Inversion"), it is nonetheless the case that in this work the very notions of a normal psychosexual development, a normal sexual act, and thus normal sexuality are inseparable from the detailed consideration of the aberrant, deviant, or perverse manifestations and components of the sexual instinct or drive [*Trieb*].

In his 1975 introductory essay to the Harper Torchbooks paperback edition of the *Three Essays*, Steven Marcus remarks on the peculiar form of this text which, "in contrast to the grand expository sweep" of Freud's major writings, is made up of "small juxtaposed blocks of material . . . fragments that are both connected and easy to separate, manipulate, revise, or delete. They function as movable parts of a system" (p. xxi). And a systematic, coherent theory is just what Freud is proposing, Marcus argues, against Freud's own insistence that it is "out of the question" that the essays "could ever be extended into a complete 'theory of sexuality' " (preface to the third edition of 1915). Freud's disclaimer notwithstanding, Marcus persists. In spite of the fact that the explosive material of the book is to be found in the second essay on infantile sexuality, he observes, it is at the end of the first essay on the sexual aberrations where, having first disaggregated the perversions and the sexual instinct into component parts, Freud can then recompose them into the neuroses. And *that is* his theory, for, after all, Freud himself remarked that "the theory of the neuroses is psycho-analysis itself" (*Introductory Lectures*, p. 379): "In a bewilderingly brief few pages on the neuroses he has recapitulated the entire structure of the earlier part of the essay, which was, one recalls, about actually perverse sexual behavior. But the recapitulation is now on the level of the neurotic symptom, of unconscious mental life, of fantasies, ideas, and mental representations. It is, in other words, on the level of theory. . . . In the neuroses the language of sexuality begins to speak articulately, coherently, and theoretically" (pp. xxxii).

If that is so, and if "neuroses are, so to say, the negative of perversions," as Freud himself put it (7.165),[2] then his theory of sexuality is based on both representations and practices of sex that are, to a greater or lesser degree, "perverse." A few paragraphs later he actually speaks of "positive and negative perversions" (7.167), so that indeed, reading this text, one has the impression that, as Jonathan Dollimore put it, "one does not become a pervert but remains one" (p. 1). And we may recall, furthermore, that the whole of Freud's theory of the human psyche, the sexual instincts, and their vicissitudes, owes its material foundations and developments to psychoanalysis, his clinical study of the psychoneuroses; that is to say, those cases in which the mental apparatus and the instinctual drives reveal themselves in their processes and mechanisms, which are "normally" hidden or unremarkable otherwise. The normal, in all these respects, is only conceivable by approximation, more in the order of a projection than an actual state of being. If "an unbroken chain bridges the gap between the neuroses in all their manifestations and normality" (7.171), as Freud states, then the gap between pathology and nonpathology is bridged at both ends: between neuroses and normality on one side and between normality and perversions on the other. That bridge is the sexual instinct in its various vicissitudes and transformations.

Freud's own ambivalence with regard to this issue—whether a normal instinct, phylogenetically inherited, preexists its possible deviations (in psychoneurotic individuals), or whether instinctual life is but a set of transformations, some of which are then defined as normal, that is, nonpathogenic and socially desirable or admissible—is a source of continued but ultimately insoluble debate.[3] For my purposes here, I will cite the concluding section of the first of the *Three Essays*, entitled "The Sexual Aberrations," which comes shortly after the well-known analysis of neuroses and perversions as the respective negative and positive of each other. It is one of many examples, in Freud's writings, of the ambiguity, inconsistencies, uncertainties, and—in his own word—ambivalence, vis-à-vis the topic at hand, that have invited passionate interpretation and made his fictions eminently open texts.

> The conclusion now presents itself to us that there is indeed something innate lying behind the perversions but that it is something *innate in everyone*, though as a disposition it may vary in its intensity and may be increased by the influences of actual life. What is in question are the innate constitutional roots of the sexual instinct. In one class of cases (the perversions) these roots may grow into the actual vehicles of sexual activity; in others [the psychoneuroses] they may be submitted to an insufficient suppression (repression) and thus be able in a roundabout way to attract a considerable proportion of sexual energy to themselves as symptoms; while in the most favourable cases, which lie between these two extremes, they may *by means of effective restriction and other kinds of modification* bring about what is known as normal sexual life. (7.171–72; emphasis added)

Shortly before this conclusion, Freud had been summarizing his first formulation of the sexual instinct ("The concept of instinct is thus one of those lying on the frontier between the mental and the physical" [7. 168]), a concept that would occupy much of his later work; and he had introduced the term *component instincts* thus: "perhaps the sexual instinct itself may be no simple thing, but put together from components which have come apart again in the perversions" (7.162). The words "have come apart again" refer proleptically to a period in the individual's psychic life that will be the topic of the next two essays in Freud's book, infantile sexuality and its transformations at puberty under the primacy of the genital organization of the sexual instincts; it is the period prior to the onset of mental forces, such as shame and disgust, which intervene to restrain the instinct "within the limits that are regarded as normal." The argument goes as follows.

Whereas in infantile sexual life the instinct had been "predominantly auto-erotic [and] derived from a number of separate instincts and erotogenic zones, which, independently of one another, have pursued a certain sort of pleasure as their sole sexual aim," in puberty, with the appearance of "a new sexual aim," the sexual instinct becomes "subordinated to the reproductive function; it becomes, so to say, altruistic" (7.207). Then the component instincts and erotogenic zones line up and combine to attain this new sexual aim, which, Freud specifies, "in men consists in the discharge of the sexual products." But the earlier aim, the attainment of pleasure, is by no means displaced by this new aim, he adds, apparently speaking from experience: "on the contrary, the highest degree of pleasure is attached to this final act of the sexual process." For women, Freud admits, it may be otherwise; in fact, he has reason to suppose that "[the sexual development] of females actually enters upon a kind of involution" (7.207). But no more is said of women at this time, except that "the intermediate steps" of the process leading from a sexuality of component instincts to one under the aegis of seminal discharge "are still in many ways obscure . . . an unsolved riddle" (7.208). And not by coincidence, perhaps, this same word *riddle* will be the leitmotiv of the psychoanalytic inquiry into female sexuality from Dora (7.120) onward.

There is a certain discrepancy of tone, a marked change in emphasis between the two consecutive pages that close the first essay and open the second. Let me attempt to point them out and suggest a possible explanation. If normal sexual life (or "what is known as normal sexual life," as Freud carefully says in the long passage already cited) could be said to be *brought about*, to be achieved, even induced "by means of effective restriction and other kinds of modification" in the first essay on the sexual aberrations (and this was an area of research hardly new or controversial after several decades of work by sexologists like Krafft-Ebing and Havelock Ellis, on which Freud admittedly drew most of his material at the time), here, on the other hand, in the second and third essays containing Freud's own, more radical and enormously controversial hypothesis of infantile sexuality and its transformations at puberty, "normal" sexual life is taken as the premise, rather than the end result, of sexual development, and assumed to be coincident with adult, reproductive, lawful heterosexual intercourse.

In the last two essays, in other words, it is no longer a matter of bringing about the normal by effective restrictions, by channeling the component instincts and realigning the erogenous zones in the service of the one socially admissible form of sexual pleasure; there is instead the posing of an ideal norm, the normal, as the a priori, the essential kernel, the original potential and promise of sexual development, the seed that will come to maturation after puberty in "normal sexuality." It is as if heterosexuality were firmly in place from the beginning, in each newborn, as the promise and fulfilment of each component instinct. This is a far cry from the hypothesis of bisexuality offered to explain inversion and from other related statements in the first essay, such as the famous footnote addition, in 1915, that "from the point of view of psycho-analysis the exclusive sexual interest felt by men for women is also a problem that needs elucidating and is not a self-evident fact based upon an attraction that is ultimately of a chemical nature" (7.146).

To account for such discrepancy, it is not altogether unreasonable to think that in setting forth his original theory of infantile sexuality, with its component instincts and polymorphous perversity, Freud saw that the sexual instinct must be theoretically restrained, rhetorically curbed, as it were, by the emphasis on an ideal normal development that will save the theory from itself partaking of the perversions that the first essay describes. I do not mean to suggest that this latter emphasis stems from expediency or is a hypocritical and merely rhetorical strategy on Freud's part. To impute this to Freud is not only a banality on the level of Jeffrey Masson's but a failure of reading, an inability to hear the difference between hypocrisy and ambivalence. I think the two emphases more likely reflect a bona fide and structural ambivalence in his thinking, due to the logic of the argument and its heuristic premise driving it in one direction and to the drift of his ideological, emotional, and affective convictions pulling in a contrary direction. In support of this reading, which is not of much consequence in itself but will become so in the development of my argument, I will cite another and more extreme example of Freud's doctrinal inconsistency, the relation between instinct and object, painstakingly analyzed by Arnold Davidson in his reading of the *Three Essays*.

Freud's redefinition of the sexual instinct, Davidson argues, was a revolutionary in(ter)vention in the medical discourses of his time, an overturning of the "highly structured, rule-governed, conceptual space" in which "psychiatric theories of sexuality had operated since about 1870" (p. 53). Freud accomplished this in the first of the *Three Essays* "by fundamentally altering the rules of combination for concepts such as sexual instinct, sexual object, sexual aim" (p. 62) and thus subverting the conceptual foundations of the notion of perversion and, in particular, its specific configuration in inversion. In order to show that inversion was a real functional deviation of the sexual instinct, rather than merely a difference in its direction or object, "one had to conceive of the 'normal' object of the instinct as part of the very content of the instinct itself" (p. 52), Davidson writes. And indeed he demonstrates that psychiatric theories of the time unanimously assumed that a specific object and a specific aim (i.e., members of the other sex and reproductive genital intercourse, respectively) were integral or constituent parts of the sexual instinct. Freud, therefore, did not just challenge the unanimously accepted view but "decisively replaced the concept of the sexual instinct with that of a sexual drive 'in the first instance independent of is object' " (p. 54).

Here is the crucial passage from the *Three Essays*:

> It has been brought to our notice that we have been in the habit of regarding the connection between the sexual instinct and the sexual object as more intimate than it in fact is. Experience of the cases that are considered abnormal has shown us that in them the sexual instinct and the sexual object are merely soldered together—a fact which we have been in danger of overlooking in consequence of the uniformity of the normal picture, where the object appears to form part and parcel of the instinct. We are thus warned to loosen the bond that exists in our thought between instinct and object. It seems probable that the sexual instinct is in the first instance independent of its object; nor is its origin likely to be due to its object's attractions.   (7.147–48)[4]

Freud's originality, Davidson remarks, is not the introduction of a new word, *Trieb* in lieu of *Instinkt*, as other commentators have suggested, for the word *Trieb* was already used by his contemporaries, including

Krafft-Ebing; the originality consists in the theoretical rearticulation that makes Freud's *Sexualtrieb* an altogether novel concept. And one whose ultimate implications Freud himself seemed unable to grasp.

Inevitably, at this point, Davidson too is led to speculate on the reasons for Freud's inconsistent reintroduction, later in the book, of notions such as perversion and genital primacy, which, on the very strength of his argument in the first essay, have been deprived of their conceptual ground and hence must now appear vacuous or nonsensical. For example, in a brilliant piece of textual exegesis, Davidson shows how Freud simply cannot mean what he says when he appears to disagree with other medical writers only to reiterate their very argument:

> [Freud's] claim that these writers are mistaken in asserting that an innate weakness of the sexual instinct is responsible for perversion, but that their assertions would make sense "if what is meant is a constitutional weakness of one particular factor in the sexual instinct, namely the genital zone," is astonishing, since this is, of course, exactly what they meant, and had to mean, given their conception of the sexual instinct. It is Freud who cannot mean to say that the absence of this particular factor, the primacy of the genital zone, is a condition of perversion. The last sentence of this paragraph reads, "For if the genital zone is weak, this combination, which is required to take place at puberty, is bound to fail, and the strongest of the other components of sexuality will continue its activity as a perversion." But the system of concepts Freud has been working with in the first essay requires a slightly different conclusion, one whose subtle modulation from Freud's actual conclusion must be emphasized. The appropriate formulation of the conclusion should read, "For if the genital zone is weak, this combination, which often takes place at puberty, will fail, and the strongest of the other components of sexuality will continue its activity." The differences between these two formulations represent what I have been calling Freud's attitude.   (p. 61)

Being perhaps of a cast of mind more philosophical than psychoanalytic, Davidson suggests that Freud's attitude or mental habits, formed in the conceptual-scientific mentality of his own time, "never quite caught up" with the new conceptual articulations he himself produced (p. 63). This does not contradict, but rather complements, my own suggestion that one's most profound ideological and affective convictions may sometimes run counter one's most brilliant critical or analytical insights. Nor, for that matter, does it contradict Freud's own view of the subject as divided between what it says and what it means, or what it knows and what it doesn't, even as, in the latter instance, it should know better.

I have stressed the obtrusive presence of ambivalence, inconsistency, and structural ambiguity in the *Three Essays* to suggest that if they do amount to a systematic, coherent theory (as Marcus asserts) or to a restructuring of our conceptual space whereby the sexual drive can be thought quite independent of its object (as Davidson argues), then Freud's theory of sexuality is not exactly the normative and normalizing synthesis of late-Victorian views that many take it to be, or a dramatic rendering of Foucault's technology of sex; but it is rather a conception of sexuality whose structural, constitutive ambiguity has *not yet* been fully taken up in its furthest implications. To this I will return, but for the moment I also want to suggest that Freud's theory of sexuality, as set forth in the early writings and never fundamentally altered in the later ones, is much closer epistemologically to his acknowledged "discoveries" or original conceptual formulations, such as the agency of the unconscious in the mind and his topographical models of the psychic apparatus, than it is usually credited to be. In particular, I find a curious resemblance between his conception of sexuality in the *Three Essays* and the configuration of the psyche in his second model, with the triad of ego, id, and superego serving as a rough analogue for the exchanges among normality, perversion, and neurosis.

Before I go on to indulge in another bit of analogical thinking, fully aware that it may have limitations, I will offer one example of the kind of statement that has instigated my speculation. In *The Ego and the Id* Freud writes: "From the point of view of instinctual control, of morality, it may be said of the id that it is totally non-moral, of the ego that it strives to be moral, and of the super-ego that it can be super-moral and then become as cruel as only the id can be" (19.54). The mind's threefold relation to morality, which evidently concerns Freud in this 1923 text as much as it did in the *Three Essays* of 1905, reproposes the three positions of the sexual instinct vis-à-vis morality in perversion, normal sexuality, and neurosis, respectively; and even redoubles the slippage of the last term into the first: the superego here rejoins the id as neurosis rejoined perversion in its negative form there. In this perspective, Freud's theory of sexuality could be seen as a system based on three interdependent agencies or modalities of the sexual, none of which has priority status with regard to causality or temporality, and one of which,

the normal, would be defined by reference to the other two (as the ego
is by reference to id and superego), rather than vice versa.

In *The Ego and the Id*, where Freud lays out his tripartite model of
the mind, the following passage appears:

> There are two paths by which the contents of the id can penetrate into
> the ego. The one is direct, the other leads by way of the ego ideal; which
> of these two paths they take may, for some mental activities, be of deci-
> sive importance: The ego develops from perceiving instincts to control-
> ling them, from obeying instincts to inhibiting them. In this achieve-
> ment a large share is taken by the ego ideal, which indeed is partly a
> reaction-formation against the instinctual processes of the id. Psycho-
> analysis is an instrument to enable the ego to achieve a progressive con-
> quest of the id.
>
> From the other point of view, however, we see this same ego as a poor
> creature owing service to three masters and consequently menaced by
> three dangers: from the external world, from the libido of the id, and
> from the severity of the super-ego. Three kinds of anxiety correspond to
> these three dangers, since anxiety is the expression of a retreat from dan-
> ger. As a frontier-creature, the ego tries to mediate between the world
> and the id, to make the id pliable to the world and, by means of its
> muscular activity, to make the world fall in with the wishes of the
> id. . . . But since the ego's work of sublimation results in a defusion of
> the instincts and a liberation of the aggressive instincts in the super-ego,
> its struggle against the libido exposes it to the danger of maltreatment and
> death. In suffering under the attacks of the super-ego or perhaps even
> succumbing to them, the ego is meeting with a fate like that of the pro-
> tista which are destroyed by the products of decomposition that they
> themselves have created. From the economic point of view the morality
> that functions in the super-ego seems to be a similar product of
> decomposition.   (19.55–56)

In contrast with the image of the ego as a poor creature in service to
three masters, and with several other equally anthropomorphic similes
that Freud uses to draw a picture of the ego (a man on horseback, a
constitutional monarch, a politician, a submissive slave, a physician-
analyst)—in contrast with these images, the metaphor of the frontier-
creature and the comparison to the protista convey the sense of an instinctual energy, a material but nonhuman living substance, rather than
a socialized or civilized person. Moreover, the figure of the ego as a
frontier-creature is reminiscent of the formulation of the sexual instinct

as one "lying on the frontier between the mental and the physical" (7.168).

In this entire section "The Ego's Dependent Relations," the frontier image seems by far the more precise in conveying Freud's concept of the ego as "a body-ego" (19.27), a physical site of negotiations between the pressures coming from the external world, on one side, and those coming from the internal world, from the id's instinctual and narcissistic drives and from their representative, the superego, on the other. For the superego is derived from the child's Oedipal object-cathexes that have been de-eroticized and transformed into identifications: the superego derives from "the first object-cathexes of the id, from the Oedipus complex," Freud says, and thus "is always close to the id as its representative *vis-à-vis* the ego. It reaches deep down into the id and for that reason is farther from consciousness than the ego is" (19.48–49). In other words, the ego is not located between the id and the superego but is the frontier between them and the external world. The dangerous and exciting domain of the real, comprising other people, social institutions, and so forth, on one side, and an equally treacherous domain, on the other—the internal world of instinctual drives, the libido with its vicissitudes, and the death drive—make that *frontier* creature, the ego, a site of incessant material negotiations between them.

If my analogy with the triad of the *Three Essays* holds, then normal sexuality there would be in a position homologous to the position of the ego here. Normal sexuality would also be a frontier creature, or a frontier concept; not a particular sexual disposition or a mode of being of the sexual instinct itself but rather the result of particular negotiations in the process of mediation in which the subject must constantly engage—the mediation between external (social, parental, representational) pressures and the internal pressures of the sexual instinct (or the component instincts). And the latter's modalities would be perversion and neurosis, two sides of the same coin, each other's positive and negative faces, the twin modes of being of the sexual instinct. In this scenario, sexuality would not come in two varieties, "normal" and "perverse" (I omit "neurotic" since neurosis is but negative perversion, as Freud implies in the section subheaded "Reasons for the Apparent Preponderance of Perverse Sexuality in the Psychoneuroses" [7.170–71]). Instead, one can imagine the sexual instinct as being made up of various component instincts—none of which would have a *necessary* priority, since no originary relation binds the instinct(s) to a particular object—and having two modalities, positive and negative perversion, depending on the presence and degree of repression. Normal sexuality, then, would name a particular result of the process of negotiation with both the external and the internal worlds; it would designate the achievement, on the part of the subject, of the kind of sexual organization that a particular society and its institutions have decreed to be normal. And in this sense, indeed, *normal* becomes totally coextensive and synonymous with *normative*.

I may put it another way by retracing my steps so far. The theory of sexuality that emerged for me from the *Three Essays*, on first reading it, seemed to consist of two theories: one explicit and affirmative, a positive theory of normal sexuality, and the other implicit and negative, appearing as the underside or the clinical underground of the first. I thought of the latter as Freud's negative theory of the perversions. However, a closer reading of the text's conspicuous inconsistencies and self-contradictory assertions (most significant in Davidson's analysis of the relation of the sexual instinct to its object[s]) has produced another picture. It now seems to me that what I have called Freud's negative theory of the perversions—that which neither he nor his followers could propose or count as a theory of sexuality—*that* is Freud's theory of sexuality. The positive theory of normal sexuality and normal sexual development that can be read, and has indeed been read almost unanimously, in the *Three Essays* now looks to me like the imposition of a historically determined social norm on a field of instinctual drives that, as Freud's entire work and the increasing fortunes of psychoanalysis go to prove, is not passible of much development, but only of shifts, readjustments, and more or less successful negotiations with a real that is always waiting around the corner, at the frontier.

In using the terms *positive* and *negative* in reference to the two theories of sexuality that coexisted in my former reading of the *Three Essays*, I was playing with Freud's characterization of neuroses as the negative of perversions; it always struck me that, by phrasing it that way, Freud was in a sense qualifying the perversions as positive. And surely, in his case histories, the actual patients, those suffering or made dysfunctional from their symptoms, are the neurotics and the hysterics, not the perverts, most of whom would or did live as well as they could without the help of psychoanalysis—think of the protagonists of "Psychogenesis of a

Case of Homosexuality in a Woman," "A Case of Paranoia Running
Counter to the Psycho-Analytic theory of the Disease," "Leonardo," and
better still, the fetishists who, Freud writes "are quite satisfied with [their
fetish], or even praise the way in which it eases their erotic life"
(21.152). With the phrase "Freud's negative theory of the perversions" I
meant to ironize on this, by reversing his own definition of psychoanalysis as the theory of the neuroses, and troping on the high-contrast
quality (as in a photographic negative) conferred to the perversions by
the highlighting that is automatically set on the normal.

Since I made the analogy between the theories of the *Three Essays*
and the economic model of the psyche in *The Ego and the Id*, however,
I must also remark on a further resonance between my terms and
Freud's notion of a positive and a negative Oedipus complex in the latter
work (19.31–34). There, as well as in the *Three Essays*, it is the case
that the negative term, the "negative Oedipus complex," designates
what is socially inadmissible (the girl's erotic attachment to the mother,
the boy's to the father) and must therefore be transformed into identification, repressed, or sublimated, or all of the above. As for the positive
term, the "positive Oedipus complex" (the girl's refocusing of her erotic
cathexis from the mother onto the father; the boy's continued erotic,
and now phallic, attachment to the mother) designates what Freud persists in calling the normal sexual development in the face of overwhelming evidence that such a development is rarer and less likely than
it ought to be. In other words, in this case as well, at least for the girl,
the positive or the "normal" is merely an approximation, a projection,
and not a state of being. Once again the positivity of the normal is a
function of social norm.

At this point, for me, the question arises, What if I were to take up
my earlier intimation that Freud's views on sexuality in the *Three Essays*
have not yet been sufficiently considered, especially with regard to the
further implications of its structural, if not structured, ambiguity? What
if, in other words, one were to follow the path of the component instincts left visible, if darkly, in the background of the picture? What if
one set out to build a theory of sexuality along the negative trace of the
perversions—let us say, fetishism? (After all, Jacques Lacan almost did.)
Such theory might not, of course, account for the majority of people,
but then the positive theory of sexuality does not either, really; and then
again, the notion of "the majority of people" is as troubled as the notion

of "the normal"—it, too, is at best an approximation and at worst a projection (of what I myself and you, reader, are not). At any rate, a theory of sexuality based on perversion, such as I have suggested, would be just as much of a fiction—and no less passionate or even true, for those who live it, than the theory of an elusive and ever more troubled "normal" sexuality.

Notes

1. This passage, only slightly modified, may be found in my article "Sexual Indifference and Lesbian Representation," first published in *Theatre Journal* 40, no. 2 (1988): 155–7), and reprinted in Sue-Ellen Case, *Performing Feminisms: Feminist Critical Theory and Theater*, 17–39.

2. Citations giving volume as well as page numbers refer throughout this paper to *The Standard Edition of the Complete Psychological Works of Sigmund Freud*, trans. and ed. James Strachey (London: Hogarth, 1953–74).

3. For example, here is one of the more liberal readings: "It is clear that when Freud attempts to ascertain the point at which the sexual instinct emerges, this instinct (*Trieb*) appears almost as a perversion of instinct in the traditional sense (*Instinkt*)—a perversion in which the specific object and the organic purpose both vanish" (Jean Laplanche and J.-B. Pontalis, *The Language of Psychoanalysis*, trans. Donald Nicholson-Smith [New York: W. W. Norton, 1973], p. 420). At this point, however, Laplanche and Pontalis are speaking specifically of infantile sexuality. In the section just preceding, "Sexual Instinct," they write: "Psychoanalysis shows that the sexual instinct in man is closely bound up with the action of ideas or phantasies which serve to give it specific form. Only at the end of a complex and hazardous evolution is it successfully organised under the primacy of genitality, so taking on the apparently fixed and final aspect of instinct in the traditional sense" (p. 417).

4. Freud upheld this view in the much later metapsychological paper "Instincts and Their Vicissitudes": "The object [*Objekt*] of an instinct is the thing in regard to which or through which the instinct is able to achieve its aim. It is what is most variable about an instinct and *is not originally connected with it, but becomes assigned to it only in consequence of being peculiarly fitted to make satisfaction possible*" (14.122; emphasis added).

Works Cited

Bersani, Leo and Ulysse Dutoit. *The Forms of Violence: Narrative in Assyrian Art and Modern Culture*. New York: Schocken Books, 1985.

Case, Sue-Ellen. *Performing Feminisms: Feminist Critical Theory and Theater*. Baltimore: Johns Hopkins University Press, 1990.

Davidson, Arnold. "How to Do the History of Psychoanalysis: A Reading of Freud's *Three Essays on the Theory of Sexuality*." In *The Trial(s) of Psychoanalysis*, ed. Françoise Meltzer, pp. 39–64. Chicago: University of Chicago Press, 1987–88.

de Lauretis, Teresa. "Sexual Indifference and Lesbian Representation." In *Theatre Journal* 40, no. 2 (1988): 155–77.

Doane, Mary Ann. "Commentary: Post-Utopian Difference." In *Coming to Terms: Feminism, Theory, Politics*, ed. Elizabeth Weed, pp. 70–78. New York: Routledge, 1989.

Dollimore, Jonathan. "The Cultural Politics of Perversion: Augustine, Shakespeare, Freud, Foucault." In *Genders* 8 (1990): 1–16.

Foucault, Michel. *The History of Sexuality*, vol. 1: *An Introduction*. Trans. Robert Hurley. New York: Random House, 1980.

Freud, Sigmund. "A Case of Paranoia Running Counter the Psycho-analytic Theory of the Disease" (1915). In *The Standard Edition*, vol. 14, pp. 261–72.

—— "The Ego and the Id" (1923). In *The Standard Edition*, vol. 19, pp. 12–66.

—— "Instincts and Their Vicissitudes" (1915). In *The Standard Edition*, vol. 14, pp. 109–40.

—— Introductory Lectures on Psychoanalysis (1916–17). In *The Standard Edition*, vol. 16.

—— "Leonardo da Vinci and a Memory of His Childhood" (1910). In *The Standard Edition*, vol. 11, pp. 58–137.

—— "Psychogenesis of a Case of Homosexuality in a Woman" (1920). In *The Standard Edition of the Complete Psychological Works of Sigmund Freud*, 24 vols., trans. and ed. James Strachey. Vol. 18 (1955), pp. 145–72. London: Hogarth, 1953–74.

—— "Three Essays on the Theory of Sexuality" (1905). In *The Standard Edition*, vol. 7, pp. 123–245.

Irigaray, Luce. *Speculum of the Other Woman*. Trans. Gillian C. Gill. Ithaca: Cornell University Press, 1985.

—— *This Sex Which Is Not One*. Trans. Catherine Porter. Ithaca: Cornell University Press, 1985.

Laplanche, Jean and J.-B. Pontalis. *The Language of Psychoanalysis*. Trans. Donald Nicholson-Smith. New York: W. W. Norton, 1973.

Marcus, Steven. Introduction to Sigmund Freud, *Three Essays on the Theory of Sexuality*, trans. James Strachey, pp. xix–xli. New York: Basic Books, 1975.

Schor, Naomi. "Dreaming Dissymmetry: Barthes, Foucault, and Sexual Difference." In *Coming to Terms: Feminism, Theory, Politics*, ed. Elizabeth Weed, pp. 47–58. New York: Routledge, 1989.

Weed, Elizabeth, ed. *Coming to Terms: Feminism, Theory, Politics*. New York: Routledge, 1989.

S A M U E L   W E B E R

Breaching the Gap:
On Lacan's *Ethics of Psychoanalysis*

I

"Lacan is a tyrant who must be driven from our shores."[1] Perhaps the most astounding aspect of this statement—and there are obviously many—is the fact that it could be, and was made, as many of you undoubtedly know, in a front-page article of a 1991 issue of the *New York Times Book Review*. There is no time here even to attempt to analyze this text in detail, although such an analysis is obviously unavoidable and urgent. I do, however, want to insist on the fact that its publication in the *Times Book Review* undoubtedly marks a new and dangerous stage in the campaign of denigration currently being directed at American universities in general, and in particular at all those who are in any way associated with attempts to introduce approaches and curricular elements that diverge from established traditions. These attacks come, as if by coincidence, at a time when the political policies of past decades have resulted in drastically reduced federal and state funding of education as well, of course, as other social services—and above all, at a time when economic recession seems on the brink of turning into full-fledged and perhaps worldwide depression. At such times, societies are called upon to reexamine just what their priorities are in order to deter-mine—or rather, more often, to sanction—the redistribution of the re-duced resources available to them. It is difficult not to see in the article published by the *New York Times Book Review*, which follows and con-tinues a series of related although not identical statements published in the *Times* and other major organs of the press, attempts to prepare influ-ential segments of public opinion to approve or at least tolerate ever-increasing reductions in state support for higher education and, in par-ticular, higher public education. And this in turn is part of a larger and ongoing campaign to discredit all institutions whose goals are not those of maximizing profit.

It is therefore not entirely without contradiction—although it is a contradiction that belongs to the traditions of this country—that it is precisely in the name of the good of all, of the nation as a whole, that the demand is made for unsavory, alien individuals to be "driven from our shores" or, if that is not possible—for instance, both because some of these individuals are no longer living and because those that remain are not "on our shore"—then the next best thing will be to drive out all those who have anything to do with their *work* by excluding them from the shores of our academic and research institutions. The fact that such an appeal, which deliberately flaunts the decorum hitherto so dear to the *New York Times*, could be published on the front page of that news-paper's *Book Review*, strongly suggests, among other things, that the idea of such exclusions, and perhaps also the reality, have already become quite respectable.

For that is undoubtedly the distinctive function of publication in the *New York Times*. Such publication rarely initiates: it *consecrates* and also propagates. It consecrates and propagates the idea, for instance, of giving money to universities in order to support the privileged and oblig-atory status of courses in "Western Civilization," as with the gift of $25 million made by a Texas oil millionaire to his alma mater, Yale Univer-sity. It underscores the ideological specificity of the gift by reprinting excerpts of the talk given to incoming freshmen by the Yale College Dean, Donald Kagan, who warned against what he described as "the assault on Western civilization" (*New York Times* [May 4, 1991], Op-Ed section, p. 15) and called for countermeasures.

One must remember that institutionally what is at stake is not the study of Western civilization as such but rather whether or not that study should be obligatory and what its relation should be to the study of other, non-Western cultures. Why, it has been asked, should one particular civilization, grandiosely called "Western" but in fact limited by and large to Europe and North America—be accorded such a privilege?

Kagan's response is both typical and instructive. He gave three reasons. First of all, Western civilization is all that Americans have in common (except, perhaps, the interpretation of the "right to life, liberty, and happiness" as the search for personal, monetary aggrandizement—but that of course was not mentioned). Needless to say, what has been questioned is the extent to which "Americans" do share "Western civilization" in common, but it is precisely the institutionalization of this question that Dean Kagan refuses to admit.

Second, Western civilization should be privileged over other cultures because of the way "it has asserted the claims of the individual against those of the state," as if the scope of human existence, and more particularly of "the democratic, liberal society" to which Dean Kagan does not fail to appeal, could be reduced to the opposition of individual and state.

But it is only in his final summing up that the third and perhaps decisive reason is named, even if obliquely: "Western culture and institutions are the most powerful paradigm in the world." That is the reason why they have been accorded a privileged place in our universities and elsewhere and also the reason why they should continue to occupy that place, at the expense of the rest of the world. All the talk about "tolerance and respect of diversity" pales before the manner in which the bottom line is defined; "the most powerful paradigm in the world." Coming shortly after the American-inspired and -led war against Iraq, this statement has a particular ring. After all the wars that have been waged and lost—the war against poverty, the war against drugs, the war for equal rights—perhaps this is a war that can be won: the war to defend Western civilization against its competitors. Western civilization is number one, and Dean Kagan now has eleven endowed professorships to help him prove it. And you can be sure that none of them will be filled by persons tainted with the alien and debilitating viruses diagnosed by Ms. Paglia.

In the light of such increasing polemics and of the increasingly unstable economic situation to which I already have alluded, all those whose work depends upon a place within the academic institutions of this country have reason to be increasingly attentive to the strategic context and ramifications of their work. This holds particularly for those who are working to transform the traditions and practices of those institutions. For whatever else one can say, there is no doubt that there *are* very real transformations taking place, both within the university and without, and it is in response to these changes that the polemical defense of the West and its America-First variant are being mounted.

It is in this context that the text that I want to discuss takes on a particularly actual significance. Delivered as lectures in 1959–60, published officially in French in 1986, and for the past four to five years undergoing an agonizingly slow process of translation into English, *The Ethics of Psychoanalysis* addresses, directly and indirectly, many of the issues underlying the controversies that have become so evident today. This can be seen from the definition of ethics with which Lacan introduces his concluding lecture: "Ethics consists essentially . . . in a judgment upon our action, with the added qualification that [such ethics] only has weight insofar as the action implied in it entails, or is considered to entail, even implicitly, a judgment."[2] If we recall that a judgment is generally understood as the process of subsuming a particular event or phenomenon under a general concept, law, or rule, then it is to be expected that the concern with ethics will increase in proportion to the difficulties involved in bringing particulars under generals or, as Lacan puts it, more concretely, in proportion to the difficulty of finding a criterion with which to "measure" our actions. In this light, what the calls to defend the authority and unity of the Western tradition paradoxically demonstrate is not simply the absence of such a criterion—which is after all a familiar enough motif in the twentieth century—but rather the fact that under the present conditions this absence has become, once again, difficult to live with. Lacan's *Ethics of Psychoanalysis* can help us to understand why this is so and, perhaps in so doing, also help us to devise strategies of meeting the dangers such intolerance entails. This, however, is only conceivable under one decisive condition: that his writings be *read* as Lacan himself read the texts with which he worked—not simply in terms of what they appeared to mean or say but in terms of what they literally do and say; that is, in terms of a literality that tends to *resist* rather than facilitate those forms of interpretive appropriation that assimilate what is read to what is expected, to what the Constance School of Reception Theory, borrowing a phrase from Gadamer, calls "the horizon of expectation."

Lacan himself is quite clear on this matter throughout his writings but perhaps nowhere more emphatically than in his lectures on the *Ethics of Psychoanalysis*. It is no accident that reading should have been on Lacan's mind in this context, since his reflections upon ethics reserve a particular place for the *text* of Sophocles' *Antigone*. Philippe Lacoue-Labarthe, whose recently published discussion of Lacan's seminar is to my knowledge by far the most incisive reading of this work, states that Lacan necessarily encounters tragedy in general, and the tragedy of Antigone in particular, along his way toward constructing an ethics of psychoanalysis, but that in *Antigone* what he encounters is "the heroine (or the figure) and the poem. Not necessarily however the play."[3] In partial disagreement, I would add that he also and perhaps above all encounters *Antigone* as a *text*. That this text and its encounter are not without a certain theatricality I will endeavor to demonstrate later on. For the moment, however, I want only to cite a long remark made in the context of Lacan's discussion of *Antigone* but that also addresses the question of reading in general and in particular as it affects his work:

> To the extent that we are not willing to scrutinize texts as closely as possible [*vouloir serrer de près les textes*: literally, to press texts as closely as possible], so as to remain within the realm of what seems to us to be acceptable, i.e. within the realm of our prejudices, [to this extent] we miss at every instant the occasion of designating, along the paths we are taking, the limits and points of crossing. If I will have taught you here nothing other than this implacable method of commenting signifiers, it will not have been in vain, at least I hope so. I even hope that you will be left with nothing else. If what I teach turns out to have the value of a teaching, I will not leave behind any of those handles which would permit you to add the suffix *ism*. In other words, the terms that I will have pushed successively in front of you, and of which your embarrassment shows me happily that none has yet been able to appear as essential, whether it is the symbolic, the signifier or desire that is concerned—in the final analysis [these terms] will never lend themselves to any sort of intellectual conjuration [*gri-gri intellectuel*].   (p. 294)

It is only insofar as one keeps in mind just how the Lacanian concern with the signifier functions not merely at the thematic level but also as a determining factor in his style of thought—which, to be consistent with itself, is inseparable from a style of *reading and reinscription*—that Lacan's effort to demarcate his kind of "commentary" from that practiced generally in the university can be properly understood, that is, clearly demarcated from the primitive and all too traditionally "American" anti-American academism such as that of Ms. Paglia. Both have a brief against professors but for very different reasons. For Ms. Paglia "the weak, anxious academic personality" is "trapped in verbal formulas and perennially defeated by circumstance" (p. 29). For Lacan, it is precisely the openness to language—not as formula, to be sure, but as signifying process—that alone can save anyone, whether academic or other, from being entrapped by formulas and by the familiar: that is, by the clichés that Ms. Paglia, for instance, identifies with what she calls the "history of civilization."

What distinguishes the Lacanian theory and practice of *commentary*, or *reading*, is precisely its concern with the "limits and points of crossing," or concern with the problematic of *articulation*. It is this that lies at the basis of Lacan's demarcation of his practice of commentary from that commonly practiced in the university:

> In this commentary to Freud's thinking I do not proceed professorially. The general action of professors concerning the thought of those who happened to have had something to teach in the course of history consists generally of formulating it so that it appears only from its most restricted and most partial sides. Whence the impression of breathing fresh air that always comes when one turns to primary texts—by which I mean those that are worth the trouble.
>
> Descartes, Kant, Marx, Hegel and several others cannot be gone beyond [*dépassé*], insofar as they mark a direction of research, a veritable orientation. Nor can Freud be gone beyond either. There is no summing up or bottom line (where would be the interest?). They are used. One moves around within [the work; *On se déplace à l'intérieur*]. As guide, one takes what directions he has given us. What I am giving you here has been guided by Freud. In no way is it an attempt to draw a bottom line. (pp. 244–45)

Thus, what might be described as a certain antiacademism of Lacan goes hand-in-hand with the affirmation of a tradition of thought consisting above all in the confrontation with texts that have had something to teach in history, texts "that are worth the trouble" of reading, worth the trouble of a "commentary" that brings to the fore the "limits and points of crossing." And since one of the most insistent motifs of these lectures concerns the question of articulating *limits*, the *Ethics of Psychoanalysis* is inseparable from an ethics of reading. One of the things that Lacan's remarks in the passage just cited indicate is that the limits in question are not simply frontiers to be *gone beyond*: "On ne dépasse pas" Descartes, Kant, Marx, Hegel, and Freud, and other texts worth the trouble of reading; "on *se déplace à* l'intérieur," literally, one *dislocates oneself* by engaging texts that themselves are on the move, since they define themselves in terms of the "limits and points of crossing" that they involve. To breach a limit (*franchir une limite*) without simply *leaving it behind*—that is, *in nuce*, the problem that Lacan addresses in the *Ethics of Psychoanalysis* and, more precisely, or more explicitly, in his commentary of, or on, *Antigone*.[4] But before we turn to that commentary, it will undoubtedly be useful—given the fact that these lectures have not yet been made available in English—first to situate it within the general argument elaborated in Lacan's lectures.

II

Perhaps an appropriate way to begin is by recounting the joke that Lacan himself uses to indicate the terms in which the question of ethics is posed, in the wake of the disclosure of the unconscious through Freud. The anecdote concerns a German émigré to America, who, when asked, "Are you happy here?" responds: "Oh yes, I am very happy. I am really very, very happy, aber nicht glücklich." And Lacan comments:

> It did not escape Freud that happiness is for us what should be proposed as the end of every search or research [*comme terme de toute recherche*], however ethical it might be. But what is decisive, and the importance of which is not sufficiently appreciated . . . is that for this happiness, Freud tells us, there is absolutely no preparation whatsoever, either in the macrocosm or in the microcosm.
>
> This is the point that is radically new. The thought of Aristotle concerning pleasure holds that pleasure involves something that is entirely beyond question, and that [guides] the fulfillment of man insofar as what is divine in man is [precisely] that he belongs to nature [*son appartenance à la nature*].   (pp. 22–23)

What is decisive, for Lacan, and what renders necessary the effort to rethink the questions of ethics in the perspective opened by psychoanalysis, is precisely the "complete overturning [*renversement*] of perspective" (p. 23) regarding the determination of the ends of human existence and, in particular, of "happiness." Far from designating a profound accord with the universe, a harmony with nature, the modern—and in particular, Freudian reinterpretation of happiness—brings out the element of chance, of happenstance, and of happening: "Curious," remarks Lacan, "that in virtually all languages the word for happiness presents itself in terms of encounter—*tuche.*" Where there is *encounter,* however, there is separation and distance, even resistance and alterity.

To describe the shift in perspective brought about by psychoanalysis (but not only by it) in such terms, Lacan remarks, may seem "banal." And indeed, he admits having heard himself belittled for, as we would say in English, having discovered gunpowder, or as one can say in French, for having announced that "le roi est nu." Lacan's response—still in his introductory lecture—turns out to be not just amusing but to anticipate much of what is to come, in particular with regard to his reading of *Antigone:* "If I say that the king is naked, it is not entirely like the child supposed to break the universal illusion, but rather like Alphonse Allais [a boulevard comedian in the first part of the twentieth century], who caused a crowd of pedestrians to assemble by crying, in a booming voice—'It's a scandal! Look at that woman! Under her dress she's perfectly naked!' And to tell the truth [Lacan concludes] I don't say even that" (p. 23). This in turn recalls another—and, I promise, final—*mot d'esprit,* this time by Nietzsche: "They say that the female is deep, but in truth it's not even flat." These all-too-macho jokes are interesting, and indeed amusing, only insofar as they tend to turn the tables on a certain machismo: "Not even flat," not "even that" (i.e., naked beneath her dress), *not even* the *second* sex, perhaps. Not even, but perhaps a bit odd, this question of the feminine—and with it that of sexual difference, which is thus posed, at least implicitly, with respect to the traditionally sexless field of ethics, as Lacan substitutes for the king stripped bare, a very different "scandal" that a woman, nude under her dress, presents to the shocked and prying eyes of a male public. And let us not forget that Lacan himself, he says, does not say "even that."

What he does say, or rather begins by saying, is that the mainstream of Western ethical discourse, originating in Aristotle, and in particular in the *Nicomachean Ethics,* construes happiness as the natural and ultimate end of man, and thus, as the "highest good" capable of orienting and guiding human action. If by "good," then—and the word "good" and "goods" (*le bien, les biens*) will be used by Lacan to characterize the object and determining value of the ethical discourse with which the *Ethics of Psychoanalysis* will take issue—(if by "good" then) Aristotle means "that at which everything aims," or an end or target or goal of activity, then happiness, as the "highest good," will be that "which we wish for because of itself and because of which we wish for the other things." Consequently, the highest good will be that which enables man not to "choose everything because of something else, since if we do, it will go on without limit, making desire empty and futile." [5] As the highest good, then, happiness is thus construed as that which imposes a limit on desire: good is something that is chosen not "because of something else" but because of itself, and therefore it can be said to "complete and perfect" the chooser. A good is a self-identical *telos*, hence something knowable and that can orient action. And the highest good is that which determines all the others.

When, therefore, Lacan describes psychoanalysis as "the experience that has returned to favor, in the highest degree, the fecund function of desire as such," and when he further asserts that "in the theoretical articulation of Freud the genesis of the moral dimension is rooted nowhere other than in desire itself" (p. 11), this implies a radical revision of the status accorded both to "happiness" and to the category of the Good in traditional ethical discourse. If the latter, as has been suggested, is defined as the goal of an aim or of a striving, and hence is determined as an object, state, or activity that may be *reached* and attained, or at least *approached*, the Lacanian notion of desire is defined not in terms of its goal or its object but in terms of the particular kind of dynamics in which it is engaged. Such a dynamics involves not a movement understood as a change of place but rather something far less linear and straightforward. If desire is above all "desire of the Other," it can be experienced only "by some sort of crossing or *breaching*[6] of borders (*par quelque franchissement de la limite*) (p. 357). Desire, in short, has more to do with the crossing of enabling limits, whereas happiness, insofar as it is understood as the highest good, has to do with containment, contentment, and completion.

This is a major reason why from its very beginnings in Aristotle, ethical discourse founded on the good displays a penchant to see its own fulfillment as closely bound up with political science and its economy. As Aristotle emphasizes from the beginning of the *Nicomachean Ethics*, the determination of the highest good is inseparable from the question of the *polis*, since the good of the collective is "greater and more complete" (p. 1094b) than that of the individual. In this perspective, ethics, as the study of the highest good and of its relation to action, thus necessarily leads to and implies political science. Lacan's evaluation of this traditional complicity between ethics and politics is, at the very least, ambivalent. On the one hand, he concedes its inevitability, as in the case of Aristotle himself: "Aristotle's ethics—go take a closer look, it's well worth the trouble—is entirely based upon an order that is doubtless contrived, ideal, but which nevertheless responds to the politics of his time, to the structure of the polis. His ethics is the ethics of the master, made for the virtues of the master, and tied to an order of power. The order of power is not to be scorned (mine are not in the slightest anarchistic proposals); simply one must be aware of its limits in regard to the field of our investigation" (p. 363). It is here, however, that Lacan situates the problem, and the manner in which he does so recalls, in certain aspects, Heidegger's discussion of modern "technics" and in particular his apprehensions with respect to the tendency of technology to disregard and dissolve all limitation. In the case both of modern technics and of the ethics of the good, what gives cause for concern is something that might be described as a constitutive incapacity to respect limitation and, in particular, *self-limitation:* both limitation of the self, qua subject, and limitation of the self, qua discourse. And it is here that Lacan situates what for him is the determining question of ethics, particularly from the psychoanalytical perspective: the question of guilt. For, as he makes clear at the very outset of his lectures, "the ethical dimension" is constituted not essentially by prescription or by what he calls "commandment" and hence not by the "feeling of obligation" that underlies them but rather by "the feeling of guilt." For such guilt is a sequel not of acts or constraints that might be avoided or circumvented, as a certain eighteenth-century naturalism might have hoped—"the naturalistic liberation of desire has historically failed," Lacan remarks[7]—but rather of the heterogeneous structure of desire itself; that is, of the fact that desire, as the desire of the Other, is constitutively involved in a debt that can never be entirely effaced. The pressing question then becomes that of the possible responses to such indebtedness. It is in this light that Lacan's contrast of desire, on the one hand, and power, on the other, is to be read. Needless to say, the prospects as he saw them in 1960, in the midst of the cold war, were anything but encouraging; unfortunately, what has occurred since its demise has hardly brightened the horizon:

> Concerning that which is at stake here, to wit, the manner in which power relates to desire, to its array and its disarray, the position [of power], no matter of what kind, has, in every circumstance or incidence, historical or not, always been the same.
>
> What is the proclamation of Alexander arriving at Persepolis or of Hitler arriving in Paris? The preamble matters little—"I have come to

liberate you from this or that." What is essential is this: "Keep on working. Work must not stop"—which means "Let it be well understood that
this is in no way an occasion to manifest the slightest desire."

The moral of power, of the service of goods, is: "As far as desires go,
come back later. They can wait."   (p. 363)

The maxim in which traditional ethics and political economy converge
can thus be described as the injunction to "keep up the good work." And
keeping up the good work means keeping out desire—which in turn
can practically only mean seeking to efface or at least to recuperate, to
capitalize upon the limitations and alterity that, in the Lacanian perspective at least, determine desire. This is why the ethics of the good, as
in Heidegger's reading of modern technics, inevitably has totalizing,
totalitarian, and indeed "planetary" or global ambitions. Like the movement of capital described by Marx, it acknowledges limits only as new
frontiers to be overcome and gone beyond.

Hence, it would be a radical mistake to see guilt as the result of the
ethics of the good or of the political economy of good works. The ethics
of the good and its political economy exacerbate that guilt by presenting
as an answer what in fact does not so much respond to the question as
obliterate it:

> Ever since guilt has existed, one has been able to see . . . that the ques-
> tion of the good motivation, of good intentions . . . has never brought
> people any further. The question that reemerged on the horizon was
> always the same one . . . For if one ought to do things for the good, in
> practice one can never avoid asking oneself, For the good of whom? And
> from this point on, things are no longer self-evident.
>
> To do things in the name of the good, and even more in the name of
> others, has never been able to protect us not just from guilt but from all
> sorts of inner catastrophes. In particular, it does not shelter us from neu-
> rosis and from its consequences. If analysis has a meaning, desire is noth-
> ing other than what sustains the unconscious theme, the proper articu-
> lation of which is what allows us to root ourselves in a particular destiny,
> one which demands insistently that the debt be paid.   (p. 368)

Thus, desire returns to remind those who might like to forget that in the
final analysis, "there is no good other than that which can serve to pay
the price for acceding to desire" (p. 371). The question that emerges,
then, is not simply what that price is but also just what such access
entails.

And it is here that the paradoxical nature of Lacan's concluding ethical propositions emerges: for if the only thing one can be truly guilty of is to have "cédé *sur* son désir," this formulation is, in French, at the very least ambiguous. "Ceder sur son désir" can mean not just "give way on" one's desire but also to "give way *to* it." And in a certain sense, the two are difficult to distinguish, given the essential heterogeneity of desire itself. For how can one give way on a desire that is, in essence, the desire of the Other? Or rather, is not giving *way on* it also giving *way to* it? To give way to the desire of *another* is to give away desire *as one's own*. If there is a solution of such a paradox, it can only be in its "proper articulation," as Lacan puts it, of the *way* itself, which grafts the two ways *on-to* one another, making way for the double, or divided notion of *Giving way on-to one's desire*. The question of course remains: Who or what is this "one" and can it be "properly articulated," for instance, in an imperative (i.e., "Act in such a way that you do not give way on-to your desire," which would be the Kantian version of the Lacanian ethics of desire)? Or, another possibility, as a question: "Have you acted in conformity with the desire that inhabits you?" (p. 362). We will have occasion to return to this question and to the question of the imperative force of desire.

For the moment, in any case, we begin to see that the question of limits may well have to be rethought in a manner quite different from that of a simple dividing line separating two, self-contained areas, orders, or entities—those designated as "the good" and "desire." This does not mean necessarily that the two will turn out to be identical but simply that their difference may not be equivalent to that of a mutually exclusive opposition involving self-contained polarities.

With this in mind, we can now approach Lacan's reading of *Antigone*.

III

During the course of his lectures, Lacan retraces a number of decisive turning or crossing points, where the effacement of the question of desire by the ethics of the good is remarked and reinscribed so as to allow its problematical status to become legible. One of these points is in Sade, where the secularized Christian conception of an immanence of nature capable of recuperating and reappropriating its own finitude is called into question by the artifice of the absolute crime of what is called "the second death." Another and related point for Lacan is to be found in Kant—first of all, in his moral philosophy, which, in separating the moral law from intuition and cognitive experience, endows moral obligation with an "unconditional" character that is in principle independent of its possible realization. This, Lacan remarks, has the effect of anchoring moral obligation in a cognitive void, one that will turn out in the light of psychoanalysis to have been the site of desire. In the Kantian categorical imperative then, the ethics of the good is ostensibly confirmed and at the same time severely undermined. A third decisive, or indecisive, turning point for Lacan is what he calls "the function of the beautiful." And although he does not give Kant the same prominence in this connection as he does with regard to the Moral Law, the *Critique of Judgment* is still the reference text for Lacan's discussion of the "singular" and "ambiguous" relation that the beautiful entertains with desire: "On the one hand, it seems that the horizon of desire might be eliminated from the realm of the beautiful. And yet, on the other hand, it is no less manifest . . . that the beautiful has the effect of suspending, degrading, disarming, I would say, desire. The manifestation of the beautiful intimidates, prohibits desire" (p. 279). In short, although the beautiful, in Kantian language, is often said to be "disinterested" in anything pertaining to the realm of desire, it nevertheless *relates* to desire in a violent way, which Lacan here describes as its tendency to "degrade" or even "prohibit" desire. If one tries to think the relation of these two "sides" of the ambivalence to one another, one arrives, Lacan argues, at the following conclusion: "This is not to say that the beautiful cannot be joined to desire at some moment, but, very mysteriously, it is always under the form that I cannot designate better than to call it by a term that carries in itself the structure of crossing some invisible line—*outrage*. It seems, moreover, that it is of the essence of the beautiful to remain insensitive to outrage, and this is surely not one of the least significant elements of its structure" (p. 280). The "joining" of the beautiful with desire is "mysterious," not least of all because it entails "the crossing of some *invisible* line," and in this, the word "outrage" also entails an outrage performed upon beauty itself. There would be much to say about this outrage, beginning with, or rather returning to, the Third Critique. For the moment, however, let me instead limit myself to noting that all these "crossings" of the good and the beautiful with desire discussed by Lacan are anticipated by tragedy in general and by Sophocles' *Antigone* in particular: the Sadian "second death" as crime against nature subverting the "natural" opposition and even distinction of "death" and "life"; the Kantian unconditional obligation to which it is impossible to give determinate, hence cognizable, form; and finally, the conflictual encounter of beauty and desire in a movement of outrage that breaches all limits. This brings me to *Antigone*.

But what is *Antigone*? A tragedy? A piece of theater? A heroine? A figure? To be sure, it is all of these, but it is also something more, and perhaps less. *Antigone* is also, and in a certain order of things, first of all a *text*. About this Lacan leaves his listeners in no doubt: "For those of you who know Greek," he tells them, "I recommend an interlinear translation, since the 'word for word' [*le mot à mot*] is immensely instructive." In French, Lacan is even more explicit: the "word for word" of Sophocles' text is *follement instructif*, literally, "madly instructive." Could he be thinking of the poet who translated this text shortly before going mad, whose translation was condemned at the time as already showing signs of insanity? Like Lacan, Hölderlin too strove to follow Sophocles' text word for word, and I will have occasion to return to those words and to their uncompromising literality as I advance in my discussion. But for now I want to follow the Lacanian word for word, which is to say, metonymical, "commentary of signifiers" as it confronts *Antigone*—not the entire tragedy, nor even the highly selective but also highly suggestive reading of it by Lacan. Rather, I want to focus upon the encounter of this commentary with one particular, if decisive, scene of the play—a scene that is undoubtedly one of those "crossings" or turning points in which Lacan locates the determining articulations of the text. But before I come to that scene, let me once again set the scene by recalling the manner in which Lacan approaches the play. If *Antigone* constitutes for Lacan "an essential moment" and a "reference" in his examination of the ethics of psychoanalysis, it is because it demonstrates just "what is signified by an absolute choice, a choice that no good can motivate" (p. 281). Is a choice that no "good" (or object) can motivate still a *choice*? Can *Antigone* be said to "choose"? And if so, what, if this choice is not motivated by a good and hence directed at an object? I leave these questions suspended, at least for the moment.

In any case, tragedy in general, and *Antigone* in particular, thus constitutes a decisive articulation of the conflict that structures Lacan's lectures: that between an ethics of the good and one of desire. That conflict is personified in the figures of Creon and Antigone: Creon, as chief of state, acts in the name of the good of all, and hence, in the name of a law that places itself above all singularity (p. 300). In so doing, Lacan argues, he commits an "error of judgment" (*hamartia*, in Aristotle's terminology) since in "seeking to act for the good of all" he inevitably presupposes a notion of a law that would be "without limit, a sovereign law, a law which exceeds and transcends all limitation" (p. 301). Lacan comments, "Thus long before the ethical progress that, from Aristotle to Kant, will lead us to discern the ultimate identity of law and of reason, doesn't the tragic spectacle show us the primary objection? The good cannot reign over everything without there appearing an excess, the fatal consequences of which tragedy alerts us to" (p. 301). This "excess" appears, in positive form at least, in the figure of Antigone herself. Her image fascinates by its beauty but above all, Lacan stresses, by its raw inflexibility: "She is *omos* . . . which literally means something uncivilized, raw" (p. 306). Like Creon, she is defined by a certain relation to the limit, but it is here that the contrast makes their distinction clear. Creon, however, sets out firm in the conviction that he is acting in the name of the norm, of the law, of the good of all—that is, in the name of an all-inclusive, universal, self-identical principle—and therefore becomes all the more distraught and ultimately disabled, even humiliated, as the course of events exceeds the bounds of that "universality." Antigone is from the very first described as subject to a movement that will impel her *ektos atas*, across the uttermost limit of human existence. It is this limit that Lacan sees articulated in the often-repeated Greek word *atè*, a word usually translated as *malheur*, and which we might render in English as "calamity," "disaster," "mishap." But all these definitions designate the effect rather than what Lacan takes to be the essence of what the word signifies: "The word is irreplaceable. It designates the limit that human life cannot breach [*franchir*] for very long" (p. 305). Antigone knows this as well as anyone else, but she also knows that after the death of her two brothers, she cannot continue to live under the authority of Creon's law, which forbids one of them, Polyneicês, to be buried with funeral honors. For the chorus, her obstinate resistance is ferocious, raw, crude. Lacan notes that the chorus fails to understand, and comments:

> That Antigone thus exceeds the bounds of human life, what does that mean for us?—if not that her desire aims precisely at this: the beyond of *atè*. The same word, *atè*, occurs in *atrocious*. . . . One can either approach or not approach *atè*, but when one approaches it, it is because of

something bound up with a beginning and a chain, [here] that of the calamity of the family of the Labdacides. Once one has begun to approach it, things occur in a chain, cascading, and what happens to be at the bottom of such goings on, the text tells us, is a *mérimna*, which is almost the same word as *mnéme*, with the accent of *ressentiment*. But it would be very wrong to translate it thus, for ressentiment is a psychological notion, whereas mérimna is one of those words [situated] ambiguously between the subjective and the objective, terms proper to [the process of] the articulation of signifiers. The mérimna of the Labdacides is what pushes Antigone to the frontiers of the *atè*.   (pp. 306–7)[9]

The untranslatable word, *atè*, then, signifies both the enabling limit of a signifying chain and also the fact that this limit is never an absolute beginning or origin but rather itself the violation of a limit, a delimitation. Or at least this is what it signifies in the exemplary case of Antigone. The "law" under which *she* labors—and this is what distinguishes it from Creon's law of the greatest good, law of the state, the law of the Labdacides—is a law that originates in a violation of law: it is a limit whose origin is a delimitation. Limit and limitlessness, law and lawlessness are therefore not simply opposed; they overlap. Hence, to seek out this limit radically, intransigently, is not really to go beyond it, since it is already *beside itself*, in and of itself, one might say. It is this that qualifies it as the "law" of desire, although it is obviously as law of a very different kind from the law of the state and of the good, which seeks to subsume the singular under the binary logic of right versus wrong, just versus unjust. This is the argument of Creon in forbidding the burial of Polyneicês: the same honor must not be done to those who betray their country as to those who defend it. A distinction must be made, he insists, between the good and the bad, the just and the unjust, the traitors and the loyal. This is his response and rejection of Antigone's position, in the scene we are seeking to "set," with respect both to the play "itself" (and yet nothing seems less certain, in the case of this play, that there is such a single self-identical self) and to Lacan's discussion of it. It is the scene in which Antigone is brought before Creon to answer for her deed. To suggest just how divergent different translations of this text can be, here is the "same" exchange between Creon and Antigone that comes toward the end of their confrontation, first as it is rendered in the contemporary English translation of Dudley Fitts and Robert Fitzgerald and then in my own translation of Hölderlin's version:

CREON. You are alone here in that opinion.
ANTIGONE. No, they [the Thebans] are with me. But they keep their tongues in leash.
CREON. Maybe. But you are guilty and they are not.
ANTIGONE. There is no guilt in reverence for the dead.
CREON. But Eteoclês—was he not your brother too?
ANTIGONE. My brother too.
CREON. And you insult his memory?
ANTIGONE. The dead man would not say that I insult it.
CREON. He would: for you honor a traitor as much as him.
ANTIGONE. His own brother, traitor or not, and equal in blood.
CREON. He made war on his country. Etoclês defended it.
ANTIGONE. Nevertheless, there are honors due all the dead.
CREON. But not the same for the wicked as for the just.
ANTIGONE. Ah Creon, Creon
      Which of us can say what the gods hold wicked?
CREON. An enemy is an enemy, even dead.
ANTIGONE. It is my nature to join in love, not hate. [10]

And now, Hölderlin:

CREON. Are you the only one of the Thebans to see this?
ANTIGONE. They see it too, but they keep their mouths shut before you.
CREON. Aren't you ashamed to interpret them thus, uninvited?
ANTIGONE. It's an honor, rather, for people of one flesh.
CREON. And of one blood also are those who died for the country.
ANTIGONE. Of one blood, children of a single stem [*Geschlechtes*].
CREON. And nevertheless you bring the godless thanks?
ANTIGONE. The departed will certainly not concede that.
CREON. Certainly. If for you the godless and the others count as one.
ANTIGONE. Not in servant's work, yet a brother he remains.
CREON. He destroyed the country, the other stood up for it.
ANTIGONE. And yet such law the world of the dead enjoys.
CREON. But like the good the bad must not be treated.
ANTIGONE. Who knows, below there can be another custom.
CREON. Never is the enemy, even when dead, a friend.
ANTIGONE. But certainly. Not for hate, for love am I. [11]

"But certainly," one is tempted to echo—with the only certainty being perhaps that of Antigone's "who knows"—who knows; perhaps the law of the dead is of a different sort from that of the living. Perhaps the relation to death—the being-to-death often cited by Lacan in these lectures, but nowhere more insistently than in regard to Antigone—introduces a different dimension into the questions of law and ethics? In any case, now that I have at least arrived at this question, the stage is now set for me to follow Lacan, as he reads, comments, or stages the first and decisive encounter of Creon and Antigone. This is how he introduces his word-for-word, metonymical commentary of the scene: "When she explains herself before Creon about what she has done, Antigone affirms herself with an 'it's like that because it's like that,' as though she were presenting absolute individuality. In the name of what? And first of all, on what basis [*sur quel appui?*] I must cite you the text" (p. 323). As it turns out, the text that Lacan thus feels obliged to cite consists of a single sentence. But this sentence is perhaps sufficient to demonstrate just what it can mean to press texts closely (*serrer les textes de près*). After he has cited this sentence, Lacan comments on it as follows: "Naturally, one understands what she thereby means to say; but I have always insisted that it is important not to understand simply for the sake of understanding" (*je vous ai toujours dit qu'il est important de ne pas comprendre pour comprendre*) (pp. 323–24). This is the linguistic and hermeneutical consequence of Lacan's more general insistence on the fact that what distinguishes psychoanalysis is the way it breaks with the habitual and instead concerns itself with the "persistence of traumas."[12] And the reminder, never to understand "simply for the sake of understanding," is no less related to Lacan's effort to delimit psychoanalysis from what is known as cognitive science: psychoanalysis is concerned with a certain form of nonknowing, with the unconscious as the memory of what has been and, in a certain sense had to be, forgotten. Psychoanalysis pursues this goal, however, not by setting itself in opposition to science but rather by repeating it and, in so doing, bringing to the fore not just a return of the same but a return of that other that lies hidden in the ostensible identity of what is "understood." This is precisely what Antigone does in Sophocles' text when she responds to Creon by echoing his words "certainly not" (*outoi*), an echo that Hölderlin's version retains at least semantically if not literally (*Aber gewiß* / But certainly . . .). This particular echo or repetition has completely disappeared in the Fitts and Fitzgerald translation.

In any case, this is precisely the aspect of Antigone's encounter with Creon that Lacan chooses to emphasize, although not so much explicitly as in his practice of paraphrase. For as we have seen, what Lacan presents as the quintessence of Antigone's response is at best a paraphrase, not something she ever actually says in so many words. And what is more, Lacan's "word-for-word" paraphrase seems to run counter to the literal Greek text of Antigone's response, which begins with a negation: "*où gar ti moi . . .*" [Not to me namely did Zeus proclaim]. Against this denial, Lacan lets Antigone counter Creon affirmatively: she does not *contradict* his charge but rather *repeats* it, a repetition that this time comes out quite clearly in the Fitts and Fitzgerald translation:

> CREON. Tell me, tell me briefly: Had you heard my proclamation touching this matter?
> ANTIGONE. It was public. Could I help hearing it?
> CREON. And yet you dared defy the law.
> ANTIGONE.   I dared. (pp. 202–3)

But Hölderlin's Antigone is perhaps even more blatantly provocative:

> CREON. How did you dare to break such a law?
> ANTIGONE. Just because [*Darum*]. My Zeus did not report it to me [*Mein Zeus berichtete mirs nicht*].

Whether Lacan had read Hölderlin's translation I do not know; in any case, he makes no reference to it or to him. Unquestionable however is the striking affinity in the way both read Sophocles' text, as I shall have occasion to point out in a moment. In the particular passage at hand, both describe a gesture of response that does not directly counter the charge of the king but rather repeats it or at least accepts it: "*Darum*"; "*C'est comme ça parce que c'est comme ça*"—that's the way it is. In this moment, at the heart of one of the most painful tragedies, something almost like a comic moment seems to surface. This would not be entirely out of spirit with the Lacanian analysis. For however much the latter places emphasis on the affinity of the tragic dimension of human existence with the psychoanalytical perspective in general and in particular with its implications for ethical discourse, Lacan also makes it unmistakably clear in his concluding lecture that this perspective also includes an irreducibly comical dimension:

> I have invited you this year to enter into a mental experience, *experimentum mentis* as Galileo says—contrary to what you believe, he had much more mental experience than those in the laboratory, without which he in any case would certainly never have taken the decisive step. The *experimentum mentis* that I have proposed to you this year . . . consists in

taking . . . , as standard for the revision of ethics to which psychoanalysis leads us, the relation of action to the desire that inhabits it.

In order to make you understand, I took the support of tragedy, a reference that is inevitable . . . The ethics of psychoanalysis is not a speculation bearing upon the organization, arrangement, or what I call the servicing of goods. It implies, properly speaking, a dimension that is expressed in what is called the tragic experience of life.

It is in the tragic dimension that actions are inscribed and that we are summoned to orient ourselves as to values. It is equally and no less in the comic dimension, and when I began to speak to you of the formations of the unconscious, it is, as you know, the comic that I had on the horizon.

Let us say as a rough approximation that the relation of action to the desire that inhabits it in the tragic dimension operates in the direction of a triumph of death [or rather] a triumph of being-toward-death [that is . . .] the negation identical with the entry of the subject supported by the signifier. This is the fundamental character of all tragic action.

In the comic dimension, at first sight, what is involved is, if not triumph, then at least the futile or ridiculous game of vision. . . . And it also involves a relation of action to desire and its fundamental failure to join up with it.   (pp. 361–62)

This "fundamental failure" Lacan identifies with the "presence" at the center of the comic of that "hidden signifier," which, however, "in ancient comedy was there in person: the phallus." The presence of the phallus, whether it is directly represented or hidden, results not so much in "a triumph of life as in its breakaway or escapade [*échappée*], the fact that life slips, slithers, flees, escapes from everything that is opposed to it as barrier, and precisely from the most essential, those constituted by the instance of the signifier" (p. 362). It is clear that one of the things Lacan is thinking of here is Freud's discussion of jokes, and he emphasizes the distance that separates the comic "slippage" of life from the tragic being-toward-death: in comedy, "life goes on, triumphs all the same." And yet, notwithstanding this enormous difference between the tragic and the comic, Lacan comes to the rather surprising although, from the analytical point of view that is his, also necessary conclusion that "they are not incompatible, since the tragic-comic exists." And it is the existence of this hybrid that enables the psychoanalytical perspective to arrive at its decisive insight in the realm of ethics, which Lacan, not without a certain irony, refers to as the Last Judgment:

It is there [in the tragic-comic] that the experience of human action lies, and it is because we are better able than those who preceded us to recognize the nature of the desire that is at the heart of this experience, that an ethical revision is possible which represents this question with the value of the Last Judgment: "Have you acted in conformity with the desire that inhabits you? It is not a question easy to support or defend [*facile à soutenir*]. I would argue that it has never been posed before with such purity and that it cannot be outside of the analytical context.   (p. 362)

However this claim may sound today, it necessitates at least two comments. First of all, we should not forget that it is once again not entirely without paradox that Lacan would vaunt the "purity" with which a question is posed that precisely concerns a certain impurity or contamination or at least combination: that of the tragic and the comic. (The question must be raised, at least parenthetically, whether or in what sense this "Last Judgment" can still be considered to be a judgment at all, insofar as the notion of "acting in conformity with one's desire" is anything but self-evident. I shall return to this question shortly.) Second, let us also remember that, as he himself acknowledges, Lacan's theory of the comic and of its relation to the tragic is, at best, preliminary. This can be seen in certain vacillations when he calls the "tragic experience of life" (echoing Unamuno) first "the triumph of death," which he then corrects to "the triumph of being-toward-death." As Heidegger's term (cited without attribution here, as often elsewhere in Lacan's lectures—and their relation to Heidegger's thought remains one of the many open questions I can just touch on here, but not explore) suggests, "being-toward-death" is very different from "the triumph of death" or from anything purporting to concern "death *itself*." What Lacan's affirmation of the factual existence of tragicomedy indicates, however, is also what his discussion of Antigone almost against its own will allows us to conceive: that "the futile game of vision" and the various slips and slides of comedy may not be as entirely foreign to the tragic as a certain pathos of negativity in Lacan's account might lead us to believe.

This brings me back to his commentary, or staging, of Antigone's encounter with Creon. Antigone, in this staging, defies Creon, not by claiming to have law on her side, or even claiming with any certitude that she is *right*, but rather in a very different manner. Here is how Lacan portrays it and how in the process he cites one line of the text word for word: "She says it very clearly—You, you have made laws. And there again one misses the meaning. To translate word or word—*For in no way was Zeus the one who proclaimed these things to me.* Naturally, one understands what she means to say, and I have always told you that it is important not to understand for the sake of understanding" (pp. 323–24). The implication here is clear: the reader, or listener, or spectator, would like nothing better than to have Antigone respond to Creon by calling his right into question, by challenging his authority directly. One would be more comfortable, more secure, if she were to make a direct counterassertion, such as "It wasn't Zeus who gave you the right to promulgate that law."[13] "But," Lacan insists, "that is not what she says." What distinguishes Antigone's discourse from that of Creon, according to Lacan, is the fact that she does not claim *to speak in the name* of any positive law, be it that of heaven or of earth, of gods or of humans. In distinction to Creon, Antigone does not speak in the name of law so much as she speaks in the name of its enabling *limits*, which at once appear to be those of lawfulness itself. Commenting on the Greek word *ôrizon*, used by Antigone to delimit the scope of human law, Lacan notes that "it is precisely the image of the horizon, the limit. What is at stake is nothing other than a limit upon which she camps, and on which she feels herself unassailable, and beyond which no mortal can ever pass. The laws, *nómma*, [of which she speaks] are not the laws, *nómos*, but rather a certain legality [or lawfulness], consequence of those [unwritten] laws . . . of the gods. What is evoked here is that which is indeed of the order of law but which is not developed in any signifying chain, in nothing [*dans rien*]" (p. 324). Antigone thus is described—in a commentary that is clearly anything but simply subservient to the explicit words of the text (but how could a commentary of *signifiers* take words at their face value?)—as "camping" out at the most extreme limits of human existence, in order to mark it precisely as a limit, as a horizon that as such cannot be inscribed "in any signifying chain" as Lacan puts it but that allows signification and law and order to take place. Antigone, in short, camps out on the breach.

If Lacan thus began his discussion, and above all his peculiar "citation," of Antigone's response to Creon in an effort to respond to the question "In the name of what?" (*Au nom de quoi?*), "and above all, with what support, on what basis" (*Et d'abord, sur quel appui?*) (p. 323), she was able to affirm her position, what his recounting of that position brings to the fore is precisely that it is grounded in nothing other than the breach itself, that is, in the relation to an alterity that turns out to be the enabling condition of significant articulation and hence of discourse itself. Whether such a grounding and its disclosure is essentially tragic, or comic, or both—tragic-comic—remains an open question. What is certain, however, is that any attempt to respond to it will have to follow very closely what it means to speak in the name of a certain breach; how this relates to language in general, and to the intransigent discourse, and then silence, of Antigone in particular. Lacan compares her intransigence in certain respects to what he elsewhere calls the "insistence" of the signifier, and he explains this relation in part as follows:

> From the moment on, where words and language and the signifier enter into play, something can be said, which says itself thus: My brother is everything you want, a criminal, he sought to ruin the walls of the fatherland, lead his compatriots into slavery; he led enemies onto the territory of the city, but finally, he is what he is, and what counts is to render him the honors of a funeral. Doubtless he does not have the same right as the other one; you can tell me whatever you want along these lines, that the one is a hero and a friend, that the other is an enemy, but I, for my part, answer that it makes little difference that this doesn't have the same value down here. For me, this order that you dare to impose upon me counts for nothing, because as far as I am concerned, anyway, my brother is my brother.   (p. 324)

Later in the play, Antigone, in a passage that will shock many readers for its apparent coldness and calculating character, explains that the loss of her brother is worse than that of a child because a child can be replaced—but a brother, once the parents are gone, cannot. Lacan underscores this passage precisely because of the fact that, far from defining the relation to her dead brother in terms of his individuality, the latter is determined by its position in a signifying chain. "The unique value of his being," Lacan observes, "is essentially [a fact] of language" (p. 325). The question is, however, just how language works to determine this position: "Antigone does not evoke any right other than that the . . . ineffaceable character of what is—ineffaceable from the moment on, when the signifier that emerges arrests it as a thing fixed through the flood of all possible transformations. What is, is—and it is to this surface that the unbreakable, inviolable position of Antigone affixes itself" (pp. 324–25). If Antigone could thus be characterized, in this perspective, as "unbreakable" in the "breach," what remains to be demonstrated is, first of all, how such inflexibility and fixation take place in and through language, and second, whether its "ineffaceabil-ity" is to be understood simply as the opposite of effacement, or, more paradoxically, its complement—its tragic-comic complement, one would be tempted to add.

For it is not just any signifier that is capable of arresting the move-ment of signification and fixing it unchanged "through the flood of all possible transformations." And, in fact, it turns out that it is only a par-ticular kind of signifier that is capable of performing this feat: "One cannot dispose of someone who is a man [*un homme*] as though he were a dog. One cannot dispose of his remains while forgetting that the order of being of someone who could have been situated by a name ought to be preserved by the act of a funeral" (p. 325). (In passing, I wonder whether the fact that "dogs" can have names would not entitle "man's best friends" to similar funereal rights as are here accorded human beings? But even more, I wonder by what right the right of burial should be limited to the recognition of a "name" in a language recognizable to human beings? And granting all this, would such a name have to be a proper name? If the name were not proper but generic—let us say, "chimpanzee," for instance—would this "situate" the named suffi-ciently so as to merit the right to a funeral? Is the being-toward-death of animals, improperly or generically named, insufficient to "situate" them? And should such a situation be the privileged access to a tomb? These are questions that are at least implicitly raised, if not answered, by the *Ethics of Psychoanalysis*.)

What its discussion of Antigone does demonstrate, however, is that she is only able to "camp" at the limits of human existence insofar as she can name the finitude of that existence in its singularity, in its uniqueness, in its irreplaceability—but it also shows that this naming is, in a very real sense, improper. She does not invoke Polynicês by his proper name when speaking with Creon but does so rather by his posi-tion in the family chain—a position that is both general, that of *a* brother, and specific, that of *my* brother. Such a brother is paradoxically both *interchangeable* and *irreplaceable*. And the same holds for the "I," whose brother he was and is. For this "I" is no less split or riven than its brother, as a play of pronouns at the beginning of the play demonstrates. Lacan does not comment on it, but it is palpable in the word-to-word, syntactically literal translation of Hölderlin, who lets Antigone report and repeat the proclamation of her uncle as follows:

Of Polynicês body they say, that
It has been proclaimed in the city, that it
Shall be sheltered in no grave and not mourned.
It shall be left unwept for and without grave,
A sweet meal for birds, out for a good bite
This, they say, is what good Creon announced
To you and also to me, for me too, I mean . . .

The last two lines of Hölderlin's German almost defy translation insofar as they seek to render the wordplay of Sophocles' Greek—*kàmoi, légo gar kàme* [to me, I believe, for to me as well was this announced]."[14] Lacan in his lectures notes a related phenomenon when he recalls that the French word, *même* [same], etymologically develops from the Latin *metipsemus*, out of what might be called a lexical redundancy. Lacan interprets this as a linguistic indication of the fact that it is a certain repetition, an "excess" of identity—a *plus moi-même de moi-même*— that lies at the origin of the self (p. 233). In this redundant, excessive return, the "I" arrives, or "comes to," inevitably too late. The "news from home" it receives comes from a home it can never inhabit and yet never leave behind either. This is precisely the position of Antigone, receiving the terrible news: "And me, for I too, I mean, am meant by this message" (*Und mir, denn mich auch, meine ich, kund gethan*). It is perhaps no mere accident that it is the figure of a woman that emerges in this repetition, as what we call "the first person," almost plural and yet still highly singular, a person—or *persona*—who would be capable of receiving and relaying the message of the other, of the ethics of psychoanalysis. It is a message on the border of redundancy and yet challenges the logic of identity by eschewing a discourse of imperatives and prescriptives, which might turn out to be more tragic-comic than tragic. For the message that Antigone receives comes, first of all, from Creon, the head of the state, figure of the good, in Lacan's terminology. Does this suggest that the ethics of psychoanalysis, with its maxim of desire, is necessarily dependent upon precisely the Good to which Lacan seeks to oppose it? And that the "Other" of desire—as desire *of* the Other— would turn out to be precisely the good, the state, and all the rest? In that case, indeed, the tragic pathos of the injunction not to "give way on/to your desire" would indeed acquire a comic note. And we might begin to understand just why, at the conclusion of his *Ethics*, Lacan leaves us not with this imperative form of the command but with the twice-repeated statement that "the only thing one can be guilty of is to have given way on/to one's desire" (pp. 368, 370). The "Last Judgment" would be not a command or an interdiction but a statement that "that's the way it is." Would this still be an *ethics*? An ethics without imperatives? And if so, where would it leave us?

Perhaps in the same place that we are left at the end of *Antigone itself*, when the chorus gives us its "last judgment." This is how it is rendered by Hölderlin:

> Um vieles ist das Denken mehr, denn
> Glükseeligkeit. Man muß, was Himmlischer ist, nicht
> Entheiligen. Große Blike aber
> Große Streiche der hohen Schultern
> Vergeltend,
> Sie haben im Alter gelehrt, zu denken.
>
> (vol. 5, pp. 405–7, lines 1397–1402)

I translate:

> Thinking is by far more than
> Happiness. What is heavenly must not be
> Desecrated. Great glances however
> Great blows [fall] on high shoulders
> Paying back,
> They have, in aging, taught to think.

Notes

1. Camille Paglia, "Ninnies, Pedants, Tyrants, and Other Academis," in *New York Times Book Review*, May 5, 1991, p. 33.

2. Jacques Lacan. *L'ethique de la psychoanalyse: Le Seminaire VII* (Paris: Seuil, 1986), p. 359.

3. Philippe Lacoue-Labarthe, "De l'éthique: à propos d-Antigone," in *Lacan avec les philosophes* (Paris: Albin Michel, 1991), p. 23.

4. It is also the result of Heidegger's reading of the first ode of the chorus in *Antigone*, in the *Introduction to Metaphysics* (1935), and expanded in his lectures on Hölderlin's poem *Der Ister*, which constituted his seminar in the summer of 1942 (cf. *Hölderlins Hymne "Der Ister,"* in the *Gesamtausgabe* (Frankfurt am Main: Klostermann, 1982), vol. 53, pp. 69–152). In the Introduction Heidegger interprets the chorus as defining the *Dasein* of historical man as a "breach" (*eine Bresch*) "into which the overwhelming power of being bursts in

its appearing, in order that this breach itself should shatter against being. The Lacanian emphasis upon the notion of *franchissement* must be read against the background of Heidegger's discussion of the breach (a discussion that Heidegger could easily have known and probably did, since it had been published in a French translation several years earlier). The significant differences between the Heideggerian and the Lacanian readings of *Antigone* occur not so much at the level of theme or statement—although Heidegger's emphasis on ontological difference and on Being causes him to reject any reading of *Antigone* that, as Lacan will do, interprets its decisive articulations dependent in terms of "familial blood relations" (Heidegger), since the latter pertains not to Being but to entities, *Seienden* (cf. *Der Ister*, p. 144), as in the manner of reading the text itself, i.e., as *énonciation* rather than as *énoncé*.

5. Aristotle, *Nicomachean Ethics*, trans. Terence Irwin (Indianapolis: Hackett, 1985), section 1094a. pp. 1–2.

6. Heidegger, in his discussion of the first chorus from *Antigone* (polla ta deina . . .) in *The Introduction to Metaphysics*, sees man defined in terms of a "breach" (*eine Bresche*), and Lacan's emphasis on the *franchissement des limites* is very much in this spirit. Although Lacan nowhere refers specifically to this text of Heidegger's in his lectures, they could not follow its spirit and letter more closely in this respect.

7. "A certain philosophy, in the eighteenth century, had as its aim what could be called the naturalist liberation [*affranchissement*] of desire. One can characterize this reflection, this time entirely practical [in spirit], as that of the man of pleasure. Well, the naturalist liberation of desire has failed. The more the theory, the more the work of social criticism, the more the filter of an experience tending to trace obligation back to precise functions in the social order, called up the hope of relativizing the imperative, constraining, indeed conflictual character of moral experience, the more we have seen accumulate, in fact, authentically pathological incidences of this experience. The naturalist liberation of desire has historically failed. We do not find ourselves before a humanity less weighed down with laws than before the great critical experience of the thought called libertine" (p. 12).

8. "Word for word," *mot à mot*, is of course Lacan's formula for metonymy, the "properly signifying function" as he puts it in *L'instance de la lettre ou la raison depuis Freud, Ecrits* (Paris: Seuil, 1966), pp. 505–7.

9. It should be noted in passing, at least, that this emphasis on memory or *mérimna* should not be interpreted in a historical manner, according to Lacan. What is involved is the constitution of signifying processes, which require a certain concatenation of signifiers in order to operate but that operate according to laws that are not genetical or teleological but rather, as Lacan states, "synchronic": "Antigone, in face of Creon, situates herself as synchrony opposed to diachrony" (p. 331). See also p. 308: "One says—tragedy is an action. Is it

agein? Is it *prattein?* One has to choose. The signifier introduces two orders in the world, truth and event. . . . In tragedy, generally speaking, there is no sort of veritable event. The hero and what surrounds him are situated with respect to the point aimed at by desire. What happens are collapses, accumulations of different levels of the hero's presence in time." The "question of temporality" is thus described as "decisive, essential" but only when understood as concerning "the manner in which threads that are already prepared converge."

10. *Sophocles: The Oedipus Cycle*, trans. Dudley Fitts and Robert Fitzgerald (New York: Harcourt Brace), pp. 205–6.

11. Translated from Friedrich Hölderlin, *Sämtliche Werke* (Frankfurt: Roter Stern, 1988), vol. 16, pp. 315–17.

12. *L'ethique de la psychanalyse,* p. 323–24.

13. This is, in fact, how Heidegger translates the passage in his 1942 discussion of the text: *"Nicht nämlich irgend Zeus wars, der mir geboten dies, / noch auch, die heimisch bei den unteren Göttern, Dike / wars, die unter Menschen setzten dies Gesetz"* (p. 145).

14. In German: *"So etwas, sagt man, hat der gute Kreon dir / Und mir, denn mich auch mein' ich, kund gethan"* (vol. 1, p. 267, lines 33–34).

Community After Devastation:
Culture, Politics, and the
"Public Space"

All post-Auschwitz culture, including its urgent critique, is garbage. In restoring itself after the things that
happened without resistance in its own countryside, culture has turned entirely into the ideology it had been
potentially. . . . Whoever pleads for the maintenance of
this radically culpable and shabby culture becomes its
accomplice, while the man who says no to culture is
directly furthering the barbarism which our culture
showed itself to be.
—Theodor Adorno, *Negative Dialectics*

I

It is not simply by chance or due to a superficial, surface change in
intellectual fashion that there has been a widespread renewal of interest
in recent years in the Shoah as well as in the origins and growth of
fascism throughout Europe. I would argue that such interest is due, first
of all, at least in part to the difficulty we have in understanding the
attraction of extreme forms of nationalism, of fascism, and even of National Socialism and anti-Semitism to a such a wide and diversified
public, one that certainly included major writers, artists, and intellectuals. Second, it is also due to the number of fundamental and as-yet
unanswered questions about politics in modernity this attraction continues to raise for us today. Certainly one of the most obvious questions
it raises is whether the so-called postindustrial, postmodern, hyperreal
age of information in which we supposedly live is not also and more
fundamentally still an age "after devastation," an age that has not and
perhaps, as I shall argue, should not ever put the devastation it has

produced and lived through simply behind it—an age that, no matter how it is characterized, must understand that it also carries within it the potential for its own form of devastation.

To begin to address questions such as these, I turn first to the work of Hannah Arendt, a thinker who is decidedly out of fashion today and who may seem to most to be much too traditional and abstractly philosophical in her approach to political questions to be of much interest in an infinitely more complex, postmodern, computer-based, and simulacrum-defined world. And yet, in terms of the phenomenon of the renewed interest in fascism, Nazism, and the Shoah that I have just described, it seems to me absolutely essential that a reconsideration of Arendt's work play an important part in the general reevaluation of totalitarianism. For it could be argued that no important political theorist of the postwar period was marked more by the horror of political devastation than she and that no one has done a better job analyzing the modern political phenomenon of totalitarianism and its effects on the way we conceive of the possibilities and limitations of the political in general. Whatever the limitations of her work, I would argue that she is one of the figures from the recent past that it would be a mistake to continue to ignore or take too lightly, precisely because of the way her work continues to remind us of fundamental questions concerning the political that have been forgotten in our haste to keep up with, analyze and explain, and finally justify the informational, technological, and media transformations, which appear from a certain perspective to dominate and define contemporary life and politics, and thus render all questions not defined in the terms they dictate irrelevant.

In her preface to the first edition of *Totalitarianism* (New York: Harcourt Brace Jovanovich, 1973), which was first published in 1950, Arendt acknowledges that even though her own goal is to write against both "reckless optimism and reckless despair," which are in fact "two sides of the same medal" and both "articles of superstition," she senses in the work of many of her contemporaries an understandable feeling of the inadequacy of historical and political thought to measure up to the horror of the recent past. What was once taken for granted—the ability of culture and civilization to avoid, or, if not, to respond to, make amends for, and overcome even the most hideous crimes and injustices—she asserts can no longer be assumed: "On the level of historical insight and political thought there prevails an ill-defined, general agreement that the essential structure of all civilizations is at the breaking point. Although it may seem better preserved in some parts of the world than in others, it can nowhere provide the guidance to the possibilities of the century, or an adequate response to its horrors" (p. vii). The terror of Nazism (and Stalinist communism) was of such an unimaginable, radical, total nature, Arendt implies, that the very foundations of the political sphere were shaken, if not irreparably damaged, and that in a period after devastation neither culture, politics, nor history can be taken for granted anymore, for no moral code, historical schema, or political doctrine can in fact provide guidance for the century or respond adequately to its horrors. After devastation, that is, so long as the horror of the recent past is seen as something more than a momentary and irrational aberration from the rational, evolutionary or dialectical course of history, we are all in the position of not being able to take "progress" for granted anymore. We are not necessarily without guidance or direction but severely limited in our attempts to account for or respond to the horror of the past and establish a future radically different from it.

But what could be called Arendt's critical pessimism concerning "politics" cannot be considered only as an effect of her sensitivity to and study of the injustices and horror of what in her later work she called the "banality of evil." Her pessimism also has to do with the perception that what she refers to as the "public space" is never public and open enough but always menaced by social, political, economic, and cultural forces that act to mold and reduce this space in order better to define it in terms of particular practical needs and specific functional ends. Totalitarianism is the total mobilization of all these forces for the same idea or end, but even outside of this extreme situation, where it is in danger of being destroyed, the public space is constantly being threatened and reduced. The reduction and control of the public space affects both politics and art in similar ways: it makes each a *product* of whatever historical, economic-political or cultural factors determine (or are thought to determine) society in general, an expression of what those participating in the public space decide they share in common and what gives this space its form and identity.

If Enlightenment values have frequently been radically questioned by a wide rage of recent theorists,[1] there is no general agreement (nor should there be) over what could replace them as political ideals or even how a critical sense of the political can be articulated without such ideals. Unlike many conservatives and traditionalists who also bemoan the so-called decline of culture and values in mass society, Arendt does not attribute the "lack of standards" or the "capacity for consumption accompanied by inability to judge, or even to distinguish" to "mass man" alone.[2] For her, "all these traits first appeared in good society, where there was no question of masses, numerically speaking."[3] Her "pessimism," then, concerns not just contemporary, postindustrial, mass society but society in general, in both its modern (or postmodern) and traditional forms. It is a form of "pessimism" that is not motivated by the usual nostalgia for a preindustrial past free of all modern forms of the corruption of judgment and values, or by the utopian desire for a postindustrial future, which would transcend the political and cultural inadequacies and injustices of modernity. For her, the threat to culture and thus to critical judgment in general is—and, one could say, will always be—constant. Throughout Western history, it has taken many forms, from the "philistinism of good society" (that is, traditional society)—including, we should add, the reactionary contemporary nostalgia for a world in which Western (read American) values dominate and are considered integral and absolute—to the consumption of culture as entertainment in the modern world. Culture, therefore, has always been menaced by either the threat of conservative, if not reactionary aestheticism, on the one hand, or, on the other, by what Arendt calls functionalism and what could be called in the present context the politicization of the arts—so long as politicization is seen both as the direct determination of culture by political ideologies and ideologically driven groups, parties, or state apparatuses, and as the determination and severe limitation of culture to so-called neutral, universal principles or values. One should naturally expect this threat to continue to take other forms in the future.

If, in Arendt's sense, the place of culture is increasingly being reduced in modern society, that is, more and more determined by the marketplace and consumer values and thus constantly at great risk, it follows that one would be right to be cautious about its impact. At the same time, were the place of culture to be inflated and projected as an ideal or model of either "refined behavior" and taste, as it was in certain forms of traditional society, or as a meta- or apolitical, transcendent ideal, as it still is in certain traditionalist, aestheticist approaches, then one would have to be equally critical of its place. A certain dose of pessimism seems necessary for the critical evaluation of culture, for the place of culture always appears to be too reduced or too inflated, culture itself, either massively determined by sociohistorical needs and concerns or excessively determining as concerns social ideals, behavior, and values. In other words, culture, for Arendt, never seems to find its proper place in relation to society as a whole; and I would add that it may even be important that it not have such a place or even aspire to have one. In other words, the public space of culture should never be *a place*.

If, in Arendt's view, society has always in some sense been at odds with culture and culture with society, this mutual antagonism should itself be taken not as something to be overcome but rather as a sign of the potential critical force of art. Her pessimism concerning the place of the arts in society is thus countered by a certain optimism about the critical potential of the antagonism between society and culture.[4] For Arendt, mass society's desire for entertainment rather than culture is not itself a threat to art, for, as she says, the entertainment industry "produces its own consumer goods" and "we can no more reproach it for the nondurability of its articles than we can reproach a bakery because it produces goods which, if they are not to spoil, must be consumed as soon as they are made" (p. 206). In such a situation, the arts and sciences, "goods" produced by other means and in order to endure, could even flourish on their own, in some sense protected or at least set aside from the products of the "fast-food" entertainment industry, which provides an overabundance of consumer goods and thus fulfills all society's consumer (or consumptive) needs.[5]

The real danger to culture, then, is not the mere existence of popular entertainment and the mass media but rather that the latter will stimulate consumers' appetite for junk food rather than satisfy it, that "the life process of society (which like all biological processes insatiably draws everything available into the cycle of its metabolism) will literally consume the cultural objects, eat them up and destroy them" (p. 207). The endurance of the arts thus depends on consumption being confined to its own sphere and on cultural goods continuing to be "deliberately removed from the processes of consumption and usage and isolated against the sphere of human life necessities" (p. 209). Something else besides consumption, then, has to exist within consumer society to counter its insatiable desire to consume. The public space, for Arendt then, unlike the marketplace or the stock exchange—or Disneyland, for those who find it an appropriate metaphor for contemporary society—is a space that must be set aside and protected from speculation and the consumption of the entertainment industry, because it has other ends and purposes than those of the marketplace. For Arendt then, the public space necessary for culture marks the limits of consumerism and indicates the possibility of a world not free of consumption but not totally determined by it either. Culture is the critical counterforce to the hegemony of the marketplace, the possibility of alternative forms of exchange and production that are meant to endure insomuch as they have a purpose and function outside of the space(s) and time(s) in which they are produced (and bought and sold).

For if there were no longer to be any counterforce to consumption, then society, in Arendt's view, would in fact be reduced to a state of ruins: "The point is that a consumer's society cannot possibly know how to take care of the world and the things which belong exclusively to the space of worldly appearances, because its central attitude toward all objects, the attitude of consumption, spells ruin to everything it touches" (p. 211). The question remains as to what exactly would be lost if such a state of absolute consumption were ever achieved or approximated—assuming that it has not already been achieved in a world of junk food, and, if I may extend the metaphor, junk politics. The answer Arendt gives is that we would not just be in a state of ruin as concerns art, that is, totally indifferent to art as such and treating it as just one more object to be consumed, just another investment to be bought and sold in the hopes of making as large a profit as possible. For with this particular form of the end or destruction of art, we would also find ourselves in a state of ruin and indifference as concerns critical judgment and politics. In other words, the end of art would also bring about the end of the political, at least in any critical sense, that is, the end of the resistance to the specific politics of the state or the dominant political party or parties as well as to consumerism and the reduction of all aspects of life to entertainment (to hyperreality?).

It seems clear that, for Arendt, the Greeks in some sense best understood that art and politics are interrelated through conflict and that neither can be accounted for in purely functionalist (in the modern period, consumer or even informational) terms. Art and politics both in fact benefit from the conflict between them, and Arendt argues that Athens had enough concern for each that it "never settled the conflict between politics and art unequivocally in favor of one or the other—which incidentally may be one of the reasons for the extraordinary display of artistic genius in Classical Greece—and [it] kept the conflict alive and did not level it out to indifference of the two realms with regard to each other" (p. 216). Greece will serve as a kind of model for Arendt—something for which she has often been criticized—but at least in this instance, it is a very unstable model.[6] Greece does not represent a *state* of affairs or a proper balance between the forces of art and politics but rather a dynamics of conflict without resolution. No specific political model and no specific aesthetic-cultural model can, therefore, be derived from Greece. The public space of politics and art is thus conceived as a heterogeneous, divided space characterized by and constantly being re-formed in terms of a nonviolent form of conflict and dissent concerning the proper place, character, and relation of art and politics. Art and politics are not identified with each other or derived the one from the other in Arendt's version of Greece quite simply because neither has a fixed identity ·or place in the conflict linking and separating them.

What Arendt "learns" from Greece is that the conflict between art and politics must be *public* and that they thus share in spite of their differences the need for a public space:

> These [aesthetic] things obviously share with political "products," words and deeds, the quality that they are in need of some public space where they can appear and be seen; they can fulfill their own being, which is appearance, only in a world which is common to all; in the concealment of private life and private possession, art objects cannot attain their own inherent validity, they must, on the contrary, be protected against the possessiveness of individuals. . . . Generally speaking, culture indicates that the public realm, which is rendered politically secure by men of action, offers its space of display to those things whose essence it is to appear and be beautiful. In other words, culture indicates that art and politics, their conflicts and tensions notwithstanding, are interrelated and even mutually dependent.   (p. 218)

Traditional political theories and strategies—from the most idealist or utopian to the most pragmatic or materialist, from the most conservative to the most liberal or revolutionary—in one way or another assume or explicitly posit a "world which is common to all" and project an ideal or real public space in which such "commonness" could or must inevitably manifest or realize itself. What is different about Arendt's position lies not in her projection of a "common world," then, but in how she goes about defining it. The problem is how to conceive of the interactions between and the mutual dependency of art and politics without

diminishing or resolving the differences and conflict between them—
that is, without making the public space more the realm of one than the
other.

The problem of how and on what basis theories of art and politics
can legitimately assume or posit either what is common to all or what
constitutes the publicness of the space in which this commonness re-
sides or is projected is, if we take Arendt's formulation seriously, very
difficult if not impossible to resolve, at last in any definitive way. An
important sign that an approach to politics is in fact critical might even
be the care it takes in addressing these issues, the difficulty it has resolving them or, even better, its reluctance to resolve them. If politics and
art both have something essential to do with the formation, manifestation, and questioning of the public space, I would argue that in their
critical forms they do not define or determine this space conceptually
but rather keep it open and not really undetermined, if this implies a
complete break with determination, but rather always to be determined
again and otherwise.

Arendt turns to Kant and the problem of critical judgment in order
to pursue the question of the public space and link politics and art to
each other in terms of, rather than in spite of, the irresolvable differences and conflicts separating them. In "The Crisis in Culture" and
many other works, she especially emphasizes those moments in the *Critique of Judgment* when Kant links judgment directly to the "presence"
of others and to the "potential agreement" with them. For Kant, critical
or reflective judgment consists in the capacity to judge without criteria.
To judge something to be beautiful, for example, means not to apply
predetermined concepts or rules to a specific case, as in determinant
judgment, but rather to judge when there are no determined rules,
"subjectively"—that is, in terms of a subjectivity emptied of subjective
determinations—based on one's own experience or feelings but in anticipation of or, more precisely, with the demand for universal agreement. Universality can thus never be assumed or posited as such; it is
not the ground for critical judgment but rather its anticipated but un-
programmable and undemonstrable end. What is "common to all" can
thus never be known or determined; it never takes the form of an identity or image of a people, state, collectivity, or class.

When one emphasizes in Kant the indeterminacy of what is common to all and of the public space in which such commonness manifests itself, the demand for universal agreement as such can in fact never

be met. It could even be said that such a demand takes its critical force from the very fact that it cannot be met or satisfied but must be continually responded to anew. From the perspective of someone like Jean-François Lyotard, whose recent work in large part consists of a rereading of Kant, it is even possible to argue that when the demand *is* met, when a particular form is given to the public space and a nature or identity given to "commonness," then this should be taken as the sign that the universal is nothing but a mystification of the particular, that the Kantian Idea is nothing but another form of idealism or, even worse, the support for one form or other of political dogmatism that claims to embody in its reality the true universal. As is the case for art, in politics, the public of critical judgment is, for Lyotard, always *to be formed*; it is never the already-existing public of the state or nation or international community, never the property of any particular form of government, any group, class, or fusion of classes.

As Lyotard has shown, such an argument can be derived from Kant, even if it may be at odds with the traditional readings of Kant. Arendt, too—at least at certain moments of her analysis—could be considered to imply that a nondetermined notion of community is at the heart of Kant's view of reflective judgment and thus of his notion of *sensus communis*. But it must also be said that she constantly reduces the potential critical impact of a notion of undetermined publicness by directly linking it to a determined public. She does this by focusing on the section of Kant's *Critique of Judgment* in which he treats most directly the problems of commonness and publicness in terms of critical judgment: section 40, entitled "On Taste as a Kind of *Sensus Communis*." It is also the section that raises the most questions for Lyotard's "transcendental reading." In it Kant defines *sensus communis* in the following way:

> We must [here] take *sensus communis* to mean the idea of a sense *shared* [by all of us], i.e., a power to judge that in reflecting takes account (a priori), in our thought, of everyone else's way of presenting [something], in order, *as it were*, to compare our own judgment with human reason in general and thus escape the illusion that arises from the ease of mistaking subjective and private conditions for objective ones, an illusion that would have a prejudicial influence on the judgment. Now we do this as follows: we compare our judgment, not so much with the actual as rather with the merely possible judgments of others, and [thus] put ourselves in the position of everyone else, merely by abstracting from the limitations that [may] happen to attach to our own judging.[7]

The problem raised by this passage is how to "take account of . . . everyone else's way or presenting" and avoid the illusions arising from both subjective and so-called objective judgments, that is, how to complicate, undercut, and transgress subjective experience in the name of universality without predetermining the form of this universality and in this way defining our own "commonness" in terms of the actual or actualizable instead of the "merely possible." To put it in words that are certainly not those of Kant but not necessarily opposed to his either, how is it possible to transgress subjective and collective experience in the name of an open, radically heterogeneous universality, of a potential being-together without the assumption or projection of a determinable common being?

In all her work on Kant, Arendt clearly emphasizes what would probably be called today the communicational side of the Kantian abstraction from the limiting conditions of subjectivity.[8] For her, Kant's notion of the "enlarged mentality" necessary for critical judgment means above all the capacity to think in the place of specifically defined others, and in this way she clearly emphasizes the actual over the merely possible:

> That the capacity to judge is a specifically political ability in exactly the sense denoted by Kant, namely the ability to see things not only from one's own point of view but in the perspective of all those who happen to be present; even that judgment may be one of the fundamental abilities of man as a political being insofar as it enables him to orient himself in the public realm, in the common world—these are insights that are virtually as old as articulated political experience. . . . Judging is one, if not the most, important activity in which this sharing-the-world-with-others comes to pass.   (p. 221)

The "presence" of empirical others and the ability to take on their perspective thus constitute the means for overcoming the subjectiveness of judgment. In this way, a collective subject, a community of "all those who happen to be present," is postulated as already existing as the support of judgment. The chief political issue, therefore, becomes how to identify and communicate with others and judge from "their" perspective.

The first problem with this reading of Kant is that the group of "all those who happen to be present" could be said to *provide specific criteria*, as it does, for instance, for Habermas, for a form of judgment that Arendt acknowledges must remain without criteria. The second problem has to do with the fact that this empirical collectivity is exclusive insofar as those who do not happen to be present are by definition irrelevant, not involved in any way in the process of critical judgment, and thus they do not participate in the public space. It should be added that Arendt indicates neither whether they are absent by choice, chance, necessity, or exclusion nor what the effects the various forms of absence might have on those others deemed to be present. All those who happen to be absent or not fully present thus do not participate in what is common to all, which means that commonness is in fact postulated at their expense. For the sake of the possibility of effective communication, the public space is seriously reduced and in fact determined—or at the very least, determinable—by those "present," no matter how complicated the notion of "presence" evoked here might be.

There is perhaps no communication-based theory of the political—whether privileging "conversations," open, noncoercive dialogue or even conflict, dissent, and the clash of opinions (as is the case for Arendt)—that does not depend on some sort of prior reduction of the possibilities of the public space, that is, on giving the public space a real or ideal form. The question of who is admitted into conversations or dialogue and according to what rules, logic, or ends (consensus, universality, rationality, emancipation, etc.) always constitutes a serious limitation to the proclaimed openness and general communicability of such theories. Hierarchies implicitly or explicitly present in the rules structuring communication also make the public space of communication or communicability less public and open than is claimed by those defending the universality or rationality of communication.

Arendt's reduction of Kant's transcendental analysis of critical judgment to a form of ideal communication is even more evident in her references to section 19 of *The Critique of Judgment*. Focusing on the status of agreement and the means to achieve it in judgments of taste, Arendt argues that critical judgment is chiefly a matter of nonviolent persuasion.

> Taste judgments . . . share with political opinions that they are persuasive; the judging person—as Kant says quite beautifully—can only "woo the consent of everyone else" in the hope of coming to an agreement with him eventually. This "wooing" or persuading corresponds closely to what the Greeks called πειθειν, the convincing and persuading speech which they regarded as the typically political form of people talking with one another. Persuasion ruled the intercourse of the citizens of the polis

because it excluded physical violence; but the philosophers knew that it was also distinguished from another non-violent form of coercion, the coercion of truth. . . . Culture and politics, then belong together because it is not knowledge or truth which is at stake, but rather judgment and decision, the judicious exchange of opinion about the sphere of public life and the common world.   (pp. 222–23)

The public space necessary for and assumed by critical judgment in both art and politics is therefore constituted by a clash of opinions, out of which agreement is, at least ideally, always to result through nonviolent persuasion. Critical judgment could in both instances therefore be considered fundamentally "conversational" for Arendt, for, after the "judicious exchange of opinion," a consensus must actually be reached or at least be possible in principle. The community implied by critical judgment is thus for her one rooted deeply in the potential actuality of consensus, and one can certainly wonder what would happen to the "common ground" of the community and to the various minority parties or groups if the conflict between them and the majority was so fundamental that consensus was impossible, when it had the status of a *différend* rather than a simple disagreement or difference of opinion— that is to say, in a situation where persuasion could only take the coercive form of the suppression of the demands of one of the parties involved in the "discussions."[9]

Arendt seems here to be proposing the type of communicational model of social interaction oriented toward consensus that is today associated with the work of Jürgen Habermas. In terms of this issue, it seems obvious that their work in fact does overlap in important ways. But in his essay on Arendt, "Hannah Arendt: On the Concept of Power," Habermas distances himself from Arendt, in spite of the similarities between their positions, because he finds her notion of power to be antiquated:

I will only recall the peculiar perspective by which Arendt lets herself be guided: A state relieved of the administrative handling of social affairs, a politics cleansed of all questions of social politics, an institutionalizing of public liberty that is independent of the organization of welfare, a radically democratic formation of consensus that puts a stop to social repression—that is not a conceivable path for any modern society. So we stand before a dilemma. On the one hand, the communications concept of power discloses modern limiting phenomena to which political science has become practically insensitive; on the other hand, it grounds a conception of the political that, as soon as one approaches modern societies with it, leads to anomalies.[10]

Of course, Habermas' critique is valid as far as he goes. But if we begin to question the specific communicational ideal regulating and determining the context of his own position and if we challenge as well whether the primary or exclusive criterion for judging a perspective on politics should be its immediate, practical applicability to contemporary society, that is, whether it constitutes a "conceivable path for any modern society," then the interest in Arendt's work remains, in spite of the pertinence of Habermas' critique but not necessarily for the reasons he gives. Arendt's "anomalies" may have a more critical and even more "practical" value than Habermas allows; they may in fact help us understand the limitations of thinking the political solely in terms of what is a practical, conceivable path for modern societies.

A critique of Arendt could be formulated, however, not necessarily in Habermasian terms but rather in terms of her reading of Kant. For Kant does not say exactly what Arendt makes him say, and the differences between them are in fact significant. Kant insists that the demand for agreement remain *a demand* and that it can only be made conditionally:

> A judgment of taste requires everyone to assent; and whoever declares something to be beautiful holds that everyone *ought* to give his approval to the object at hand and that he should declare it beautiful. Hence the *ought* in an aesthetic judgment, even once we have all the data needed for judging, is still uttered only conditionally. We solicit everyone else's assent [*Man wirbt um jedes andern Beistimmung*—which Arendt translates as "we can only woo the consent of everyone else"], because we have a basis for it that is common to all.   (*Critique of Judgment*, section 19, p. 86).

What is missing from Kant is the actual process of "wooing" or persuading others, a process of practical, public exchange that for Arendt is essential for critical judgment in general and that she finds most fully embodied in the political exchanges of ancient Greece.

According to Kant, however, who is not quite so "Greek" as Arendt makes him, in the name of common *ends*, we insist that everyone *ought* to judge an object to be beautiful if we judge it to be so. We demand that agreement in principle, but we cannot in fact act to convince others by rhetorical or any other means that the object is in fact beautiful or that they *must* agree with us. Critical judgment demands that there be a public space, but this public space cannot be modeled after that of an idealized Greek public space or, in contemporary terms, after the spaces devoted to the exchange of information and opinion provided by the town forum, the legislature, newspapers, electronic media, or even computer networking—although a good sign that the public space is in grave danger would be the destruction or monolithic control of all forums and other means of exchange, something repressive political regimes always make one of their top and most pressing priorities. In fact, when any authority—state or private—attempts such control, unauthorized, unofficial networks of exchange inevitably emerge, no matter how great the repression and how extreme the risks that need to be taken to institute them, and for this reason alone Arendt's insistence on the strictly *public* aspect of the public space must be considered seriously. But at the same time, persuasion, no matter how nonviolent and non-coercive, cannot in fact occur without the public space being limited to one of its components: the rhetorical-political arena as such.

Our "conversations" with others, then, not just with those "present" but with others in general, remain virtual as concerns beauty. They are, therefore, not so much conversations with those present as the indirect evocation of a nonpresent and nonpresentable universality with which and on which we cannot in fact converse directly. We can only suggest indirectly the possibility of a commonness in diversity and heterogeneous public spaces in which this commonness could manifest itself, but we can never point to it as such or actually come to an agreement as to what it is. This is equally true of a sense of the political from the perspective of critical judgment; the public space(s) it implies should never be reducible to any particular social space or practical politics, no matter how judicious the exchange of opinions taking place there. The political in this sense thus always points beyond the limitations of "practical politics" as such—just as the sense of the aesthetic is never equivalent to any specific artistic production—not because the actual practice of politics is irrelevant (or the art object insignificant) but because more is at stake in politics (and art) than what is practical or practiced in its realm. The critical demand we make of the political should also challenge what is accepted or acceptable as "practical politics" by constantly making possible other forms of political practice than those practiced as politics. Culture in this sense could be seen as the manifestation of the heterogeneous public spaces in which the alternative "products" and practices of art and politics are produced, put on display, and responded to, that is, discussed and judged.

II

Kant holds such an important role in Arendt's later work precisely because he is for her the philosopher of publicness, sociability, and openness; because he represents a position that is the extreme opposite of the destruction of the public space (and therefore the destruction of both the aesthetic and the political that are both guarantees of publicness and manifested in it) that totalitarian movements strive for. Near the end of *The Origins of Totalitarianism*, Arendt describes the effects of total terror precisely in terms of the destruction of the public space: "By pressing men against each other, total terror destroys the space between them" (p. 466). For Arendt, there is a fundamental and radical difference between tyranny and oppression, on the one hand, and the total terror of totalitarian movements, on the other. As she puts it, in tyrannical governments that are not totalitarian, "not all contacts between men are broken and not all human capacities for action and power are frustrated. The whole sphere of private life with the capacities for experience, fabrication and thought are left intact." In totalitarian governments, on the contrary, "We know that the iron band of total terror leaves no space for such private life and that the self-coercion of totalitarian logic destroys man's capacity for experience and thought just as certainly as his capacity for action" (p. 474).[11] Private life in this sense does not refer to the secret, intimate life of the bourgeois individual but rather to the more fundamental capacity to experience, feel, respond, act, and so on, which itself implies not the freedom of the isolated individual but the freedom that depends on access to and participation in a nondetermined, open, public, and in this sense "common" space, a "common sense" that is not a shared identity but a sense of the heterogeneity of all experience.[12]

One could conclude from this that Arendt's insistence on developing the capacity for reflective judgment (as concerns both politics and art) is itself not only an argument against totalitarianism but an indication of a possible critical sense of the political in the aftermath of totalitarian devastation. Kant represents for her not a way of nostalgically returning to a pretotalitarian world but rather a way of emerging from a world

devastated by the terror of totalitarian movements. Her references to
Kant thus serve as a kind of starting point for a critical approach to the
aesthetic and the political in which private life is inextricably connected
to public life and subjective experience and judgment are tied to the
demand for universal agreement, but without the private or the subjective being swallowed up or determined in advance by the public, the
common, or the universal. In making critical or reflective judgment the
key to both his aesthetic theory and his political philosophy, Kant, for
Arendt, defends both the "spontaneous," undetermined character of experience and the fundamental "sociability" of human existence, the necessity that we live "in common" and judge in the name a possible public "commonness" that itself cannot be determined. It could be argued
that what separates us most radically from Kant (and also from Arendt)
today is that this "commonness" can only be thought in terms of a radical heterogeneity or alterity, of a potentially infinite number of common
or public spaces—and, in spite of appearances, this is not necessarily
an anti-Kantian or anti-Arendtian position but one that owes much to
both.

What creates the public realm, then, is not what we supposedly share
in common or even what we do together in the name of a common
cause or project but rather the fact that no action can be considered an
end in itself, that all political actions must be critically judged.[13] The
critical position is that of the spectator and judge, not because thought
is a higher calling than action but because action is not autonomous
(nor is thought) nor can it be considered truly historical or public until
it meets the test of critical judgment.[14] In this sense, political action and
critical judgment should always be linked the one to the other. Ultimately, then, the public "formed" or demanded by each could be considered, then, not to be the empirical public actually present at the
moment of action or judgment as Arendt frequently states, but, as she
also argues (as does Kant), a public of the future. An event's importance,
for her as for Kant, "lies precisely not at its end but in its opening up
new horizons for the future" (p. 56). Because we are, "after devastation,"
"between past and future," rather than in a present determined by the
past and anticipating a particular future, these horizons can never be
determined. The very possibility—the possibility, not the actuality—of
an age that could truly be considered post-totalitarian, an age *after* devastation, depends on such anticipation, on the continual demand for

critical judgment and the alternative horizons it makes possible, given the fact and continual possibility of devastation.

III

If the aesthetic and the political—at least in their critical forms—can be linked to each other, it is because each demands a critical (reflective) rather than determinant form of judgment. Each thus both depends on and points to the necessity for a notion of public space of a very particular kind. It could be said that the "commonness" in question in this space is not that of the identity of a people or a particular form of society but rather of a community always in formation, always in search of or even without a project that unites it. Nevertheless, it seems inevitable that we ask what kind of community that would or should be. In "Sensus communis," Jean-François Lyotard claims, however, that all questions of this type are quite simply false:

> What kind of a *communitas* is it which would not be unified by a project? What kind would have no Idea as to what it wanted and what it should be? What kind does not have the Idea of its unity even as a horizon? These are false questions governed by an unquestioned line of reasoning, by the prejudice that it is diversity, chaos, which comes first . . . and that what is necessary is a principle which would unify it.[15]

The questions are false because they all still demand an answer in the form of a synthesis "between what one is an what one wants or desires. And even if we are told that it does not exist, that it is always lacking, . . . this does not in any way change the principle that community is the desire experienced by diversity" (p. 71).

What Lyotard calls the different "philosophies of the will" still then determine the form of the community in question in terms of the desire for community, for a common project. That is to say, community is constituted by the desire for community, even if this desire is seen as impossible to realize. Lyotard's critique of the desire for community leads us rather to ask whether it is not necessary, for reasons having to do with the future of both politics and art, to begin to think in terms of a notion of community that does not depend on such a synthesis, whose explicit or implicit project is not the unification of the diverse. To pursue this line of questioning, it is necessary to challenge in more detail the specific characteristics of the notion of the public space that Arendt derives from Kant and even the undetermined synthesis of the common or the communal it proposes.

Lyotard's reasons for criticizing any form of synthesis, whether explicit or implicit, have largely to do with the political dangers of anthropologizing the *sensus communis* (as Kant himself, at least in part, does) and giving it an empirical or sociohistorical interpretation. Collectivities formed in the name of either a commonness of nature, being, class, sex, or race, or, in the case of Kantian aesthetic of the beautiful, taste and the capacity to feel, all present the same problem. If, as we have seen, *sensus communis* is to be understood in a Kantian sense as "the idea of a sense *shared* [by all of us]," one that demands that "we compare our own judgment with human reason in general," Lyotard warns against the dangers of this comparison being made in terms of any form of collectivity of determined others, even if what Kant himself seems to indicate at times is that such a comparison with others is basic to critical judgment. "This operation of comparison is directed at a collectivity of individuals, or so it seems. Interpreted in this way, it induces a realistic, empirical, anthropological definition of the *sensus*. And how many political illusions and crimes have been able to take nourishment from this supposed immediate sharing of feelings" ("*Sensus Communis*," p. 86)! As much as the demand for universal affirmation must accompany critical judgment in order to move it outside the realm of subjective taste, Lyotard insists that the common element of *sensus communis* can never be articulated or projected onto any specific community but must remain unknown and unpresentable.

Lyotard sees the possibility of political crimes lurking behind all political projects that depend on or whose explicit aim is the unification of diversity in the name of community, group, class, state, people, or, of course, race. Such totalizing political projects work to diminish sensitivity, the capacity to feel and respond in each instance to what Lyotard calls "events"—that is, unanticipated, undeterminable occurrences, whether historical, political, aesthetic, or simply "phrasic" in nature. Such projects also entail the destruction of critical judgment itself and thus signal the impending "end" of both art and politics in any nondogmatic, critical sense. Arendt and Lyotard both return to Kant in order to argue that radically different futures are both possible and necessary in the wake of (because of) totalitarian devastation. But Lyotard, because he argues that there are serious limitations and dangers in a notion of publicness or commonness that is "communicational" or "consensual" in nature, uses the idea of a *sensus communis* he derives from Kant against the anthropological, humanist side of Kant and all post-Kantians—and thus against Arendt as well. His is thus a very uncommon (perhaps even un-Kantian) sense of Kant's "common sense," a *sensus* without *consensus*.

"This *sensus*," Lyotard insists, "isn't a sense [meaning], and the feeling that is supposed to affect it . . . isn't common, but only communicable in principle. There is no determinable community of feeling, no de facto affective consensus. And if one claims to have recourse to it, or a fortiori, to create it, one is the victim of a transcendental illusion, and one is encouraging deception" (p. 87). One form of political deception is certainly rooted in the premise that the community or public of critical judgment is determined or at least in principle determinable, that art in fact has a specific public—either preexisting or determined by art itself—and that this public should serve as a model for the political community as well. Another form of deception is that of the notion of communication itself: that is, that art demands an ideal form of free, uncoerced communication, judgments concerning the beautiful (or the political) that are exchanged, bartered, used in open dialogue to persuade those with different opinions, all in the name of an eventual, noncoercive consensus.

Read from Lyotard's perspective, the critical (political) function of art is to indicate the limits of communication and therefore the limits of any and all notions of publicness and commonness. Or to put it another way, the notion of critical judgment Lyotard in his turn "derives" from Kant is always an indication of other communities, other publics not yet formed, possibilities lying outside or at the limits of the formed and the formulatable—and thus outside or at the limits of the communicable. Critical judgment indicates, among other things, that no notion of community can ever be diverse or heterogeneous enough, that any concept of community carries within it the possibility that deception, crimes, and even the project of total mobilization and devastation could be carried out in its name. It could even be argued that for Lyotard the principal problem for us today, "after" the devastation of totalitarianism—assuming we are in fact "after" or even know what it would mean to be "after"—would be not to formulate and work toward realizing an ideal unity of humanity but rather to forge links among profoundly and irresolvably contradictory elements of the various public spaces, without at the same time either destroying their openness or publicness or attempting to postulate or forge a unity in the name of a particular real or ideal community or public.

What makes Kant's work still relevant for us today, then—a way, as Arendt puts it, of "opening up new horizons for the future"—is its formulation of a critical (i.e., reflective) form of judgment. Critical judgment makes it possible (and necessary) to continue to raise the issue of community (and make demands in the name of community) in an age where traditional (all?) foundations for community have proved inadequate, illusory, oppressive, antiquated, or even terroristic and criminal. Critical judgment also implies that the issue of the public space is fundamental to all politics, and this in an age when the modern forms of publicness are perceived as superficial, degraded, staged, coercive, monolithic, and, more often than not, even irrelevant—having more to do with the advertisement of products and the imposition of uniformity and controlled taste than with the possible linkages of differences and heterogeneity in critical reflection. The continued insistence on a "Kantian" notion of critical judgment is thus in the work of both Arendt and Lyotard a sign that for them the possibility of alternatives to existing notions of community, whatever their form or concept, no matter how "democratic," egalitarian, or open they are considered to be, must be a fundamental component of any critical approach to the political.

In *Peregrinations*, Lyotard in fact claims that "by taking seriously into account the main characteristic of reflective judgment, which is not simply involved but maximized (or minimalized) in taste and which is to judge without a concept, one is led to the idea that the community required as a support for the validity of such judgment must always be in the process of doing *and* undoing itself . . . always remaining *in statu nascendi* or *moriendi*, always keeping open the issue of whether or not it actually exists."[16] In the face of the continual threat of new forms of totalitarianism, devastation, and "democratic" homogenization, the critical judgment demanded by art can (should) serve to unform (or even deform) the already-formed sense of community motivating the different contending political theories, to resist the imposition of a mythical, historical, or natural identity onto the public as the sign of its publicness—that is, in a sense, to resist the determination or theorization of the political itself.

I would argue that it is still possible, even "after" the repeated devastations inflicted on specific communities or religious, ethnic, sexual, or political groups, which have in large part defined the history of this century, to argue that there is no critical sense of the political that does not respond to the call for or the obligation to community, that does not work toward reinaugurating, fostering, and ensuring the continuation of some form (or various forms) of open, public space. The dilemma we face today, however—one whose fundamental significance for critical thought the work of both Arendt and Lyotard emphasizes in different ways—is that the notions of community and public space, at the same time that they might be considered necessary for maintaining an open, critical sense of politics or the political, inevitably impose restrictions and limitations on the political. Thus no approach to politics can be considered just if it is not driven by a sense of and desire for community, but at the same time no theory of politics or political strategy can be considered truly critical if it is determined or regulated by a particular practical or ideal form of community. Community and publicness, therefore, cannot be considered resolutions to political questions or the ends toward which the political process—if it is a process—should be directed. They are rather demands made on the political that must be responded to but that can never be met in their entirety without perpetuating the very devastation they are meant to counter.

IV

I am arguing, therefore, that if we take seriously the devastation that has already occurred to community, that has repeatedly been inflicted on various communities in this century, we cannot assume that we still "have" community or, if we are assumed to have "lost" it, that we will be able to regain it in the future. We cannot assume that the public space is guaranteed by any political system and the form of community and communication it makes possible—that is to say, that any form of politics can be considered to be a sure protection or safeguard from the threat or possibility of devastation. Quite simply, what the history of this century should have taught us is that there are no longer any safeguards, no longer any limits to horror and devastation. The impossible, in fact, is possible; it has already (repeatedly) occurred and therefore could occur again in the same form or in some other, as-yet not imaginable form. If Adorno is right to say that we can no longer assume the survival of art, for similar reasons, is it not necessary to argue that the survival of the community, of the public space, is anything but unproblematic?

Are these grounds for melancholy or even despair? Not necessarily, and what interests me in Arendt and Lyotard (not to mention Adorno and numerous others) is the way in which such despair is challenged. Because the understandable "mourning and melancholia" in the wake of devastation in fact tends to perpetuate the very devastation it bemoans by treating it as an insurmountable tragedy, a critical rethinking of the possibilities of community must be rooted precisely in the rejection, as Arendt argues, of both naive optimism and despair. "After devastation," a more complicated, critical sense of the political, a more nuanced, heterogeneous, open sense of community must emerge in order for the seeds of a new form of totalitarian devastation not to take root once again as a response to the increasingly complex crises of modernity, so-called postmodernity, or the age of information, which carry within them their own very particular potential for totalitarian devastation.

What (of) community is left to us then? And what kinds of de-mands—political and other—does the desire or necessity for commu-nity make on us? In a recent work, *La Communauté Désoeuvrée*, Jean-Luc Nancy has attempted to respond to these kinds of questions,[17] in part through an extended reading of the political texts of Georges Ba-taille. The title of the work itself indicates how problematic Nancy finds the notion of community to be. The word *désoeuvré* should be taken in Blanchot's sense of *désoeuvrement*, so that the title of Nancy's text could be translated as the nonworked, nonfashioned or nonmodeled com-munity, the community that is not a work or product, a community that has not and will not fashion or fictionalize itself as *a* community.[18] This notion of "community," if it is still a notion "*of* community"—and in a certain sense, Nancy's title is an oxymoron, for how can there be com-munity if it is not "worked," that is, if it does not have *a* form?—is certainly one that could be related to what has been called the general "crisis of foundations," which is for Nancy a crisis of ideals and ends as well. The question that emerges from this crisis, or as this crisis, be-comes how to think community, how to act in the name of community, in the absence of any reliable foundation for community and without recourse to an ideal or myth of community. Rather than attempt to resolve the crisis or move beyond it, Nancy's work tends to exacerbate it, to attempt to think community in crisis or to think this crisis as the possibility of community. In this context, the crisis is without end and community without finality.

For those who are sure that a solid, irrefutable foundation for community exists—in human nature, in the individual or collective subject, in a class, social structure, or political ideal designated as universal, or in a form of metaphysical or religious destiny, or even in history itself considered as a secular form of destiny, an evolutionary or dialectical process whose end is the establishment of a world community—a text such as Nancy's must seem at best irrelevant and at worst to constitute a dangerous threat to community itself. One can always dismiss the kind of radical critical questioning Nancy proposes by refusing to admit that concepts such as man, the subject, history, community, progress, and so on, can or should ever be critically analyzed or questioned—a practice that is certainly all too common today. But if one takes seriously the philosophical, historical, and political imitations of these concepts, then it becomes necessary to attempt to avoid falling back on them and naively using them as if they had never been undermined or seriously put into question. At all times acutely aware of these limitations, Nancy offers a critical approach to community that refuses to presuppose the existence of community—its being or ideal form—at the same time that it refuses to abandon the question of community. His work could also be considered to constitute an approach to the question of what is left of community after devastation, for it focuses on how the question of community persists even in the midst of its own devastation or undoing, how it persists in fact as the resistance to devastation as such.

Nancy argues that the problem of community should not be approached as if community were something that had been lost in the course of history and that history, in its modern, progressive form, has as its ultimate goal to reestablish. Not only should this form of retrospective approach be challenged because it presupposes that we know what community is or what it ideally was and thus should be once again, that an ideal of community exists (once existed) to determine and give meaning and direction to history, but it should also be challenged because "it seems to accompany Western thought since its beginnings" (p. 31). That is to say, this presupposition has something to do with the very limitations of Western thought itself, the difficulties it has in thinking radical alternatives to itself, or even in thinking and allowing there to exist alternatives within itself and at its margins.

To counter this retrospective tendency, Nancy goes so far as to say—

naming various mythological, religious, historical, and anthropological projections of what an ideal community, at various moments of history, was supposed to have been—that "community did not occur" precisely where and in the form of the "projections that we have made onto these different societies" (p. 33).[19] Community did not and does not occur in the form it has been assigned: in other words, no form of society can be considered a true community, a model for community, a successful embodiment of the true sense of community, that is, the realization of the ideal of the immanent and transparent communion of all its members. All such attempts to refer to an ideal (of) community—and there is certainly no shortage of them in history, philosophy, literature, anthropology, or political theory—are limited by the very form of the projection (fiction) they impose. The problem is, of course, how to move beyond such limitations without rejecting the entire question of community at the same time. Nancy's work is an attempt to do exactly this, for he challenges all projections or ideals of community in order to raise the question of community outside the limitations imposed by such ideals.

One temptation specific to modernity is the mythologization of a certain form of the premodern, that is, the attempt to locate true community before industrialization and the complications and injustices capitalism and modernization impose on society. Arendt, as Habermas has argued, in an indirect way partially gives in to this temptation. Nancy argues against all mythical projections of community—whatever their specific political orientation—not only because such communities never existed as such but also, and more important, because these projections are necessarily reduced and simplified versions of the critical potential of the notion of community as a nonworked, unformed, nonmythical possibility:

> Gesellschaft did not come along, with the State, industry, and capital, to dissolve a preexisting Gemeinschaft. It would be undoubtedly more just . . . to say that Gesellschaft—"society," the dissociating association of forces, needs, and signs—replaced something for which we have neither the name nor the concept, something that originates at the same time in a communication much more vast than that of the social space . . . and in a much more distinct segmentation. . . . Society was not constructed on the ruins of a community. It was constructed in the disappearance or in the conservation of what—whether tribe or empire—had perhaps no more relation to what we call "community" than to what we call "society." (p. 34)

Nancy attempts to break with the way of thinking that treats community as the process of recovery of what society has supposedly lost in order to be receptive to and pursue the possibilities of what has not yet occurred to, or as, community.

Nancy argues that community, far from being what society would have lost or broken with, is *what happens to us*—in the form of questions, expectations, events, demands—from the time of society on" (p. 34). For Nancy, then, the question of community should also not take the form of the unifying project of what society will or should be.[20] It should rather have the unformed "shape" necessitated by the fundamental impossibility of total communion and immanence, the "shape" of a being-together that does not assume or project a being-one-with-each-other. Or as Nancy puts it, "community assumes and inscribes . . . in some sense the impossibility of community" (p. 42). How to live "together" with or as this impossibility becomes, for Nancy, the task that community assigns us, what it demands from us today. It would not be enough, then, to grant autonomy to and enfranchise, in the name of liberal pluralism, the plurality of groups and collectivities demanding to be recognized and legitimated as communities—even though in situations of political and economic injustice and disenfranchisement, this is unquestionably an important and necessary step—for Nancy demands the opening up and undermining of the work of community in general, of community as a work, as the fashioning of a collectivity, in each and every instance.

Nancy asserts that Bataille, more forcefully than any other modern thinker, revealed that the terms of thinking community and living "in community" have radically changed, that community is no longer a question of finding or thinking a profound interiority or immanence of a collective subject but is rather more to be thought in terms of a radical Otherness. Bataille, argues Nancy, "in the most acute way revealed the modern experience of community: neither a work to be produced nor a lost communion, but the space itself and the spacing [*espacement*] of the outside, of the outside-the-self" (p. 50). Such an "outside" is not that of a loss of self, a form of alienation from self and other that would fall within the retrospective illusion of community. Rather this "outside" must be thought as the possibility of links and relations to others and to alterity in general that are not rooted in or dependent on any sense of the interiority, immanence, or essence of the self to itself or to others—links that are not postulated in terms of the ideal of a community present and transparent to itself.

This is a further reason that we cannot lose community (even in order to regain it). We can lose (and have from the start lost) community that has the form of immanence; we can lose (and have from the start lost) community in the form of a specific fashioning, work, or project; we can lose (and have from the start lost) community as the ideal of communication. But we cannot lose, even in the most extreme situations, this "outside-the-self" in which, no matter what else we are deprived of, we in some form or other must still "appear-together":

> It is impossible for us to lose it. A society can be as little communitylike as possible, it is still impossible, even in the social desert, that there be no community, no matter how minuscule or even inaccessible. We cannot not appear-together. At the extreme, the fascist masses tend to annihilate community in the delirium of a communion incarnate. Symmetrically, the concentration camp—and the extermination camp, the exterminating concentration camp—is in its essence the will to destroy community. But, never, even in the camp itself, did the community completely cease resisting this will. It is in this sense resistance itself: that is to say, resistance to immanence.   (pp. 87–88)

As resistance to the fashioned or worked community, the "nonworked" community—for Nancy, the only "critical" sense of community, if it is possible to say this—persists as the possibility of an other relation to others than that already formed and established, or, in extreme situations, violently imposed. Resistance in its strongest sense means the possibility of a constant undoing of the type and form of communion and communication chosen, imposed or projected as community or as the devastation of community. It is the recognition that the *escapement* of the subject, its appearing-together-with-others, precedes and founds the individual subject and not the reverse, that the subject is first in relation with others, with alterity, before being self.

It is in this spacing, the space "outside-the-self," the space of *désoeuvrement*, that Nancy also locates the question of literature, thus linking together—though in no sense equating or deriving the one from the other—the "political" question of community (if it is still or ever was primarily a political question) and the "literary" question of writing (if it is still or ever was primarily a literary question). In a certain sense, before such linkage can be envisaged, Nancy must distinguish both the question of community and that of literature from the myths governing them, in both their history and their concepts. He must distinguish them from myth in general. In a section of his book entitled "The Interrupt(ion)ed (of) Myth," after describing the unifying and establishing effects of the "original scene" of myth, Nancy has this to say about myth in general, in all its diverse forms:

> The idea even of myth perhaps contains in itself what one could call, on the one hand, every hallucination, on the other, every imposture of the conscience-of-self of a modern world which has exhausted itself in the fabulous representation of its own power. The idea of myth perhaps concentrates in itself every pretension of the West to appropriate its own origin, or to recover its secret from it, in order finally to be able to identify itself, absolutely, in terms of its own articulation and its own birth. (p. 117)

As Nancy repeats more than once, defined in this way, we "have nothing more to do with myth"; we have, or should have, nothing more to do with this search for and obsession with a defining and determining origin. Our age—after devastation—is the age not just of the end of myth, which could itself be another form of myth (as any search for a new mythology undoubtedly is), but that of the interruption of, and as we shall see, the active resistance to myth. The nonworked community and the "unworkness" (*désoeuvrement*) of literature are in Nancy's argument interconnected in their resistance to myth and its effects.

We should have nothing more to do with myth for many reasons, but perhaps the most forceful and unquestionable historical-political reason is that we find ourselves in the world we inhabit today "after devastation," after the devastation provoked by an ideology, a political movement, a mobilization of a people, and a "final solution" all conceived in the name of and driven by the most lethal of all myths. As never before, Nazism revealed once and for all the lethal powers of myth in modernity. By constituting itself as and thus realizing in its totalitarian project the power of myth, it went the farthest in the fabrication of an absolute (mythic) collective subject, a community fashioned ("fictioned") in terms of a mythic origin.[21] The mutual recognition of those whose place was assigned to them in terms of this mythical origin was intimately connected to the project of extermination of those who had no place assigned to them, not only whose place was denied by the myth but whose very being was also considered a threat to the integrity and purity of the mythical community.[22] Mythical thought, defined as the "thinking of a founding fiction or of a foundation by fiction" (p. 134), must, according to Nancy, not just be denounced as a fiction, for this fiction has a specific function. It should rather be resisted as an *operation* with potentially lethal effects and rejected as a way of making (or even of projecting the making of) a world and, therefore, a public space.[23]

In his analysis of the *work* of myth in politics and poetics, its power to make *a work* of community, art, and literature, Nancy is aiming not just at myth per se but at "every idea of a guiding or regulating fiction," even of the Kantian "regulating Idea," insomuch as it too functions as a myth. "One must go as far as to think an interruption or a suspension of the Idea as such: what its fiction makes visible must be suspended, its figure kept unfinished" (p. 141). It is clear here and at other moments that Nancy has less confidence in Kant than either Arendt or Lyotard, no matter how different their respective readings of Kant are. For Nancy, the question of community after devastation is itself devastating because it cannot rely on (even if only in the form of a demand) the Kantian notion of the Idea but must suspend (resist) even the unrepresentable "guarantee" of universality implied in the Idea. Even though Lyotard (and Arendt, up to a point) would acknowledge that the universal market economy and consumer society separate us from Kant and the idea of an emancipated, cosmopolitan citizenry—that is, that Marx comes between us and Kant—Nancy makes of this distance a much more radical problem than they do.

For Nancy, this distance from Kant also means that the modern notion of the "*work* of art," which is still in large part indebted to Kant, must also be resisted because it remains determined to a large extent by a notion of fabrication (creation) or making (production) as an expression of freedom, modeled after an ideal or idealized nature. Nothing seems left for community, no space open for it, no means—practical or transcendent—available in which to strive for it or respond to the demands made in its name. It might even seem to some that Nancy has given in to devastation, that he has accepted it as inevitable, that the absence or destruction of community is all that his critique of community leaves us.

Such is not the case, however, for Nancy also argues that "the pure and simple obliteration of the community is a calamity (*malheur*). It is not a sentimental or ethical calamity but an ontological disaster. It is the deprivation of being for a being that is essentially and more than essentially a being *in* common" (p. 146). Nancy implies, then, that the resistance that constitutes a response to the demands of community must be double: first, a resistance to community as work or to the working (fashioning) of a people, an identity or a social space, which inevitably moves toward and operates as devastation by imposing immanence and *a* form of communicability at the expense of other forms and of the Other in general; and, at the same time, second, a resistance to the obliteration of community, which is already in itself the extreme form of devastation. After reading Nancy, not only does one better appreciate the difficulty of practicing effectively this double resistance but also one is led to ask whether any resistance to myth could avoid perpetuating what it attempts to resist, that is, whether it really is possible to think community without giving in to one or another of the fictions or myths that have always been associated with it.

Nancy himself has difficulty at this point articulating the forms of this resistance, but this difficulty, it seems to me, is not specifically a limitation or weakness of his thinking per se but a limitation of critical thought in general. This limitation is also what continues to make community a vital and pressing question, and it should not be seen in any way as encouraging the abandonment of critical thought or action—an abandonment that would take the form, on the one hand, of an extreme pessimism or despair or, on the other, of a nonreflective activism or pragmatism, regardless of its form or intended ends. It certainly in no way encourages the abandonment of community in the name of the individual or individualism. What continues, what must continue in the absence "of the work of community, of community as work," is what Nancy calls "the unworked passion of community, demanding, calling us to pass beyond every limit, every accomplishment that delineates the form of an individual." Nancy thus considers the response to the call to move outside of self and beyond the limits of community in the name of another, unformed community to be not an abandonment but "a movement" of community, "unworkness in its singular activity" (p. 151). Such an activity and resistance can obviously have no specific end but rather demand a constant receptiveness to the call of community to resist and exceed its own limits and ends, to be constantly undone by an alterity it cannot and should not attempt to contain or incorporate into itself.

The community of "being-in-common without end, of this being *in* common which is not a 'common being' " (p. 156), if it cannot have *a* form, does have a "voice" of sorts, a voice of interruption or an interrupted voice. The name that could be given to this strange voice, Nancy claims, is literature. He immediately admits, however, that the name is not right; no name would be (p. 157). And yet he continues to use the name literature rather than some other and in spite of what he agrees with Blanchot is its "inconvenience." The name literature is inconvenient first of all because, in its critical, "nonworked" sense, it is not suitable for the mythical ideal (of) community that has the form of the public space of communion or communication—it resists being reduced to what it says, the message or content it conveys. This could be considered in this context to be its positive, critical inconvenience. But literature is also inconvenient in another, opposed sense: it cannot be easily separated from its own myth, the myth of literature, which in fact does posit it as an ideal form of communication, as work, creation, genre, vision, and voice, to name only these. Nancy admits all of these inconveniences, but he nevertheless still considers "literature" in his sense, borrowing from Blanchot and Bataille as well as Derrida, to be what in literature interrupts and resists the myth of literature, what writes or traces this resistance. This "voice" called "literature," therefore, is not a voice but a complication of voice, something at the same time less and more than a voice or a fusion of voices. The question is not even what this voice says but what takes place, that is, what is written in or as this voice: not the sharing of an identity but the partition and sharing, sharing as the partition of nonidentity. For Nancy, the voice of literature in a critical sense is always and must remain *partagé*.[24]

"The stakes of literature," Nancy claims, "are not itself, and this is different from myth, which communicates itself, thus communicating its own communion" (p. 163). In other words, literature, when it does have itself—that is, the production, reflection, and mastery of self, perhaps even the deconstruction of self—as its end or its stakes, is in his sense not literature but myth. And it could certainly be argued that from the romantics through structuralism, as well as within important currents of what is called poststructuralism, literature remains more mythic than *literary* (or what I would call critical). Not only does there exist, admits Nancy, "a myth of the text," but accompanying it "there exists a text of myth, which interrupts it at the same time as it partitions/shares it and reinscribes it in 'literature.' The latter is perhaps nourished only by myths, but it writes only of their interruption" (p. 163). What is partitioned/shared in (as) literature is a profound nonidentity: of the work, of literature as such, and of each individual (as author, character, figure, persona, reader, etc.) with him- or herself and with others. Nancy finds that at this extreme limit of literature, which is also for him the nonoriginal origin of literature, literature functions not as work but as the complicated and incomplete process of partition/sharing itself. In this sense, literature is not in any way a model for community but already community itself, that is, the partition/sharing of nonidentity, which constitutes and deconstitutes community in the absence of community, which constitutes community after devastation as the partition of identity and the sharing of nonidentity.

It seems clear that Nancy's "nonworked community" has little directly to do with the notion of community rooted in the "public space" of Arendt; in almost all of its characteristics it is in fact explicitly opposed to both the notion of the commonness of the public and that of the integrity of space implied in Arendt's writings. At the same time, however, it is equally true that Nancy proposes fundamental links between literature and (nonworked) community that parallel the nondetermined links, which, Arendt (after Kant) suggests, exist between the aesthetic and the political. But it is not critical judgment and the absence of criteria per se that link literature and community for Nancy but their (un)common unworkness. "There is the unworkness of the works of individuals in the community, . . . and there is the unworkness of the works that the community carries out as such by itself. . . . It is the same unworkness: the work in the community and the work of the community" (p. 180). Nancy argues that the unworkness of literature is in fact "offered to the infinite communication of the community" (p. 181) but not as *a* communication as such. He thus claims that the only form of "communication" to be associated with the literary (non-)work is potentially infinite, and this means that literature marks the noncommunicable limit of communication, a fractured form of (non-)communication that is "presented, proposed, and abandoned on the common limit where singular beings are partitioned and shared [*partagés*]" (p. 182). It is also in terms of this kind of partitioned/shared offering (rather than communication) that community, for him, must be thought.[25]

Quite simply, there is no common space in which the work (or community) can be located, for "only the limit is common, and the limit is not a place but the partition/sharing of places, their spacing" (p. 182). What is common and thus "public" for Nancy is not space but spacing, not identity but difference or differentiation, not an identical historical destiny and direction that one shares with others but an alterity from self and an openness to others that one shares only as a partitioning or differentiating that is both in and outside community, continually being displaced at and as its limit.

If Nancy's notion of resistance to community (that is, to myth, devastation, totalitarianism) can still be compared both to Lyotard's critical strategies—with which it shares a radical distrust of any realization or actualization of the Idea—and to Arendt's, it is insomuch as there is a political demand being made by his text that is not derived from or regulated by any specific politics as such. This "irrepressible political demand," if it does not define a specific politics, does provide a critical perspective on politics and thus is "political" in another sense. It persistently reveals what limits the forms of politics and literature with which it refuses to make any accommodations: all forms that attempt to ignore or repress this resistance to the commonness, immanence, and worked finitude demanded by community. "A politics that wants to know nothing of this is a mythology, or an economy. A literature that wants to say nothing about it is a diversion, or a lie" (p. 198). As can be seen, for Nancy the demands made by, or as, the nonworked community tolerate no compromises or half-measures.

It may seem, then, that with Lyotard and certainly with Nancy we have moved far away from Arendt's demands for community after devastation. On the one hand, Arendt's notion of the public space as an actual or actualizable space, a polis or forum, a place of the potential exchange of opinions among individuals sharing an immanence and commonness (even if unpresentable as such) and united in a common project or uncoerced communication, is directly challenged by both Lyotard and Nancy. On the other hand, from Arendt's perspective, Nancy's and, in a slightly different way, Lyotard's critiques of the potential of uncoerced communication and of a general communicability as the basis of community could only appear as impediments to her general project for defending and developing the aesthetic-political capacity for and potential of critical judgment. And yet Arendt's work, in terms of both its connections to and its differences from that of Lyotard and Nancy, also never loses sight of the limitations of politics and the necessity to offer alternatives to the delineation of the political as such. Her notion of the public space, if pushed just a bit, could even be considered as the unformed "space" of these alternatives.

The conflicts and irresolvable demands and counterdemands of Arendt, Lyotard, and Nancy thus all point to the heterogeneous stakes, possibilities, limitations, and even dangers of the demand for community after devastation. From their diverse perspectives, the demand for (of) community is considered constant and without end, for both the absence of such a demand and the "successful" and total fulfillment of its requirements are indications of potential devastation. One of the most important tasks the notion of community after devastation imposes on critical thought, then, would be how to find ways to respond to this double and contradictory demand of community, that is, how both to respond to and to resist community at the same time. This is, I would argue, undoubtedly one of the principal reasons why, at the present time, it is so difficult and, I would add, so necessary to continue to question and critically rethink the political in terms of the irresolvable contradictions, heterogeneous demands, and multiple possibilities and ends constituting and deconstituting it at the same time.

Notes

1. This is not to deny that they are being staunchly defended by others, the most obvious case being that of Jürgen Habermas, who situates his own critical endeavors in terms of rationality, progress, and the general Enlightenment project of emancipation.

2. The more contemporary form of this debate might be the controversy surrounding curriculum reform at various universities. The attacks by professors and politicians on the right, in the name of higher standards and moral values, of all those who are attempting to "politicize" the study of "Western civilization" by introducing works into the canon from outside the Western tradition as well as works by women and minorities "within" the tradition but for the most part ignored, assumes that what traditionalists and reactionaries call the partisan, politicized act of opening the canon is the origin and cause of the "decline in standards," if decline there is. Following Arendt, it would be easy to show that the "decline" being denounced is much more fundamental than that and evident from the start, long before anyone challenged the Eurocentrism of such courses, and that the process of politicization begins with the notion of Western civilization itself.

3. Hannah Arendt, "The Crisis in Culture: Its Social and Its Political Signification," in *Between Past and Future: Eight Exercises in Political Thought* (New York: Penguin, 1977), p. 199.

4. In *Aesthetic Theory*, trans. C. Lenhardt (New York: Routledge, 1984), Theodor Adorno takes a similar position concerning the antagonism of art and society: Art "is social because it stands opposed to society. By congealing into

an entity unto itself—rather than obeying existing social norms and thus proving itself to be 'socially useful'—art criticizes society just by being there. . . . This social deviance of art is the determinate negation of a determinate society. . . . Art will live on only as long as it has the power to resist society. . . . What it contributes to society is not some directly communicable content but something more mediate, i.e., resistance" (p. 321).

5. Arendt thus has a very traditional, one could even say "predevastation," view of art: that, no matter what, endurance must be assumed to be a defining characteristic of art. In terms of this issue, Adorno's position is quite different, for he attacks the notion of endurance as being antiquated: "Aesthetics, or what is left of it, seems to assume tacitly that the survival of art is unproblematic. Central for this kind of aesthetics therefore is the question of how art survives, not whether it will survive at all. This view has little credibility today. Aesthetics can no longer rely on art as a fact. If art is to remain faithful to its concept, it must pass over into anti-art, or it must develop a sense of self-doubt which is born of the moral gap between its continued existence and mankind's catastrophes, past and future" (Aesthetic Theory, p. 464).

6. Arendt's "pessimism" concerning the present could in fact be argued, then, to be rooted in an "idealization" of sorts, not as concerns preindustrial society in general, however, but specifically in terms of the ancient world. Nevertheless, the question of her constant references to Greece and Rome cannot be casually dismissed as "nostalgic," as some of her critics claim, for these references are an integral part of her relentless historical investigation of political, aesthetic, and philosophical concepts and terminology, whose purpose is not in any way to encourage the mystification of or a return to "Greece," whatever that would mean, but rather to understand our historical indebtedness to "Greece" and "Rome" and, more important, our differences from what they represent. This is the aspect of her critical strategy that is undoubtedly the most clearly marked by the thought of Heidegger, who, in passages such as the following, strongly advocates such critical-historical investigation: "The more clearly and simply a decisive inquiry traces the history of Western thought back to its few essential stages, the more this history's power to reach forward, seize, and commit grows. This is especially the case where it is a matter of overcoming such history. Whoever believes that philosophical thought can dispense with its history by a simple proclamation will, without his knowing it, be dispensed with by history. . . . He will think he is being original when he is merely rehashing what has been transmitted and mixing together traditional interpretations into something ostensibly new. The greater a revolution is, the more profoundly must it plunge into its history" (Nietzsche, vol. 1, trans. David Farrell Krell [San Francisco: Harper and Row, 1979], p. 203).

7. Immanuel Kant, Critique of Judgment, trans. Werner S. Pluhar (Indianapolis: Hackett, 1987), p. 160.

8. In her *Lectures on Kant's Political Philosophy* (Chicago: University of Chicago Press, 1982), Arendt constantly stresses this side of Kant's thought. For example: "We were talking about the political implications of critical thinking and the notion that critical thinking implies communicability. Now communicability obviously implies a community of men who can be addressed and who are listening and can be listened to. To the question, Why are there men rather than Man? Kant would have answered: In order that they may talk to one another" (p. 40).

9. Jean-François Lyotard's "defines" a *différend* in the following way: "A differend [*différend*] would be a case of conflict between (at least) two parties, that cannot be equitably resolved for lack of a rule of judgment applicable to both arguments. One side's legitimacy does not imply the other's lack of legitimacy. However, applying a single rule of judgment to both in order to settle their differend as though it were a merely a litigation would wrong (at least) one of them (and both of them if neither side admits this rule). . . . The title of this book suggests . . . that a universal rule of judgment between heterogeneous genres is lacking in general" (*The Differend: Phrases in Dispute*, trans. Georges Van Den Abbeele [Minneapolis: University of Minnesota Press, 1988], p. 9).

10. Jürgen Habermas, *Philosophical-Political Profiles*, trans. Frederick G. Lawrence (Cambridge: MIT Press, 1983), pp. 178–79.

11. Arendt's analysis of totalitarianism is very detailed and specific and can in no way be confused with the liberal, cold war use of the term to refer to fascism and communism in general as equivalent ideologies opposed to liberal democracy. She gives the following brief definition of the term, which she develops throughout the last sections of *The Origins of Totalitarianism*: "The struggle for total domination of the total population of the earth, the elimination of every competing nontotalitarian reality, is inherent in the totalitarian regimes themselves. . . . Totalitarianism in power uses the state administration for its long-range goal of world conquest and for the direction of the branches of the movement; it establishes the secret police as the executors and guardians of its domestic experiment in constantly transforming reality into fiction; and it finally erects concentration camps as special laboratories to carry through its experiment in total domination" (p. 392). For Arendt, all these elements have to be present for a regime to be considered totalitarian. The project for mobilization and domination must be *total*.

12. Arendt argues that sensual experience itself depends on the existence of others: "Even the experience of the materially and sensually given world depends upon my being in contact with other men, upon our *common* sense which regulates and controls all other senses and without which each of us would be enclosed in his own particularity of sense data which in themselves are unreliable and treacherous. Only because we have common sense, that is only because not one man, but men in the plural inhabit the earth can we trust

our immediate sensual experience" (p. 476). Perhaps one could say that, for Arendt, the most intense and complicated form of sensual experience is that of art, but the argument that there is no aesthetic judgment that does not imply the irresolvable plurality of others and their judgments is already an argument about the sensual experience of the material world in general. This is why total terror destroys experience itself, why the absence or reduction of aesthetic experience is in itself a devastating *political* phenomenon.

13. If publicness for Kant is, as Arendt claims in her *Lectures on Kant's Political Philosophy,* the "'transcendental principle' that should rule all action" (p. 60), she goes to great lengths to distinguish between the actor and the fabricator, on the one hand, and the spectator, on the other, only then to link them to each other again in terms of the judgment necessary to produce and act in a public way. What is *essentially public* for her is not that actions are taken by individuals or groups in the name of a collectivity or that an art object is produced for or received by a plurality of spectators or critics, and even though this initially produces a clash of opinions among them, their differences are expressed with the ultimate goal of agreement: "The public realm is constituted by the critics and the spectators, not by the actors or the makers. And this critic and spectator sits in every actor and fabricator; without this critical, judging faculty the doer or maker would be so isolated from the spectator that he would not even be perceived" (p. 63).

14. Arendt distinguishes between Kant and Hegel in terms of the question of the spectator: "The spectator, not the actor, holds the clue to the meaning of human affairs—only, and this is decisive, Kant's spectators exist in the plural, and this is why he could arrive at a political philosophy. Hegel's spectator exists strictly in the singular: the philosopher becomes the organ of the Absolute Spirit, and the philosopher is Hegel himself. *The Life of the Mind* (New York: Harcourt Brace Jovanovich, 1978), p. 96.

15. Jean-François Lyotard, "Sensus communis," in *La Cahier du College International de Philosophie* (March 1987), no. 3, p. 71.

16. Jean-François Lyotard, *Peregrinations* (New York: Columbia University Press, 1988), p. 38.

17. Jean-Luc Nancy, *La Communaute Desoeuvree* (Paris: Christian Bourgeois, 1986).

18. See Blanchot's own reading of Georges Bataille and his response to Nancy's notion of community as a "nonwork" in the first chapter of *La Communauté inavouable* (Paris: Minuit, 1983), which is entitled "La Communauté négative."

19. Nancy lists the following projections of community that in each case he rejects: community "did not occur among the Guayaqui Indians, it did not occur in the age of huts, it did not occur in the Hegelian 'spirit of a people,' nor in the Christian *agapé*" (pp. 33–34).

20. Nancy thus argues that "a community is not a unifying project, nor in a general sense a productive or operative project—nor a *project* at all (that is its radical difference with the 'spirit of a people,' which from Hegel to Heidegger has figured the collectivity as a project and the project, reciprocally, as collective" (p. 42).

21. See Philippe Lacoue-Labarthe and Jean-Luc Nancy, "The Nazi Myth," trans. Brian Holmes, in *Critical Inquiry* 16 (Winter 1990), for an analysis of what they call "the myth of Nazism, or of the National Socialist myth *as such*. We will speak, in other words, of the fashion by which National Socialism constitutes itself, with or without the use of myths, in a dimension, for a function, and with a self-assurance that all three can be properly called mythic" (p. 292).

22. Nancy is not arguing that mythological thought in general is responsible for Nazism but that all mythological thought and all thinkers of myth have some connection to it, that Nazism exploited the power of myth: "This does not mean that all thinkers of myth, from the nineteenth century on, are responsible for Nazism: but it does mean that there is a connection between mythical thinking, mythical 'scenographics,' and the working through and staging of a 'Volk' and of a 'Reich,' in the sense that Nazism gave to these terms" (*La Communauté Désoeuvrée*, p. 117).

23. For further analysis of the devastating effects of what is usually referred to as the aestheticization of politics under National Socialism, but what in this context should be called the operation of fiction as politics or the fiction of the political, see Philippe Lacoue-Labarthe, *La Fiction du politique: Heidegger, l'art et la politique* (Paris: Christian Bougois, 1987), translated by Chris Turner as *Heidegger, Art, and Politics: The Fiction of the Political* (Cambridge: Blackwell, 1990). Lacoue-Labarthe characterizes National Socialism as a "national aestheticism" (p. 58), which "does not merely mean that the work of art (tragedy, music, drama) offers the truth of the *polis* or of the State but that the political itself is instituted and constituted (and regularly regrounds itself) in and as a work of art" (p. 64). "It is the community itself, the people or the nation, that is the work [*oeuvre*] following the conception acknowledged by Romanticism of the work as subject and the subject as work. . . . The infinitization or the absolutization of the subject, which is at the heart of the metaphysics of the Moderns, here finds its properly *operational* manifestation: the community in action and at work [*à l'oeuvre et au travail*] (National *Socialism* as National *Aestheticism*) works itself into a work [*s'oeuvre*], if this can be said, and works (on) itself [*se travaille elle-même*], thereby accomplishing the subjective process par excellence, that is, the process of self-formation and self-production" (p. 70, translation modified).

24. See Nancy's *Le Partage des voix* (Paris: Galilée, 1982), which is a provocative critique and recasting of hermeneutics whose concluding words an-

nounce the project of *La Communauté Désoeuvrée*: "Community remains to be thought according to the partition/sharing [*le partage*] of the *logos*. This can surely not provide a new *foundation* for community, but it will indicate perhaps a new task in terms of community: neither its reunion, nor its division, nor its assumption, nor its dispersion, but its *partition/sharing*. . . . We have been communicating in this partition/sharing and announcing this partition/sharing to each other ever 'since we have been a dialogue and have been listening one to the other' (Hölderlin)" (p. 90).

25. Theodor Adorno argues in a similar vein that "art maintains its integrity only by refusing to go along with communication" (*Aesthetic Theory*, p. 443). In the same work, Adorno characterizes the way art communicates as a "lack of communication. . . . This noncommunication points to the fractured nature of art" (p. 7).

Back from Moscow, in the USSR

J'avais . . . trop lu de récits de voyage [I had . . . read too many travel narratives]
——Gide, *Retouches à mon Retour de l'U.R.S.S.*

For the moment don't expect any attempt on my part to describe my stay here
——Benjamin to Scholem, from Moscow,
December 10, 1926

Travel Agency (Preamble and Prospectus)

Fort/Da (Back from/Back in the U.S. . . . .)

This title, "Back from Moscow, in the USSR," is a consortium of citations. You will have been quick to identify them.

What I would like to propose to you under this false title, will it be a sort of narrative? Will it be the narrative of a trip I made to Moscow from February 26 to March 6 of this year [1990] (at the invitation of the Institute of Philosophy of the Academy of Sciences of the USSR)? A travelogue [*un récit de voyage raisonné*]?

Yes and no. Yes because in a certain way, directly or indirectly, I will not be able to do otherwise. No because, without being capable of it, I would like to avoid the risks of every travelogue. You know them as well as I do. The first is that of selectivity, especially for someone who has

Translated by Mary Quaintaire. I thank Peggy Kamuf for her help in the final preparation of this text.

never known how to tell stories—and that is the case with me. A *récit raisonné* is a narrative that, more than others, filters or sifts out the supposedly significant features—and thus begins to censor. The second risk results from the first: *raisonner* also signifies, in this case, to *rationalize*. In the code of psychoanalysis, this at times connotes active over-interpretation: it imposes order *after the fact* where there was none before, to draw a certain benefit, if only that of intelligibility or simple meaningfulness.

I still hesitate to propose a travel narrative for a less general reason. Here it touches on my very topic. It is a matter of nothing less than a certain relation between the literary genre and history, notably political history. We have at our disposal, in this century, a particularly striking example of works whose formal "genre," "type," or "mode" (I do not know which of the categories proposed by Genette is the appropriate choice here), along with a certain thematic generality, are essentially linked to a finished sequence of the political history of a country, of more than one country, a sequence that also marks a decisive moment in the history of humanity. I am talking about the rich, brief, intense, and dense tradition of *back from the USSRs*, a tradition to which, by metonymy, I propose to give the title that André Gide chose in 1936 for his famous work. Before the October Revolution, there were no such works. There will be no more tomorrow; there can already be no more after the end of the struggles and hopes, the anticipations and debates to which this revolution will have given rise [*donné lieu*]—and *donné lieu* from a unique geographic and political *lieu*, from an irreplaceable geo-political event, held to be *exemplary*, namely Moscow in the USSR (here we should emphasize in passing another paradox: as it has often been remarked recently, just when certain republics of the USSR have begun to claim their independence, in what is apparently a constitutional manner, the very name of the USSR is the only name of a state in the world that contains in itself no reference to a locality or a nationality, the only proper name of a state that, in sum, contains no given proper name, in the current sense of the term: the USSR is the name of an etatic individual, an individual and singular state that has given itself or claimed to give itself its own proper name without reference to any singular place or to any national past. At its foundation, a state has given itself a purely artificial, technical, conceptual, general, conventional, and constitutional name, a common name in sum, a "communist" name: in short a purely political name. I know no other example of a comparable phenomenon in the world and we will surely have to return to this from another point of view; the case of the *United Kingdom* no doubt remains to be analyzed separately since it is not the only name for that ensemble, if I am not mistaken. In any case, one of the differences between the U.S.A. and the USSR is that the first confederation claims to give itself—with the name of a place, America—the name of a people).

It certainly seems to me that there is no other example, in the history of human culture, of the type of works that, like these *back from the USSRs* from October 1917 until recently, are linked with a unique, finished, irreversible, and nonrepeatable sequence of a political history—and are linked with this sequence in the very respect that welds foundation to form, semantics or thematics to the structure of the narrative of autobiographical-travel-testimony. When I describe this appearance or advance this hypothesis, is it a naive proposition on my part? A proposition that exposes itself to counterexamples and calls for a more patient historical examination, a more rigorous historiographic reflection?

Perhaps. In any case, I submit this hypothesis for your discussion. Everything that I will say from this point on should nonetheless tend to put the hypothesis to the test, that is, to isolate the singular and pertinent features that would forbid or in any case limit any analogy between the type of works I am talking about and some other type to which one might be tempted to compare it. Here I am thinking of pilgrimage narratives, of every poem in the direction of a "paradise lost" or a "promised land," of all utopias, of old or new Jerusalems, Athenses, Romes (Moscow was also the other Rome of Christianity) as well as of, for example, witness accounts of the French Revolution, all of which are so many reflective, historical, philosophical narrations signed by foreign travelers.

But here the hypothesis and the appearance do not concern only the type, the goal, or the confines of certain writings in an essential relation to the singularity of a historical sequence. It is not simply a matter of circumscribing the now-exhausted possibility of certain "travel narratives" of the *back from the USSR* type. It is also, perhaps, a matter of becoming conscious or taking the measure of a fact as formidable as it is provocative, by turns paralyzing and imperious for whoever would like in his turn to tell his little story and add his little version to the venerable archive of *back from the USSRs*: unless they conceive in its fullness and radicality the unique seism that is now shaking the history of the world—and whose epicenter, after all, may not at all be in Moscow, supposing that there even is an epicenter somewhere—unless they try to become conscious or take the measure of what Perestroika is at least a flagrant symptom of, a symptom that *destroys at its root* the possibility of all *back from the USSRs*, which from now on are out of date; unless they try to say something momentous and new on this subject, all narratives by travelers (like me, for example) risk being either mediocre and belated apings unworthy of their proper canon or, in the best of cases, a "private" travel diary, published by accident and into the bargain, recounting things that are sometimes interesting or picturesque, sometimes complacent anecdotes, but whose singularity has no essential relation with the political history of the world.

After all, one could do such a reading of Benjamin's *Moscow Diary* (English translation in *October*, 1935 [I also stayed at the grand "official" hotel *Oktober* in Moscow] of 1986, with a preface by G. Scholem dated Jerusalem, where Benjamin so often wrote to him). I also emphasize these facts to usher in a certain *ellipse with two focal points*, Moscow and Jerusalem, which in traversing our discussion will not fail to cross another ellipse, if that is possible, the one that stretches between a para-Oedipal Greek mythology and a revelation of the Mosaic or messianic type: in 1926–27, Benjamin finds himself between Moscow and Jerusalem, between the German communist party that he hesitates to rejoin at the time and the Zionism to which he will never adhere, as between two brothers—the two Scholem brothers, Werner and Gershom—and two influences as well, his two friends the communist and the Zionist. Instead of interrogating this two-month diary as a historical document or a literary and philosophico-political work, one could also in fact compare the *Moscow Diary* to the interrupted memoirs of an intense and tragic passion for Asja Lacis, the woman whom Benjamin describes in a letter to Scholem as a "Russian revolutionary from Riga, one of the most remarkable women I have ever met" and who opened up in the very body of his life a wound so profound and uneffaceable that he dedicated *One-Way Street* as follows: "This street is named Asja Lacis Street, after the engineer who laid it through the author."

Next to these grand examples, and after a ten-day trip, I ask myself if I have something to say that merits being read or heard, and that would be up to the measure of a great historical event, a great private passion, even less to the crossing of the two. I have perhaps learned less, and you will as well perhaps, from my trip to Moscow than through good read-ings, and thanks to the work of competent journalists or historians, of involved and informed political analysts. And if I had something very "private" or "new" to say on the subject of my recent trip to Moscow, perhaps I am not yet ready for it. Perhaps its form is not yet accessible to me. Perhaps it can have no relation to a paper destined for my friends in Irvine's Critical Theory Group, who no doubt expect something else from me.

As Walter Benjamin's *Moscow Diary* (1926–27) could have done ten years earlier had it been published at the time, the title of André Gide's book, *Retour de l'URSS, suivi de retouches à mon Retour de l'URSS* (1936–37), could thus serve as a metonymic and generic title for a whole series of analogous works (narratives, diaries, reflections) that, from 1917 until our time, have limited politics to literature. I do indeed say "to literature" for these works are signed by writers and are integrated into corpuses taken to be literary; they have a specificity, whether it is a matter of formal structure, rhythm, temporality or internal dramatiza-tion, and I will speak of this later. They also belong to the space called autobiographical and thus pose all the now-canonical problems of the relations between autobiography and literariness, autobiography and fictionality, autobiography and referentiality. These autobiographical sequences interest us; we generally accord them credit and authority in the first place and perhaps uniquely because such "testimonials" are also the doing of already "legitimate" writer-intellectuals whose princi-pal commitment is at once literary and political. No doubt better in-formed, more lucid, ultimately more interesting analyses and descrip-tions concerning "the thing itself" (the USSR, Moscow, and the course of the Soviet Revolution) are perhaps destined not to appear or to reach only the "biodegradability" of the archive; and this is because of their authors' lack of credit on the scene of public legitimation or the condi-tions of their publication, supposing that they have even crossed the threshhold of the public space. This last problem is always serious, but it is particularly and originally so when the regimes or the societies in question are those we are going to talk about. Under what conditions does one publish today in the USSR? I will evoke the new particulars of this question later; they concern less directly an explicit policy of cen-sorship than one of a political economy of paper, of a certain relation-ship between "memoirs" and paper.

I will limit myself for the moment to a few examples—Gide or Benjamin, to begin with—so as not to lose myself in too rich a corpus, one hard to delimit and that I know less well, especially when it is not French (here let me indicate in passing a whole program of study for the future, if it has one, of a department of comparative literature in expansion) and especially so as not to entangle myself in problems of delimitation that are certainly interesting but on which I must economize here, such as the question of knowing where to place, in this rich corpus, less clearly "literary" works like the Beatles song or the book-diary of my compatriot "comparatist" Etiemble entitled *Le meurtre du petit père (ligne d'une vie ii)*. I would like nonetheless to say a few words about these two works, so different from each other and so different from the others.

The Beatles song is perhaps what finally must have given me the idea to write these few pages several weeks after my first—and so, for the time being, my only—trip to Moscow, and to do it the moment I was back in the U.S., when, having barely unpacked my bags and with a case of the flu, I wrote this and destined it first for my American friends or colleagues of University of California–Irvine's Critical Theory Group. This decision was announced more than made, not only because, sharing it a bit in my fashion, I am well acquainted with your political concern, your interest in the historical thing, your legitimate desire not to pass by real history, but also because I ask myself what I am doing with my life today when I travel between Jerusalem, Moscow, and Los Angeles with my lectures and strange writings in my suitcase at this very precise moment of History, as one rightly says, which I want to talk about, to talk to you about a little. This project was formed within me at the very moment my plane touched down in Moscow after flying very low over the snow-covered plains. The Beatles song deserves to be cited here, at least because it inverts the Gidian title to which it seems to refer. It does not in fact say, like Gide, "Back from the USSR," but rather "Back in the USSR." And moreover, as I am doing here between Irvine and Laguna Beach, it commemorates the return *to* the U.S., by playing on the initials—the initial initials. This is the second verse:

> Been away so long I hardly knew the place
> Gee it's good to be back home
> Leave it 'til tomorrow to unpack my case
> Honey disconnect the phone
> I'm back in the USSR.
> You don't know how lucky you are boy
> Back in the U.S. Back in the U.S. Back in the USSR.

The reference is all the more tempting at the moment of my return to the U.S. in that the Beatles are not content to play on the homonymy or the metonymy between U.S. and USSR (impossible to play on in my language, where one says URSS) or between the two Georgias ("And Moscow girls make me sing and shout / That Georgia's always on my mind"). They are not content to stage a twinning or a specularity, more and more interesting today, between U.S. and USSR. They do it while inscribing in their song the citation of a Beach Boys Californian melody. All this is good reason for me to address this postcard from Moscow to Californians and for me to address it a little late in California, from Laguna Beach in Southern California. (And then, I could not help thinking of the Beatles the moment I left Moscow, when I went through customs without any problem at the airport. Ten years ago in Prague, just before being taken to prison and just after an eight-hour official interrogation, I asked the commissar in an aside, "Come on, just between us, tell me, do you really believe, deep down, that someone like me—an intellectual, a philosopher, an old prof—is going to amuse himself by coming to Czechoslovakia to undertake some drug trafficking?" (Production and traffic of drugs were the charges that had just been officially brought against me.) The commissar's response: "Yes, yes, exactly, we are used to it; it's people like you who do that, most often, well-known intellectuals, artists—look what happened to the Beatles in Japan. Listen, I tell you this to reassure you, they also were indulgent with them precisely because they are very well known."

Oedipus and the Jewish Question

Etiemble's double diary could also have interested us from several points of view. It is a diary of travel in the USSR covering several periods, that of the naive enthusiasm in 1934 (after Benjamin but before Gide, then) and that of disappointment and severe judgment in 1958. Between the two, the man who passes or would like to pass for the master, indeed the founder, of comparative literature in France makes two trips to the United States in 1937 and 1943; and he inserts the two American "diaries" between the two Russian "diaries." The comparatist notes in Chicago that "culture determines the man more strictly than 'nation' or 'race,' more strictly even than 'class' of origin" (p. 149). He was inspired to make this remark, interesting on the part of someone who calls himself and still at this time believes himself a Marxist and a revolutionary, by the time he spent with certain of the writers and comparatists that were his colleagues:

I feel fraternal with my colleague Weinberg: more than with French bourgeois, more even than with French workers. We have the same profession, he and I; Liautey felt more affinity for a Prussian officer than for a chimney sweep from Auvergne. It would be quite foolish to be indignant at this. The *technopsychology* everyone used to talk about so much does not seem to be progressing at all; in any case, in the essentials, there exists no divergence between Weinberg, for example, and myself. We have read the same books, listened to the same records; *we test our merits on the track—we aren't worth much* [this reminded me of jogging sessions with Hillis Miller, Frank Lentricchia, David Carroll, and Richard Regosin]—for our profession stiffens the legs and contracts the rib cage. Thus I felt fraternal [second occurrence of the word "fraternal": for Etiemble too the friend, the *semblable*, the neighbor is a brother—I venture this remark in the margins of a seminar given at Irvine last year on the "politics of friendship" that made us attentive to that old virile scheme of fraternity that dominates the canonical model of friendship, private and political, between men] with Tai Wang-chou, who taught at Nankin, before revealing himself to be one of the greatest Chinese poets of the twentieth century. Culture determines the man more strictly than "nation" or "race," more strictly than "class" of origin.

Three remarks, in passing, on this diary note dated Chicago, April 7, 1937:

1. First of all, it invites any traveler to be prudent who, in Moscow, this country, or elsewhere, ends up fatally enclosed in a single sociocultural milieu: interests and points of reference tend by definition to become identified with one another and thus to efface differential features. In Moscow, with two or three exceptions that I will get to later, I could only talk with intellectuals, mostly with intellectuals of the Academy of Sciences—that is, with a very select group of researchers, rather privileged from a certain point of view and, generally speaking, foreign to the university if not hostile or vaguely condescending with regard to most academics. But also, more narrowly, within Moscow's Academy of Sciences, whose official guest I was, I had substantial exchanges only with the members of a subgroup of the Institute of Philosophy, the recently created semiofficial "Laboratory for Studies of Postclassical Philosophy," about fifteen or so young researchers who were sometimes joined by intellectuals from the same milieu, who shared the same interests but came from Minsk, Leningrad, or Riga. In any case, with all their irreplaceable qualities in this situation (taste for hospitality; intelligence; generosity; the desire to inform me on everything I could not

directly see, which is to say almost everything; multilinguism; etc.), these interlocutors, who were also fervent friends, were nonetheless by definition the intellectuals closest to me, the least likely to make me feel out of my element, those who in this country shared or wished to share the most with me, inscribed as they already were on a map linking Moscow to the United States, via Paris (where one of these colleagues had already gone and would return to participate in a colloquium, "Lacan with the Philosophers," at the International College of Philosophy the following May), Yale (one among them being able, for example, to allude to Hillis Miller's Presidential Address at the MLA on the topic of deconstruction in America!), Cornell (via Susan Buck-Morse, who visits them often in Moscow), and Duke University (where three of them had just spent several days at the invitation of Fredric Jameson, with whom they share certain projects). Thus, despite all the windows that they did open for me on the country and on what is happening there now, they enclosed me in the specular circle of a complicity against which, while recognizing with gratitude what could be helpful and gratifying in it, I had to try to defend myself.

2. Etiemble's note involves another paradox. Someone who called himself a Marxist in 1937 needed a certain independence of mind to say, or in any case to think and to write in his diary, that "culture determines the man more strictly than . . . 'class' of origin"; but as for saying, in the same sentence and the same breath, that "culture determines the man more strictly than 'nation' or than 'race,'" that is what our times—and notably what is happening this very day, I will say at once in the USSR, around Russia, and in the world in general—ought to oblige us to think about anew.

3. Whatever may be determinant today about "culture" (what I would still call here, to move quickly, by this confused and problematic word) notably in the seism that is so heterogeneously shaking all the countries of the East or of South Africa, is in fact becoming more apparent than ever, on the condition that we profoundly revitalize the approach to the structures, the media, the operation, the "causalities" in general of everything filed away under the old concept of culture or, again, of what would formerly have been called "ideology."

There is something that is generally interpreted (crudely but not necessarily erroneously) as a "movement of democratization," as "democratization in progress" in many countries. This is no doubt what calls for profound, difficult, and new analyses of "infrastructural" causalities (which are too often given up, as is a Marxian theoretical approach capable of transforming itself—that is, worthy of that name), whether they concern markets, the forces and relations of production, their mediated or immediate links with the technosciences, which is also to say with the laws of the militaro-industrial field and "culture."

But these "movements of democratization," in all their diversity, in the too-often-neglected difference of their style and their rhythm, would not have been possible without a profound and, I believe, determinant transformation of causalities said to be cultural. To recognize this massive fact is facile and trivial. It is well known that without the ultimately irrepressible circulation of techniques of reproduction, of televisual images, music, and film, discourses that could be achieved according to new modalities, without the circulation of scholars, intellectuals, indeed athletes themselves, and above all of images of these producers of discourses and images, the sociopolitical models, the scenes of everyday life of peoples, the schemas of what we call "material culture" could never have given rise to this more-or-less spontaneous comparative analysis that made their own way of life intolerable to certain peoples or to certain majority segments of certain peoples. We know all this, of course, but the appropriate analyses of this type of phenomenon are far from being up to the task. We lack not only refined conceptual instruments but also a more "general," "fundamental," "radical" vigilance as to the very axiomatics that would come to support these analyses. To say, for example, that a "democratization" is in progress and to mean by that all the movements in progress in the East is not perhaps false but it is surely very confused. Especially when this supposes that we have a rigorous model of democracy, an assured experience, a frozen concept, at home, *chez nous* in the West; and especially, therefore, when a naive euphoria or a very calculated strategy tries to credit the idea that what these peoples want (which is sometimes but not always true), what they ought to want in any case, is to rejoin us and resemble us by taking part in the great space of liberalism, both political and economic.

So how does one dare say something of a recent trip to Moscow if one does not give oneself the time, the means, and the conditions necessary to think and begin to say "that very thing," *cela même*—that which this word "democratization" so confusedly covers with all the investments capitalized in it? How else does one avoid peripheral chatter, unless one tells the story of a "private" trip that has nothing to do—if at least that were possible—with the historical and political thing. But this is no less difficult and it is not what is expected from me here.

I do not wish to advance any farther on this path for the moment. I was simply commenting on the word "culture" in a sentence by Etiemble. I underscored some precautions to be taken when one recognizes (legitimately, up to a certain point) that culture played an apparently determinant role in the movements of democratization that have accelerated in these last few months. People have been gripped with enthusiasm before spontaneous and nonviolent revolutions whose leaders have sometimes been intellectuals or poet-playwrights who had always resisted in legality (this is eminently the case in the Czech "revolution," with the militants of Charter 77 and Vaclav Havel; we would also have to speak of Sakharov and of a professor at the University of Moscow, great scholar, historian, expert on icons, and currently a deputy in parliament). But it goes without saying (and we forget or pretend to forget this) that without Soviet Perestroika and therefore the awareness of the Czech, Hungarian, Romanian, and East German armed forces (for the military has been too little spoken of in this phase), without an assurance that they had to have received from the Soviet military officials and politicos, concerning the nonintervention of tanks in Bucharest, Prague, Budapest, East Berlin, or Warsaw, none of all this would have been possible or thinkable, in particular that most often nonviolent "spontaneity." This should not at all diminish our admiration for the conditions in which the peoples and their new leaders often engaged this democratization, notably in Czechoslovakia. But shared admiration or enthusiasm should not blind us to the effective conditions of these immense events.

I will not leave Etiemble's book without first taking from it several other preliminary benchmarks. Still letting myself be guided by the same hypothesis, I select another essential feature. Etiemble's diary is written with a double urgency, as are all the other *back from the USSRs*: an account must be given of a unique process in which the fate of human society is at stake *in a place, in an exemplary country* but also of the fact that the very period of this experience, or rather of this experimentation, is structurally provisional—and apprehended as such. This is what Etiemble writes in Moscow on August 13, 1934:

> The idea of dictatorship:
>
> 1. The proletariat is the only force that dares—that has the frankness to proclaim dictatorship (everything that this implies for a [illegible word] bourgeois). All egotistical and bourgeois dictators camouflage their dictatorship under less frightening names. "Duce," "Führer,"

"Leader." The proletariat, on the other hand, knows that it can affirm *its* dictatorship, because it is not that of a man.

2. This dictatorship, it must not be forgotten, means to be only *provisional* [my emphasis].

Hitler and Mussolini are dictators for life. Mussolini already knows that his son-in-law will succeed him . . . unless . . . and Hitler, after the death of Hindenburg, has conferred upon himself the privilege of choosing the next Reichsführer.

Here, a *transitory* [my emphasis] period in any proletarian revolution. And to appreciate the Russian Revolution better, let us refer to the Chinese revolution of Sun Yat-sen who foresaw, before the constitutional period, a period of "military trusteeship." The latter still remains, because of the egoisms of the generals. There is nothing of the sort in Russia, which is accused of militarism.

Lenin's mausoleum and the crowd that waits to file by.

This admiration for a dead man, isn't it better than the adoration for who knows what saint?   (pp. 66–67)

I interrupt the citation of this 1934 text for a moment to make two remarks; not on what we might be tempted, with a certain historical ingenuousness, to consider in Etiemble as a rare historical ingenuousness (which it certainly was not at the time—rare, that is). Rather, on the one hand, I want to recall that even today the crowd—I saw it a few weeks ago—"waits to file by" "Lenin's mausoleum," whose image seems not yet to have suffered too much, at least in the official ideology, in the imagery of public places and in something like popular consciousness. On the other hand, I want to sharpen my hypothesis a bit on the historical unicity of the series of works of the *Back from Moscow, in the USSR* type. Since they are not narratives of travels "abroad," to distant countries with an unfamiliar culture, but rather of travels toward a new model of "home" to come, of the Revolution to be imported, toward what Gide, as we shall hear in a moment, calls a "chosen fatherland," the historicity of these works resembles certain paradigms without resembling them. At the moment that it marks the experience, that it is even constituted by the historical experimentation of a revolution whose event is both past and present, in progress and in the process of repeating itself, renewing itself, through a "period," as we just read, that is essentially "transitory" and "provisional," the original historicity of these works seems to me incomparable to anything but narratives of pilgrimage—for example, to Jerusalem.

But this analogy would be limited by two essential features:

1. The place is not the archive or the seal of an event that has already taken place but rather of a process in progress, though the dimension of promise, of eschatology or messianism could save the analogy (I also believe that one could and should push the analogy as far as possible, if only to refine the difference, however minute);

2. The Revolution (of men for men) wants to be, it *claims* to mark the end of religion and pilgrimage, of myths and sacralization: Stalin is in the process of destroying hundreds and hundreds (four hundred in Moscow, I am told) of sites of a cult whose locations are sometimes shown still today beneath horrible architecture, swimming pools, or offices. They even say that the ground has not stopped dissolving there where Stalin wanted to replace a church with who knows what socialist construction that he finally had to give up. Above all, it is clear that for Etiemble, Lenin's mausoleum is not the tomb of Christ: Lenin is no more a saint than Moscow is Jerusalem. But because he points out that this "adoration" of a dead man is worth still "more," it will always be easy to decipher this discourse as raising stakes of religious sublimation and thus to inscribe the texts we are speaking of in the tradition of pilgrimage novels. And what can be said of these "narratives" can be said first, a priori and a fortiori, for the "Revolution" itself.

I return to this citation to take from it, beyond the evocation of what one could call the Holy Face or Holy Shroud of Lenin, two allusions to the *Jewish question* and to the *question of nationalism*, since we will have to come back to them more than once, as to *three* major questions in the USSR today (the memory or the body of Lenin, the Jewish question, and the question of nationalisms). It is not necessary for me to add to the following passage the cruel or painful commentary that it calls for:

Nightclub. Eisenstein.

Dynamo Stadium: it is more beautiful than the arena at Nîmes.
Removing oneself from the inanities of one's friends, it is very nice.
A party at the House of the Red Army. Strange that this house of the Red Army is a place of culture, music, and dance.

1. Chopin, Beethoven.
2. Kirghiz songs (the warrior mounting his horse),
Jews (philosopher with a rat's brain),
bachkir (sic): love and spring that come but once.
In the language in which they were composed.
There's good nationalism!

The moment the Jews have no more right to the city in "kulturesque" Germany, Russia organizes a Jewish socialist republic and gives recitals of Jewish songs. Which reminds me of the story of Brunot [a great professor and author of, among other things, a monumental history of the French language] at the Sorbonne: explicating Garnier's *The Jews*, he proposed to have the choruses sung by Jewish choirs to give his students an idea of what that might produce. A tide of opinion among the nationalist student groups caused this attempt to fail. Here then is a bourgeois France that gets put in its place by the USSR!

Mausoleum. I would like to be one of the soldiers of the Red Army who have the honor of keeping their watch at the head and feet of the glass "coffin" in which V. I. [Vladimir Ilitch, i.e., Lenin] lies embalmed. I always envy the one who, at Lenin's feet, always sees this face from the front. . . .

Here, an old nightclub under the tsars.

Today, it is where Eisenstein works.

Moscow, August 14

The force of *La Marseillaise* and the weakness resulting from the fact that we no longer perceive its meaning! *San-gimpur, sillon*, everything is blended as if in a magic formula of syllables that have no intelligible import.

What makes for the import of the *Internationale* (beyond the beauty of the couplets) is that it is understood by those who love it and by those who hate it. Proof of its still-fresh vitality.

La Marseillaise, which was revolutionary, has aged. The bourgeois cling to old debris.

In the USSR, many people are especially alarmed by the beauty of the women and the firmness of their breasts.

Why, at the risk of stretching out the preliminaries indefinitely, am I thus tempted by these long citations?

No doubt, first of all, before the enormity of this credulous passion that was so widely and so painfully shared by so many intellectuals and writers, I cite certain passages, almost at random, to recall from what a distance *one had to come back*. Etiemble had to come back—not come back from Moscow but come back from his first return from Moscow. In French, as you know, there are at least two interesting idiomatic locutions around the word *revenir* and they would be very useful here. "On n'en revient pas" means that one is stupefied, amazed, one can scarcely believe what one sees as it is so enormous, disproportionate, indeed obscene. In this case, "on n'en revient pas" faced with an Etiemble who himself "n'en revient pas" from his trip to Moscow: he is in a perpetual state of blessed astonishment. Then he had no choice but to "en revenir," from Moscow and the Soviet Revolution. The other locution of the French idiom "en revenir" means "to lose one's illusions," "lose faith," endure the cruelty of a disappointment. And the moment that one "en revient" is here all the more serious in that one "revient de loin" [returns from afar], as a third French expression would have it, and in that one returns from a moment and a place where one could not be done with "ne pas en revenir." At bottom, this is perhaps the trajectory of most of these *back from Moscow, in the USSRs*: one goes there ready to explain, upon return, to friends and sympathizers, why and how one "n'en est pas revenu" given it was so wonderful; then one "en revient" and it is necessary to "retouch" and to say at what point it very much became necessary to "en revenir en revenant de loin." It is always a bitter pill, and all the more so because one thought one did not have to come back since one did not go there, abroad (*fort*) but here, home (*da*), to a "chosen fatherland."

If I am accumulating all these signs of faith or of enthusiastic credulity before sketching my own phantom narrative (since I went to Moscow at a time when it was no longer permissible for anyone not to "en revenir" and when everybody "en est revenu" from the Revolution, without knowing in what direction), it is to specify a "background": I shall soon have to describe in what respect, even though I have never been either a Marxist or a communist, *stricto sensu*, even though, in my youthful admiration for Gide, I read at fifteen (1945) his *Back from the USSR*, which left no doubt as to the tragic failure of the Soviet Revolution and today still seems to me a remarkable, solid and lucid work and even though, later, in Paris in the 1950s and 1960s, I had to resist— and it was not easy—a terrifying politico-theoretical intimidation of the Stanlinist or neo-Stalinist type in my most immediate personal and intellectual environment, this never kept me from sharing, in the mode of both hope and nostalgia, something of Etiemble's disarmed passion or childish imaginary in this romantic relation with the Soviet Revolution. I am always bowled over when I hear the *Internationale*, I tremble with emotion and then I always want to "go out into the streets" to fight against the Reaction. And despite so many differences, particularly that of generations, the history of my relations with communism, like his, passes by way of childhood (of which he speaks at the beginning of the book) and of the experience of the *Ecole normale supérieure* (the two pages of the forward of his book are entirely devoted to scenes on the *rue d'Ulm* and to his war against *L'Action française* and Brasillach, whom he calls "Robert the Devil" and forces to cross the street every time their paths cross. I would not be able to describe what my trip to Moscow was, in full Perestroika, if I had not said at least something about this revolutionary pathos, about the history of this affect or this affection, which I cannot, and in truth do not want to, give up completely. And so I will have to come back to it.

The other reason that I cited such a passage from Etiemble's diary is that I still must emphasize—it is an essential feature of this tradition of *back from Moscows*—that they claim to relate something quite other than a trip to a particular country or a determined culture. Rather, we are talking about a quest—as one says, a quest for the Grail, but this time the quest for the universal, for universally human meaning, for the human species speaking "in languages," without language or in a universal language. In this sense these trips are not trips; they are the end of the trip, if a trip leads one from a particular country toward another or from one culture to the other. Here one goes toward absolute human culture and, on return from the trip, one claims to report to the uncultured, to the barbarians still enclosed in their particular language, news of the absolute culture speaking in an absolute language that speaks, by way of Russian, the universality of ultimately human meaning, of the "human species," of the "internationale" *realized* at last, realized beyond verbal or linguistic formality. And at once the work itself—this event of language, the discourse of testimony, the travel narrative—must *efface itself in the service* of this universal cause. On the page that follows the passage I just cited, you can read:

> Morality and aesthetics
>
> The Pharisee, the bourgeois says: "Lord, you bear witness that I am just, moral order, etc." The other, the communist, clamors against aestheticism and verbal moralism—but realizes morality and aestheticism.
>
> The words whose meaning we do not understand, because we don't know Russian, these examples whose import we, Westerners, do not understand, because we don't know the human   (p. 71)

This appears to be in contradiction with the encomium for "good nationalism" that, a few pages earlier, applauded the use of the "language" of origin. The contradiction is only apparent: as in "good nationalism," as, since forever in all self-respecting "good nationalism," the Russian language bears witness to the universal; it finds itself bearing responsibility, at the heat of this revolutionary situation, for a universal meaning, message, future, in truth a universal discourse. We would soon see, if I were able to recount my own trip, in what respect the Russians and all the citizens of the Soviet Union are today, like everybody else, but at a more critical moment of this universal experience, torn not between nationalism and its opposite (supposing it has one) but among various *types* of nationalism, of memory or national affirmation, the "good" and the "bad" type.

We are not going to abandon Etiemble in the middle of his watch. He has "confessed" his errors (I purposely use this language that is as religious as that of the "autocritique": these discourses belong not only to the arena of faith—what discourses escape it?—but also to an *ecclesiastical* arena, and we should never forget that. All the more so in that we often live, still today, in intellectual or academic communities where the true fault consists less in committing a crime, in having, for example, written something abominable fifty years ago, than in not having confessed to it after the fact and humbling oneself before one's peers). From this autocritique as literary confessional, which covers hundreds of pages, I can only take two particularly symptomatic signs. One concerns Stalin and the national question, the other Gide's *Back from the USSR*, which we are thus approaching little by little. What allows the passage between the two is the *time of avowal*—the confession, one could say, the history of the interdiction that weighs so long on an avowal concerning the sin of the father, Stalin, the "little father of the people," the father of assassin of Jews. The avowal ultimately consists, after a long period of latency that is nothing other than that of Nazism, in the accomplishment of parricide. And the avowal itself is avowed, confessed in 1990, when the author declares, as the first sentence of the book, "I am eighty years old."

1. Etiemble's book is very recent. It was just published (January 1990) under the intentionally oedipal title *The Murder of the Little Father*. Far be it from me to try to minimize Stalin's crimes and the evil of what today is so facilely called Stalinism. But one day it will really be necessary to analyze the operation by which from this point on all the responsibilities are concentrated in the person of the "little father," that is, the operation by which they are expurgated, exorcized, objectivized, kept at a distance, and thus neutralized, if not annulled, in the body of the

despot-*pharmakos* (which furthermore cannot be found, I was told in Moscow: "burned, no doubt, and thrown no one knows where"). Finding myself in Moscow during the anniversary of Stalin's death, and at the same time recalling the scenes of distress at the Ecole normale in 1953, among the Stalinist students who since have become stars of the world intelligentsia and sometimes of anticommunism, I watched television in my room at the *Oktober* hotel: they were showing newsreels of the period, millions of Soviets in tears in Red Square, the spectacle of a collective sorrow the extent of which and, let us say to move quickly, the "spontaneity," the "sincerity" of which, in any case the not immediately "manipulated" character of which certainly has no real equivalent in the history of humanity, especially if one takes into account the structure of "specular" resemblance guaranteed by the filming and the televisual archive. I know of only three rivals to Stalin's telegenic body: the bodies of Nasser, Mao Tse-tung, and Khomeini. A rigorous comparative analysis would be necessary here. But I now know less than ever if the concept of "comparatism" can sustain the necessity and the dimensions of such a task.

And so, rereading in 1989 what he does not hesitate to call (p. 105) these "ridiculous notes" (which he could just as well not have published and which he doubtless published less out of a concern for confessing the truth than, when one knows Etiemble and the logic of confession, in the hopes of reaping, as always, some small narcissistico-exhibitionist benefit: look at me beat myself, I did not wait for you to do it, pity me and admire me, will you finally pay attention to me? and so forth. There, it is done), he accuses himself first of all of not having adequately accused Stalin and the "Russian nationalist" Stalin, executioner of nationalities and in particular of Ukrainians (you know that today it is not only the Baltic countries and Azerbaidjan that are reclaiming their national independence but also a very powerful Ukrainian movement). Here, then, is the last paragraph of this 1934 diary:

> Rereading these notes in 1989, what troubles me the most is that I made no allusion to a lavish feast in a Ukrainian kolkhoz: astounding quantity and quality. A little while ago I learned that in 1933, and thus the preceding year, Stalin starved to death millions of Ukrainians, guilty of indocility: of wanting to be Ukrainians and not dissolved in the turbid absence of a Russification and an extremist Stalinism. Thus does one travel in a country of tyranny, seeing nothing, knowing nothing, understanding nothing. Enslaved, and completely enlivened to be so.

2. When Gide published his *Back from the USSR* in 1936, two years after Etiemble's trip, the latter had already established his distance from the French party. Fascinated by Trotsky and the theme of "permanent revolution," he was becoming what he calls a "touristo-Trotskyist" in the "heteroclite band" of his political friends in Paris. The share of tourism in the expression "touristo-Trotskyism" would call for a systematic reflection on the relations between tourism and political analysis, notably in this century when tourism is, from every angle, more "organized" than at other times (which can both better enlighten and further blind the visitor). Such an analysis would have to allow a particular place to the intellectual tourist (writer or academic) who thinks he or she can, in order to make them public, translate his or her "travel impressions" into a political diagnostic.

The assumption is that the operation of a political and social apparatus phenomenalizes itself or the essential (this does not go without saying; far from it) and that its supposed phenomenality is accessible to the traveler (which goes even less without saying), even when this traveler does not speak the language, the languages and the subdialects of the country of the state visited (which seems to me to be completely out of the question; yet, it is the case with most of these travelers, in particular with Gide and Benjamin).

Because this assumption is neither totally and in all cases well-founded nor totally and in all cases false, it is necessary to reelaborate the whole problematic. After such a recasting (another joint program for our group and the department of comparative literature, once it is understood what "comparative" and "literature" mean in some sort of "comparative literature as a rigorous science"), it would be necessary to adjust the analysis to take into account all the differences in tourists, times, and places. It is difficult to create a series, on the same plane, of Benjamin, Gide, or Etiemble for "Moscow in the USSR," Barthes for Japan, or Baudrillard for America. (Here allow me to reserve all my personal evaluations and not even to evoke the still-recent examples, at once sinister and ridiculous, of certain *back from Chinas* in the 1970s.) That is why, at the moment I am writing these lines, I do not yet know if I will make up my mind next week to speak to you of my trip to Moscow. It will always be easier to quote Etiemble than to speak of myself—and it is doubtless more interesting for you.

And so Etiemble confides to us after his "second trip to Moscow, 1958," that after this he became a sort of "Touristo-Trotskyist," which leaves us to understand that he had until then been something else:

Between 1930 and 1934, Marx and Freud lit up a world for me that my whole education had somehow obscured in clouds. I had read *Mein Kampf*. Hitler to me was absolute evil. Without having read much of him, I admired Vladimir Ilitch and, for his genius as a writer, Leon Trotsky. I believe that the "permanent revolution" still had more power over me than *My Life* or than *The History of the Revolution*. Trotskyizing, I was at the time, in the manner of Malraux, in sympathy with "heresy." . . . And so I became the "touristo-Trotskyist" of this heteroclite band.

This lasts until the Moscow trials that push him in particular to resign as secretary of the International Association of Writers for the Defense of Culture (Malraux had offered him the position and he worked there with communists like Aragon, Ehrenbourg, etc.). What strikes him above all in the Moscow trials is the *anti-Semitic* fury. I insist on it because, as one can see if one reads a little, and as this was more than once confirmed for me in Moscow (I may return to this), the new public legitimacy (I do not say legality) conferred upon itself by Russian, indeed Soviet anti-Semitism, what allows it to display its old tradition in new, more arrogant and menacing forms, is sometimes the paradoxical amalgam of Stalinism and Judaism. The same projection—that is to say, the same rejection—now identifies with Stalinist power, indeed with the Revolution itself, "the Jews" that Stalin had persecuted.

In his indignation over the Moscow trials, which he describes purely and simply as anti-Semitic trials, Etiemble avows the murders of the father (objective genitive), moves on to the murder of the father (subjective genitive), and gives the reasons for which he did not "dare avow" what Gide, for his part, dared to publish in his *Back from the USSR*. (The question always is, At the end of what trip, what expedition, what pilgrimage, what *travel*, what *travail*, what labors of childbirth, what *tour* and *retour* will the tourist be ready to avow? And here to avow the father, to face up to the murder of the father? The heart of the drama is that there is always more than one place, more than one country, more than one bad father. The misfortune is that it is necessary to pass through Nazi Germany to go to the USSR or to return from it, and this pair of terrible fathers is not done with conditioning so many rending contradictions, so many collective and individual tragedies: one need only think of the totalitarian Stalinist model evoked today by the so-called revisionist German historians of the Germano-Soviet pact, of all its effects on the launching and unfolding of the Second World War, on the communist culture and the Western communist parties, on the fate of the Baltic countries, on so many individual destinies and on so many indeterminations in the stakes of today's geopolitics.) Here, then, is Etiemble in 1958; here is the avowal of what he did not avow, could not "dare to avow," the avowal of the impossible avowal, the disavowal and the "vow" reaffirmed:

> But the Moscow trials affected me to such a degree that I submitted my resignation and took on a sixth form at the Beauvais *lycée* that hardly suited me; but anything seemed preferable to what might seem like complicity with the assassin of the Jew Zinoviev, of the Jew Kamenev, of [sic] the eviction of the Jew Radek, of so many others . . .
>
> Gide published his *Back from the USSR*; I recognized more than one grievance that I had formulated during my 1934 trip, though without avowing it because of the Nazi peril; the cult of the leader especially revolted me, the exaltation of warrior values, which our pacifism and, let us not be evasive, our cowardice in the face of death made particularly unpleasant. From that point on, without renouncing my vow for a liberal and aristocratic socialism, I separated myself from the Stalinists. To become a Trotskyist? No indeed!   (pp. 205–6)

The theme of anti-Semitism returns regularly in Etiemble's narrative and always in order to define the determinant motivation of his rupture. I will not try to interpret this recurrence on Etiemble's part. Perhaps it would be necessary to interrogate it on my part if I said, as I am in fact tempted to do, that the Jewish question remains a "red thread" or a flashing red light for the reading of the process that is under way today. And so I will return to it. For the moment, then, I will somewhat arbitrarily close *The Murder of the Little Father* by evoking the moment in which Etiemble, when he could not return "in the U.S."—because of some problem with a visa refused, then granted too late through the intervention of American colleagues (this can always happen again)—finds himself invited to come "back in the USSR" of Khruschshev. I cite another long passage, by way of preface and for all the resonances it sets off:

> First I thought it was a mistake, a joke: for twenty years, I had been one of the little bêtes noires of our Stalino-Jdanovians, and here was Moscow calling me to teach there! For as long as Stalin's power had lasted, for as long as the Russians and their colonies had endured it, I felt very little concern to see the Soviet Union again. In addition, the idiocy of the French party, piling up baser and baser actions, saluting as so many vic-

tories of socialism the assassination of clearly innocent (and since then, rehabilitated) victims, gave me but a lukewarm desire to degrade myself with anti-Semites who applauded the assassination of the Jew Slansky, the Jew Rajk, the liquidation of the Jewess Pauker, and to top it all, hideous trophy, who demanded the skin of the "assassins in white shirts," all of the great Jewish doctors of Moscow. With Stalin dead, the self-proclaimed communist world was so clearly changing bases, at least in the Soviet Union, that I again had the desire to see what was happening there. Just when the United States refused me their visa, Khruschshev, to repay me for having fought against Stalinism, had me invited in 1958 to the Slavic and communist world. As soon as I arrived at the Moscow airfield . . .   (p. 210)

Demeter, or the Annunciation of the Superman

I could, if I were ready, here attach my own "travel narrative" and say in my turn, "As soon as I arrived at the Moscow airfield . . . ," from Paris, after having explained, as I will do later, why I accepted an invitation that I had refused for a long time. But I am not ready to begin such a narrative nor even to decide if and how I would do it. These last citations will thus have helped me, among other things, to make the transition from decade to decade, to go back from 1958 to 1936–37, toward Gide, then to 1926–27, toward Benjamin, which is also to say, without claiming to exhaust a typology, from a French Catholic obsessed by Soviet anti-Semitism to a French protestant rather indifferent, not to say more, to the Jewish question in the USSR, to a German Jew very closely frequenting the Jewish milieu at the time of his trip (Scholem even claims that he only met Jewish intellectuals and artists) and offering multiple notes on this subject.

Unlike Etiemble, Gide names (p. 117) a good number of victims executed in the Moscow trials, he condemns the "cowardice," the denunciation of and informing on "friends," but without the least allusion to the fact that Zinoviev, Kamenev, and Radek (three of the five names he cites) are Jews. This should not keep us from seeing the fact that Gide's *Back from the USSR* remains—this at least is my hypothesis—not only the prototype of the series of publications we are sketching here and thus the paradigm of a finite tradition, after which it is very difficult to write without laughter or shame one's own "back from the USSR," but also a *prototype that defines itself*. Benjamin, as we shall see, will have made the same gesture more interestingly and more ambitiously, but in the name of an unrealized project, and furthermore the material of this project itself was not published in his time. That is why I have said that *Back from the USSR* no doubt remains the prototype of *publications* in the series that we are studying. Gide in fact interprets the original space in which his own writing moves here: no, not his own writing, not the method or even the epistemology chosen for this descriptive or narrative writing (as Benjamin had expressly tried to do ten years earlier) but the mythico-historical field in which this writing is advanced. The mythic note is given right from the epigraph, which, before the narrative is broached and even before the foreword, tells in short what is going to happen through the detour of a Homeric hymn to Demeter. She is seen "leaning forward, as if over future humanity, above a radiant nursling" in whom something "superhuman is being prepared." Metaneira interrupts the experience, "pushes aside the goddess and all the superhuman that is being forged, thrusts aside the coals, and, to save the child, destroys the god."

The new space in which the writing of *Back from the USSR* is advanced is a mythic (ahistoric, *in illo tempore*) *and* eschatological (Mosaic or messianic) space to the very extent that it remains to come, like the promised land and the future of a chosen fatherland—myth, religion, pilgrimage, and hope but also end of myth and origin (promised, indeed in progress) of history itself. Which corresponds, you will say, to the very structure of messianism (and certain texts of Benjamin, like *The Critique of Violence*, could correspond to the same schema: the destruction of [Greek] myth in order to bring history to light through a messianico-Marxist revolution). At the outset—and I do say the outset [*départ*]—what inspires "love" and "admiration for the USSR" in Gide is an "unprecedented experience" and, through that very experience, the singularity of a place determined, identified, assigned by the future of a promise. In other words, like all those making this round trip at the time, Gide does not leave his country; he does not leave *home* for the USSR as one would go abroad, to a distant or eccentric country, in order then to return *home* and give news from "over there." No, Gide leaves to go *home*; his trip, his visit, is already a return (back home) toward what should be a "home" or, better, toward a place, the USSR, that is "more than a chosen fatherland: an example, a guide" (p. 18). The "over there" is the future of the absolute "here" toward which this voyage tends. The messianic or eschatological dimension of the trajectory toward that which is not by chance named a "land" offers itself from over there, from this there (*fort*) as here promised for election: "What we dreamed, what we scarcely dared to hope but toward which all our will, our force tended, *took place over there*. And so it was a land in which utopia had a good chance of becoming reality" (p. 18, my emphasis). Utopia, nonplace, was on the point of or in the process of taking place on this "land" (if I emphasize the word *land*, it is not only to reawaken the memory of the promised land—and Gide speaks later of "promises" kept or not kept—through the paradox that consists in still calling a country a "land," *plural* countries whose industrialization or deagriculturization already stands out so tragically, I want to anticipate what I hope to say later about the specificity of the *ecological* theme in the current experience of perestroika).

The return *from* the USSR will first of all have been a mythico-messianic return *to* the USSR, like home, in the "chosen fatherland": *Back in the USSR*, the Beatles would have said. And if the Frenchman that I am still winks toward the America where he finds himself, it is also to point out that at the end of his foreword, coincidentally or not, Gide cites Tocqueville, *Democracy in America*. It is at the moment he reminds us that we should never recoil, on the contrary, before the vulgar cowardice of enemies who hasten to exploit an advantage when we ourselves are facing up to a wounding truth:

> I do not disguise from myself the apparent advantage that the enemy parties—those for whom "the love of order is confused with the taste for tyrants"*—will claim to draw from my book. And that is what would have kept me from publishing it, even from writing it, if my conviction did not remain intact, unshaken, that on the one hand the USSR will end up triumphing over the grave errors I am pointing out; on the other hand, and this is more important, that the particular errors of a country can never be enough to compromise the truth of an international, universal cause. The lie, be it that of silence, may appear expedient, and expedient the perseverance in lie, but it gives the enemy too good a hand, and the truth, be it painful, cannot wound except to cure.

> *Tocqueville, *Democracy in America*, introduction.

It will not have escaped you that this end of the foreword has already displaced the initial logic put into place several pages earlier. According to the hypothesis of a failure or of "errors" of the revolution in the USSR, the latter will no longer be the "chosen fatherland" in the "destiny" of which "the fate of culture" is played out ("The fate of culture is linked in our minds to the very destiny of the USSR. We shall defend it." [from a speech by Gide in Red Square on Gorky's death]). In case of failure, the USSR will only have been "a country" among others. The "particular errors of a country" are incommensurable with "the truth of a universal cause" that this country will nevertheless have incarnated, in the singularity of its body, of its place, of its advent (internationality being here the intermediary scheme between a nation that is further-more already abstract, international—the USSR—and universality, from which we get the clumsiness of a false redundance: "international, universal cause"). But we cannot say that the logic has contradicted itself or vacillated from the beginning to the end of a foreword whose movement mimes in advance the experience of the whole book, from immense hope to the terrible diagnostics that I will not enumerate, sup-posing them known, but that I will collect in a single citation; I choose it for a reason that should now be obvious, the fatal "comparatist" strat-egy of this time: "I doubt that in any other country today, even Hitler's Germany, the spirit is less free, more broken, more fearful (terrorized), more enslaved" (p. 108). There is doubtless, then, an interval between a logic of the concrete universal (the incarnation of the cause in the singular history of a "chosen fatherland") and a logic that abstracts the universal from all national particularity. But this interval is experience itself: it is the experience in progress in the "chosen fatherland" and the experience of the book that lives at the same rhythm. This experience is that of a "construction" of which it is impossible to decide in advance whether or not it will deliver the "future," whether or not the incarna-tion of the universal will take place in it. The true intermediary *scheme* between the universal and the national particularity, for the USSR as for Gide's book, will be this "construction."

And the process of this "construction," of this "being in construc-tion," is suspended, as is for that very reason the breathless writing of this *Back from the USSR*, of these *back from the USSRs*; it remains as undecided and undecidable as the future of a promise and the birth of the future, of this "radiant nursling" of "future humanity" spoken of in the mythological and Homeric epigraph before the foreword. The being "in construction" of the Gidian text, the map and chart of its course, of its voyage, of its trajectory, of its transfer, is analogous to the being "in construction" of the USSR, on land and on the "land" of the USSR: "The USSR is 'in construction,' it is important to tell ourselves incessantly. And hence the exceptional interest of a stay on this immense land in childbed: it seems that one is witnessing at the parturition of the future" (p. 17).

The "parturition of the future," the conception, gestation, and delivery of the future—all this is an insistent rhetoric that, even beyond the "radiant nursling" of a Homeric Gide and the "murder of the little father" of an Oedipal Etiemble, would lead us very far from the area in which this experience of *travel* intersects the labor of *travail*. The revolutionary voyage is the voyage toward the "chosen fatherland" of work where the *travail* has begun, because the Earth-Mother is in the process of delivering, unless the stepmother Demeter comes to kidnap the "superhuman" child.

Why insist on this being "in construction"? Is it to better specify the status or the *travail* of these "voyages," of these "returns," and of the texts that arrange them? No doubt, but also, indissociably, it is to remark on something like a strange paradox of *anticipation*. On the one hand, at an initial level, we are talking about a *travail* of time to come, of an uneasy anticipation of the future: will the promise be kept? But from another perspective, we can say today that, this "construction" having failed, the supposed taking into account of this failure opens the era of perestroika, a word that also means "construction"—"reconstruction," construction that begins or rebegins after a new departure. This new departure supposes that the first construction has failed or been undone—I would not myself have dared to say "deconstructed" if certain of my interlocutors of the Institute of Philosophy of Moscow's Academy of Sciences had not told me in all seriousness that in their eyes the best translation, the translation that they were using among themselves for *perestroika*, was "deconstruction." If I manage to someday, I will relate and later perhaps comment upon this exchange, the reflections, questions, or perplexities inspired in me when a Soviet colleague said to me, scarcely laughing, "But deconstruction, that's the USSR today."

This is not the point on which I would like to linger for the moment. But ever anxious to analyze the structure and the history of this finite sequence of a historico-textual *travail*, I must *nuance* and *complicate*, without simply contradicting it, what I suggested earlier—namely, that today there could not possibly be any *back from the USSRs* of the same type as those of Benjamin, Gide, or Etiemble, and so forth. I believe that there could be, that there are texts, speeches, trips, notes for *travail* that resemble the preceding ones, but on two conditions that I find very restrictive—those of both a *reversal of direction* and a very problematic *presumption*: first, that one claims to go see "over there," *fort* (and not in an ideal and future "here," *da*) if perestroika is "working," if the delivery went well, if the *travail* is happening as it should; and second, that in an inverse sense, one expects perestroika to forge a society (Russian or not, Soviet or not? By definition, we can no longer say) *on the model* of Western parliamentary democracies, liberal in the political and economic sense.

In other words, certain in the knowledge of what democracy *is or ought to be*, believing he knows its already realized model (this is what I called the *presumption*, the site of the gravest problem for us today), such a traveler would go to see if this society, there (*fort*), is or is not in the process of coming to us, to join us or at least to approach us. It is this distance that one will attempt to measure in reversing the direction of the *fort/da*. In the *fort/da* of the Gidian type, one went abroad only in the hopes of finding an end to an exile but to an exile one experienced *at home* (*da*) and not in Moscow. Today, the dominant discourse, in the West and for the travelers it dispatches in the Eastern countries, too often consists in asking oneself, Are these people going to succeed— at what cost, at what rhythm—in resembling us by entering the now more than ever assured space of democracies and their market (whether it is called capitalist, neocapitalist, or mixed or whether its autoregulation is named in another fashion)? Are they finally going to enter history? Or—and this amounts to the same thing—will they leave history by entering it, if one tranquilly believes, as does one White House thinker-adviser, that we are finally reaching the end of history with the universal realization of the democratic model? This discourse (which I would like, of course, at all costs to escape, along with what it overturns: the whole historic difficulty of the task, the difficulty of thinking the history of this history) can be maintained on occasion by the citizens of the Eastern countries, as we know so well; it almost always implies that democracy is not *to come* but already given in the presence of its concept or its fact. It is my perplexity on this subject that paralyzes me at the moment of speaking of my trip to Moscow. This perplexity does not concern only the concept or the fact of democracy; it also concerns, *and as a result*, the identification of the process that is happening and is known under the name of perestroika. In the debates that I will try to report, certain of my Muscovite interlocutors and myself rather easily fell into agreement in saying that no one yet knows what something like perestroika is, which is to say what it will have been. Its identity, the unity of its meaning, remain among the most obscure, even for the most visible of those who claim to be or call themselves its agents, for the most determined activists of perestroika: Gorbachev among others, first or last. This essential obscurity, what delivers it in its entirety to the future—now that is reason enough to remain very reserved on the subject of the translation alluded to a moment ago (*perestroika:* deconstruction), not to reckon with a penumbra that analogously stretches over the unity and identity of something like "deconstruction."

For lack of time, we must abandon Gide to the *Retouches,* in the middle of the implacable "trial" he prosecutes against Moscow. There would be too much to say. What drives me to go and look at an earlier time, 1926–27, is that Gide himself claims not to have been *dépaysé,* out of his element in the USSR, not only because he made himself *at home* in a "chosen fatherland" but, more trivially—and the argument is a different one—because he had read all the books: "I had, for three years, macerated myself in too many Marxist writings to find myself very *dépaysé* in the USSR. I had, furthermore, read too many travel narratives, enthusiastic descriptions, and apologies" (p. 136). How can one be *dépaysé* in the course of a trip, for example, to the USSR? And is there a certain incompatibility between understanding and being-*dépaysé?*

Tiresias: Phenomenologico-Marxist Clairvoyance

Through a series of *at least three* distinctive features, Benjamin's project contrasts, in the most vivid and rigorous manner, with all those I have alluded to up until now. Naturally I must distinguish here, principally, between the *project in view* of which he takes notes and these notes themselves, this material since then published under the title *Moscow Diary.* The project itself is remarkable and it is known to us in particular through a letter that Benjamin addresses to Martin Buber several days after his return from the USSR, February 23, 1927. To isolate the three distinctive features that I just announced, let me first cite a long fragment of this letter and emphasize several words in passing:

> My presentation will be *devoid of all theory.* In this fashion I hope to succeed in allowing the creatural to *speak for itself:* inasmuch as I have succeeded in seizing and rendering this very new and disorienting lan-

guage that echoes loudly through the resounding mask of an environment that has been totally transformed. I want to write a description of
Moscow *at the present moment in which "all factuality is already theory"*
and which would thereby *refrain from any deductive abstraction, from
any prognostication, and even within certain limits from any judgment*—all of which, I am absolutely convinced, cannot be formulated
in this case on the basis of spiritual "data" but only on the basis of *economic facts* of which few people, even in Russia, have a sufficiently
broad grasp. Moscow as it appears at the present reveals a full range of
possibilities in schematic form: above all, the possibility that the Revolution *might fail or succeed*. In either case, something *unforeseeable* will
result and its picture will be far different from any programmatic sketch
one might draw of the future. The outlines of this are at present brutally
and distinctly visible among the people and their environment.   (cited
in G. Scholem's preface to the *Moscow Diary, October*, 1935, pp. 6–7)

What are these *three features?* They concern the mode of thought as
well as the mode of writing; they traverse the content, be it semantic,
thematic, or interpretative (which aims, in truth, to be preinterpreta-
tive) as much as the form of what Benjamin calls his "presentation."
And they have in common an extraordinary philosophic exigency,
whose radicality allies itself to that of a sort of *phenomenological Marxism* pushed to its limit, joined to the naïveté of a historical and theoretical optimism that not surprisingly led Benjamin to disappointment,
failure—in any case, to the abandonment of the project.

The first lesson to be drawn, for me in any case, could be the decision never to dream of writing, much less to engage in writing a "physiognomy" of Moscow. That is a madness it is wiser to defer infinitely. For
if, as Scholem reminds us, Benjamin left for Moscow above all because
of his love for Asja Lacis, and doubtless also to deliberate better over his
possible adherence to the German communist party, we must not forget
that he had promised, against a financial advance, to write and publish
on Moscow when he returned, which, furthermore, he did in part, as
of 1927, in several essays including "Moscow," published in *Die Krea-
tur*. These essays have no common measure, it seems to me, with the
ambition formulated in the letter to Buber, even if, naturally, they retain traces of it and even if these traces are today, for us, of the greatest
interest.

The second lesson, once again for me at least, concerns this alliance
of Marxist and phenomenological motifs to which I will return in a

moment, the first being more overtly declared but the second also quite determinant, it seems to me. These two motifs have rarely been associated (except perhaps in France in the abortive attempt of Tran-Duc Tao, in *Phénoménologie et matérialisme dialectique*, at the beginning of the 1950s). But quite a long time ago they figured for me—and there remain many signs of this in numerous published or unpublished texts—a sort of impossible double matrix or, as Apollinaire would say, two "breasts of Tiresias" as alluring (the one as the other and the one at the same time as the other) as they are hopeless. Only by relating how I had to separate myself, wean myself from these two breasts could I attempt an anamnesis of my trip to Moscow that would be at all consistent, once I would have begun to understand what is happening or announcing itself under the name *perestroika*. The figure of Tiresias, after those of Oedipus and Demeter, signifies less in my view the tragedy or the heroico-familial mythology of the Greeks, or sexual completeness beyond all difference, or even blindness, than the irreducible teleology (ineffaceable in Marx as well as in Husserl) of someone who anticipates the future and blinds himself for the very reason that he pretends to the *lucid intuition of presence*, to the *sight* and foresight of *the thing itself*, of the referent beyond speculation, interpretation, ideology, and so on. But of course, if I have constantly interspersed references to Greek and Judeo-Christian narratives, it is also to suggest that through these historical epics—as through the historiography, implicit or not, of these "travel narratives"—we are dealing on the one hand with a constant concurrence of Greek and biblical, mythological, and Mosaico-messianic models and on the other hand with a muffled struggle both to escape them and to restore them. One seeks *in them* the reassuring truth of a language, of a significant order, of an iterable truth, but at the same time one seeks *against them, beyond them*, to interrupt repetition: to let speak itself at last, all alone, the completely new advent of the unique, of absolute singularity, in other words, alas, the most iterable thing in the world: the beginning, finally, of history.

First feature, then: a reflexive vigilance intractable as to the adjustment (adequation or truth) of the mode of *presentation* (and so of the form of writing) in the "present" of the thing itself (Moscow) as it presents itself. It is what I called the phenomenological motif. The writing must efface itself to let the thing itself (Moscow) speak for itself ("allowing the creatural to speak for itself") in a "description" that is to some extent an autodescription of the thing itself, of the referent itself in itself, by itself. And this abstention of the subject, its deference to things or "facts," this neutralization of all interpretation, of all putting into perspective, of all theoretical construction ("My presentation will be devoid of all theory"), Benjamin believes that it is made possible, in an exceptional and historically unique way, by the "present moment" of Moscow. It is because of the Revolution and what is currently happening in Moscow that such a presentation without a point of view is possible. Here Benjamin is less a phenomenologist and more of a historian and a Marxist revolutionary. For if the "present" situation allows a "presentation . . . devoid of all theory," this does not mean the purely descriptive text that results will be atheoretical. It means that the theory, the theoremes, the very meaning will not be due to the intervention, the "construction," the projection of the author-subject; in a word, they will not be constituted, a phenomenologist would say, by Benjamin. The facts are theoremes in themselves; it is enough to *describe* them, which is also to say, to *relate* the referent, since it is history that is in question, so that theory is produced by the very "object" of description, as the very meaning of the things themselves. This meaning presents itself in the presentation of self that the "presentation" of Moscow would have to be. But this is only possible thanks to the Revolution. It is the Revolution. It is thanks to the grace of the "present moment" (but *lived* and *on the spot*, in the proximity of the present, by the visitor-traveler-voyeur who has be-come there, *Moscow in Moscow*, looking at the capital in his eyes) that the immanence of theory to facts would have to pass immediately, without translation or transformation, into Benjaminian writing: "I want to write a description of Moscow at the present moment in which 'all factuality is already theory' and that would thereby refrain from any deductive abstraction, from any prognostication, and even within certain limits from any judgment—all of which . . ."

Second feature: the factuality of facts, the presence of the referent *and* of the present meaning that allows this phenomenological neutralization of interpretation or of judgment nonetheless finds itself *interpreted*, we could say "rationalized," in the name of noninterpretation, as essentially economic (economic "in the last instance" as one still said in France in the 1960s—that is to say, at a time I would have to describe interminably if I wanted to analyze with some rigor the distant premises, the resonances and the connotations of my own trip to Moscow several weeks ago). It is furthermore in the economic as such that the meaning would thus be welded, once and for all, to the referent (if at

least one still holds to this distinction). Of these economic facts that are
the infrastructural foundation of the "present moment," consciousness
does not give the measure, any more than "spirit" or even "culture" does
(though culture is, from a distance, the principal theme of the notes
and, one could say, of Benjamin's interest and experience in Moscow).
Of these economic facts of the last instance, nobody in this case has a
conscious perception or sufficient analytic, not even the Russian subjects of Moscow: ". . . all of which, I am absolutely convinced, cannot
be formulated in this case on the basis of spiritual 'data' but only on the
basis of economic facts of which few people, even in Russia, have a
sufficiently broad grasp."

Third feature: at the intersection of phenomenological and Marxist
motifs, this return of the description to the things themselves claims to
do without not only judgment and speculation but also any teleology,
indeed any messianic eschatology, any determinant discourse about the
end—which is also a choice within many possible Marxisms. Here one
might say that Benjamin is not interested in the future or indeed that he
is interested precisely in the future of the future *as in the unforeseeable
itself*. Like Gide, Etiemble, and others, he allows the space of anticipation to be shot through with an indeterminacy at the heart of his experience and his description ("the possibility that the Revolution might
fail or succeed") but he himself insists on leaving this indeterminacy
whole, on not saturating it with any prognostication or any program, on
leaving it to itself, free and different, free and different "from any prognostication," "from any programmatic sketch." Anticipation, promise,
hope, opening up to the future would have to present themselves, in
the *presentation* of the work, under the pure form of presence.

Who could be surprised that Benjamin had to defer infinitely a project so ambitious in its radicality that it seems ingenuous in its preten-
tion? But as Benjamin himself says in "The Task of the Translator," the
event of a promise must be taken into account, even when it remains
impossible, when it is not or cannot be kept: the promise takes place and
it is significant in itself, by its very nature.

If we had been given the time, we could have plunged into this *Moscow Diary*, to follow day after day the fortunes, good and bad, of Benjamin's passions, whether it was a matter of his love for Asja, of the Revolution and communism, of the projected tableau on or of Moscow.
The latter, furthermore, would also have taken a place in a sort of "gal-
lery" of portraits of cities: Naples, Weimar, Marseille, San Gimig-

nano—and of course, standing a bit apart, Paris. Benjamin himself recalls it in his diary, in a moment of optimism, when he still hopes to complete the project, on December 27, 1926. He does so at the end of a passage on language that I would like to bring up before provisionally closing here.

This passage is of interest for at least *two reasons*.

First, it recalls an essential distinction to which Benjamin holds for more than ten years—namely, that which opposes or rather polarizes on the one hand the language of *expression* or of *manifestation* that renders what it names immediately present, presenting itself without the informative or instrumental mediation of the sign, and on the other hand, at the other pole, the technical, instrumental, semiotic, conventional, mediating language of *communication,* as means in view of an end that is foreign to it. The language of *communication* corresponds to the dethronement [*déchénie*] and even the destruction of authentic language, that of *expression*: this destructive dethronement is nothing other than the "original sin" evoked by a 1916 text that he recalls in his *Moscow Diary* in 1926, "Language as Such and the Language of Man." But these two opposite poles coexist and cohabit *simultaneously* in all human language, since this original sin and this inauthentic dethronement remain inscribed in it. They are constitutive of it, they constitute an co-institute it, so to speak, from the beginning. I will simply remind you that this very rich and very enigmatic text also qualifies as "bourgeois" the communicational conception of language as arbitrary and conventional sign ("Language never provides *pure* signs") but rejects the doctrine simply opposed to bourgeois doctrine, the "mystical theory" that sees in the word the essence of the thing. What he is proposing already is thus a sort of *compromise* between the two theories and the two practices of language—and we shall hear an echo of this negotiation, which is all politics, on December 27, 1926, ten years later. But of course, the ideal language he dreams of for his text on Moscow, the one he has no choice but to renounce, is a purely expressive language that would let the thing itself speak, the thing then known and manifested in its name, "the factuality" as "already theory": as if, in this very singular moment of history, in this "present moment," what is happening in Moscow could restore a supralapsarian experience of language, a sort of redemption from sin.

Second, as he also speaks of a "destruction of language" in its communicational corruption, and of a "tendency in contemporary Russian literature," this reminded me—I will no doubt return to it—that this theme of "destruction" (so important elsewhere in Benjamin) often resurfaced in my discussions with Russian colleagues: in some of their eyes, the revolution had "destroyed" Russian language and literature, along with capacities for reading—and the task today would thus be for them to destroy this destruction, to destructure this destructuration that has taken the solid form of an institutional language, of stereotypes, of mechanical operations, and so forth.

And so here is the promised passage; it reports a conversation with Reich, Asja's lover and future husband, the whole *Moscow Diary* being written and coming to grief, we might say, in the acute angles of this internal triangle, open or closed, in this Muscovite paradise where there is already more than one couple, more than one possible father, opened and closed by the promise of the *impossible* child or work (still Oedipus, Demeter, Tiresias in a predominantly Jewish milieu, as Scholem notes: "nearly all the individuals with whom he managed to establish contact [all Jewish, almost without exception, whether or not he was aware of it] belonged to the political or artistic opposition," p. 7).

> In the evening Reich and I had a long conversation about my work as a writer and about the future direction it should take. he was of the opinion that I tended to belabor the things I was writing. In the same context he made the very pertinent observation that in great writing the proportion between the total number of sentences and those sentences whose formulation was especially striking or pregnant was about one to thirty—whereas it was more like one to two in my case. All this is correct.(. . .) But I did have to disagree with him when it came to certain ideas that have never been in doubt for me and that date all the way back to my early essay, "Language as Such and the Language of Man" (1916, posthumously published; included in *Reflections*, pp. 314–22). I referred to him the polarity that exists in every linguistic entity: to be at once expression and communication. This clearly related to something we had often discussed together, "the destruction of language" as a tendency of contemporary Russian literature. The development of the communicative aspect of language to the exclusion of all else in fact inevitably leads to the destruction of language. On the other hand, the way leads to mystical silence if its expressive character is raised to the absolute. Of the two, it seems to me that the more current tendency at the moment is toward communication. But in one form or another a *compromise* is always necessary. I did, however, concede that I was in a critical situation so far as my activity as an author was concerned. I told him that I saw no way out

for myself here: mere convictions and abstract decisions were not enough, only concrete tasks and challenges could really help me make headway. Here he reminded me of my essays on cities. This was most encouraging to me. I began thinking confidently about a description of Moscow [I have emphasized *compromise*].

Benjamin had to give up this grand work on Moscow, which would also have commemorated his love for Asja (with whom, according to all witnesses, he spent his time arguing), as he had to give up having a child by her, although three years later he divorced for her. I will not insist on comparing the work ("Moscow") and the child to be swept away (re-member Demeter) as mitigating thirds for these impossible couples, but the fact is that these two obsessions besiege the diary. For example: "To-day I told her that I now wanted to have a child by her. Certain gestures, spontaneous yet rare and not without significance given the control she has now imposed on herself in erotic matters, tell me she is fond of me." Then, the same day, December 20, speaking in short of what Gide (whom he very much admired, as is well known, and whose journal of a trip to the Congo in 1927 he praises in a February 1927 letter to Kracauer) called "the parturition of the future":

> A contributing factor is certainly the fear that in the future, when Asja is finally well again and living here with Reich on stable terms, it will only be with a considerable amount of pain that I will be able to come up against the boundaries of our relationship. I still don't know if I will be able to disengage myself from it. At this point, I have no cause to sever myself from her completely, even admitting I were capable of it. The thing I would prefer the most would be the bond a child might create between us. But I have no idea whether I could even now bear living with her, given her astonishing hardness and, despite her sweetness, her lovelessness.

The sentence that follows seems to talk, as if by chance, of the weather, of the heat and cold in Moscow, and of the people who live in the street "as if in a frosty hall of mirrors," but as always we can see Benjamin playing at the skillful composition of "correspondences" among all the places and themes of this diary. It would thus already be the childbirth, the "parturition" of a work of which one can always wonder whether it is not at this point worthwhile in itself and not simply as the ruin of an abandoned project or an unkept promise. By the same token, one can always ask oneself the same question about the desired child: once entrusted to the symbolic *destinerrance* of a remainder or a trace that, in its very finitude, outlives in advance Benjamin, Asja Lacis or Reich, this desire for a child holds, like every promise, an existence without presence that through the work and as much as a work will rival the memory of these "present" existences that Benjamin and Lacis were, not to mention Reich. For centuries, in a word, in the heritage of what is called "culture," there are chances, perhaps more and more chances, to recall this child that never saw the light of day and to remember it as well as Reich, for example, who would doubtless have been forgotten, like Asja, without this abortive project still attested by a work named *Moscow Diary*. (This work is also the most "surviving" trace of Benjamin's love and, if at least there was love, of Asja's. The latter did not entrust her love to letters, so far as I know; and Benjamin, the author of one of the first great texts on the appearance of the telephone in bourgeois houses [in *One-Way Street*] notes this revolutionary sign in the modernity of our passions a little before his departure, on January 25: "That day as well as the following ones we had long telephone conversations that recalled the ones we used to have in Berlin. Asja absolutely loves to say important things by telephone. She spoke of wanting to live with me in the Grunewald and was very upset when I told her it would not work out." [Perhaps I will speak to you of the telephone in Moscow today: it works very badly for international calls.]) And so it is as if this child from this point on had a name. We would also have to follow the seminal motif associated with that of conception (*Empfangen*) and parturition, as with that of sur-vival (*Uberleben* or *Fortleben*) throughout Benjamin's work, particularly in the 1916 text on language and in "The Task of the Translator" (1923) but also everywhere that it is a question of the name and the proper name (notably in the essay on Goethe's *Elective Affinities* (1922–25).

Among all the problematics that we could elaborate through the reading of this *Moscow Diary*—that is, of this so very successful failure, of this abortion destined to survive—there would for example be that of the *dialectic* (evoked on December 22, 1926). One of the questions would then be, What relation is there between the resolutely and explicitly "materialistic" critique proposed by Benjamin of idealism as "nondialectical" universalism and the "compromise" we spoke of earlier between the two languages (expression and communication)? Another possible problematic: that of the private/public relation, notably for a writer in a communist state. One of the questions would thus concern belonging to the party and inclusion in a communist society. On this topic one would have to read the letter of December 26, 1926, to his friend the sculptress Jula Radt or what he writes a little later in his diary on January 9: "Join the Party? Clear advantages: a solid position, a mandate, even if only be implication. Organized, guaranteed contact with other people. On the other hand: to be a communist in a state where the proletariat rules means completely giving up your private independence." A little further on, he asks himself "whether or not a concrete justification can be given for my future work, especially the scholarly work with its formal and metaphysical basis. What is 'revolutionary' about the form, if indeed there is anything revolutionary about it?" Above all, we would have to return incessantly to this essential limitation on which Benjamin often insists but that, like Gide, he seems only secondarily worried about, as if about a provisional weakness (December 25, letter of June 5, 1927 to Hofmannsthal): not knowing the Russian language. For someone who thinks of letting the "facts" speak for themselves because "all factuality is already theory," is not the claim to speak of Moscow (and especially of the Russian, Soviet, or revolutionary culture) without understanding anything of the dominant language a bit ridiculous? Benjamin had to have known that. It is because I know it too that I shall always hesitate to write about my trip to Moscow. But at least we shall evoke together, in the course of the discussion suggested in this way, questions of language: the one that was posed to me during my stay, English having been the principal vehicle for our exchanges, and the one that was posed to the "Soviets" whom I met.

Everything remains to be said about the "travel narratives" I have just commemorated, both in order to encourage me to continue by taking account of what ought to be forbidden from now on and in order to attempt to justify a no doubt insurmountable discouragement. One always stops arbitrarily. Here I do so because I have already written too much and abused your patience on the eve of a discussion that I only wanted to initiate and, furthermore, because I am tired and have been suffering, since my arrival in California, as my friends know, from a sort of persistent flu. It may be the effect of the jet lag that has continued to affect me since my return from Moscow. You recall that Benjamin had promised Buber he would write a text on Moscow upon his return. Almost a month later, on February 27, he writes to excuse himself: "My esteemed Herr Buber, my visit to Moscow lasted somewhat longer that

I had expected. And when I got back to Berlin, I then had to deal with a flu. I've been back at work for a few days now but I will not be able to send you the manuscript before the end of February."

Postscriptum: The Benjamin

If I were someday to write something on my first trip to Moscow, necessarily from dated fragments, I would try to take what precedes into account and thus to cross the criteria of an inevitable selection. What would I retain, if possible? At least this:

1. signs (anecdotes, encounters, experiences) that require, indispensably, *at least my testimony* (that to which no one could have been the only witness except for me or a witness in my place: conditions that are already quite obscure and difficult to define and perhaps impossible to fulfill);

2. sketches of responses to questions posed by the preface—or attempts to reelaborate these questions. In truth it is this anticipation that has already guided me. It will no doubt have *arranged* [agencé] things in this "travel agency." In the form of a preface that will perhaps forever remain without a follow-up or "without child," unless it be Benjamin's child or his godfather, that is, he who gives the name, in this case the name of a sort of bastard,* this *agencement* will thus have sketched the potential apparatus for a critical, indeed a deconstructive reading, a criteriological apparatus. Today any narrative of a trip to Moscow would have to be put to the test of this apparatus, particularly the one I might be tempted to sign—in writing or even in the course of a discussion. But whether we are talking about "deconstructive" reading or writing, I recall having suggested here six years ago (in *Mémoires . . . Back in the U.S. . . .*) that it was doubtless never simply possible; instead it would be a certain *"experience of the impossible."* Given this, it only happens, if it does happen, in the form of promise and of failure, of a promise that cannot be *sure of succeeding* except by succeeding in failing. One can always try to draw an advantage from it, but this would be, I believe, rather risky.

In any case, I believe that at the moment one forms the project of writing or saying anything, it is always better to go as far as possible into historical knowledge and the formalization of already available programs, set to work and finished. Infinite work, of course—but today it is better, as much as possible, to know the history and formalize the matricial logic of *back from Moscow* travel narratives since October 1917, of the kind that were already possible and have already taken place. This is always better, at least so as not to reproduce while believing oneself to innovate, not to write without knowing while letting oneself be dictated to by programs that are both already "initialized" (I borrow this word from the Macintosh code) and already exhausted or saturated. This effort at historical knowledge and interpretive formalization is the minimal condition for a "responsible" form of writing: at least as regards history and historiography, not to mention other responsibilities; and

3. propositions linked to "personal recollections" (and *only if they are linked to "personal recollections"*) and crossing with the general themes we just encountered, intentionally arranged like stepping stones or programmatic indicators, for example: the situation of philosophy (academy and university, the reception of Heidegger, relations with tradition and with the West, notably with Paris); Perestroika; Glasnost (and "deconstruction"); nationality(ies) and nationalism(s); memory (the politics of memory); censorship and paper; the figure of Gorbachev; language and languages, the question of woman and "feminism"; references to Marx, Lenin, and Stalin; the specificity of the "ecologist" thematic; the Jewish question(s). And so on, and so on . . .

Note

*I elsewhere discuss, in a forthcoming text, the signature, the proper name, and bastardy in Benjamin.

ALEXANDER GELLEY

City Texts: Representation, Semiology, Urbanism

I

In Jean-Luc Godard's *Deux ou trois choses que je sais d'elle* the principal character, Juliette (one of the *elles* referred to in the title—Paris itself is another), remarks,

> No one, today, can know what the city of tomorrow will be. One part of the semantic wealth which belonged to it in the past . . . , it will lose that, certainly . . . The creative and formative role of the city will be taken charge of by other communications systems . . . , perhaps . . . television, radio, vocabulary and syntax, consciously and deliberately. (p. 40)

What interests me in this passage is the characterization of the city in terms of communications functions. The kind of perceptual and sensory stimulation that one associates with cosmopolitan life is reduced here to "semantic wealth," and this element, we are told, is being not simply depleted but transformed into an altogether different modality, one that is no longer congruent with experiential immediacy but becomes assimilated by a new apparatus. Godard does not, on the whole, provide any explicit characterization of this apparatus. The reference to "other communications systems" is deliberately vague, and the figures for such systems that are evoked in the movie—such as the *grands ensembles*, the new satellite housing complexes outside Paris—are delineated in a fairly subdued manner. He appears to be more interested in tracking the atrophy of an older, semantic mode of urban experience than in identifying a new one. But this indeterminacy is symptomatic and it enables Godard to use the story of Juliette in order to intimate a new kind of social space.

The images of this film are saturated with texts and objects, the jumbled paraphernalia of commodity culture. Scraps of text are cited from walls, billboards, book covers—they are legible but not meaningful. They connote (in Barthes's sense)—something like "Americanization" or "commodification"—but their denotative function has shrunk. Similarly, the images are stuffed with objects, familiar objects like brand-name grocery items, pinball machines, ready-made clothes, paperbacks. And these too signify in a mediated way, as if they were being cited. In a sense the film alludes to codes aplenty, fragments of meta-discourse in the form of book titles, posters, street signs, advertising slogans, graffiti, and so on—but these too, far from contributing to the goal of cognition or enlightenment, are treated as scraps of the pervasive system of commodification. *Deux ou trois chose que je sais d'elle* is structured like a message that is rich in semantic content—plenty of recognizable names, images, icons—but diffuse and scrambled in respect to semiotic organization.

Citation functions here, in good Brechtian fashion, as both an authoritative and a distancing technique. Bouvard and Pecuchet make an appearance as inveterate, idiotic practitioners. Baudelaire, Heidegger, Marx, and other luminaries provide snatches of philosophical commentary. The actors' discourse itself seems to be spoken as if it were being cited. Correspondingly, the images allude to a repertory of familiar objects and signs. But the film goes well beyond a mere cataloging of stereotypes by putting into play the level of signifying practices itself.

Citation works by being always slightly off the mark. What is evoked does not quite match what is shown. The effect of citation is to unsettle the signifying or indexical function. In that effect of dislocation, that small shock of mismatching, we approach Brecht's *Verfremdungseffekt*, estrangement, making strange. The consequences at the level of reception—of the reader or audience—are, in a sense, perfectly familiar to us and have long been acknowledged as a feature of modernist experience. And yet perhaps we too easily take them as simply another register in the array of (post-)aesthetic options. This flattens and normalizes what, I think, Godard's cinema aims at. Its open assault on both aesthetic and fictive criteria may be understood as the search for new forms of reception. The audience is drawn into an activity that is hard to label—a kind of decoding, perhaps a form of reading. But the text has been displaced, the audience position put into question. Godard has found ways to insinuate the quotidian into the narrative so as to activate in the audience mechanisms of defense and cognition that are operative in urban life but here, in the film, without the protective aura of familiarity and routine.

Godard's is not the Paris of the grand panoramas, either historical or visual. His representation is in the form of an investigation (*recherche*) of certain typical conditions of contemporary urban existence. The two primary referents of the title—Juliette and the "Paris region"—are linked, at both a narrative and a thematic level, by the concept of prostitution. The narrative follows Juliette on what appears to be an ordinary day as she sees off her husband and children and then goes into the city from her apartment in one of the *grands ensembles* on the outskirts. The episodes and encounters that follow constitute a montage of Parisian quotidian life centered on Juliette and others in a similar situation. Juliette's engagement in acts of prostitution—apparently a routine occurrence of her trips into the city—is not treated as any kind of deviancy.

Initially Juliette seems to fill a traditional narrative function—a "character" that serves as the basis for the level of represented experience. But in place of the kind of complexity and richness that would support such a function in a realist work the movie stages a series of loosely connected vignettes in which familiar experiential categories are drained or distorted: the home—here a housing development where Juliette and her family live—is as massive and alienating as a business complex; the city neighborhoods are in the process of being destroyed for the sake of a redevelopment project; public sites usually associated with refuge and leisure—café, hairdresser, department store—appear standardized and inhospitable. Most important, Juliette is represented less as a character actuated by need or desire than as function of a system that has absorbed her subject identity. Thus her prostitution serves less as index of personal intention—and thus assimilable to realist representation—than as element of an allegorical representation.[1]

In terms of Godard's political analysis Juliette illustrates a pervasive condition of urban dwellers in contemporary capitalist society. She serves as an agency whose attempts to "read" the city by negotiating it, and negotiating with it, betray a desire that is incommensurate with the possibilities available to it. To paraphrase a remark by Walter Benjamin that I shall return to later, Juliette "is not a flaneur," instead "one may rather see in [her] what would become of the flaneur when the context in which [she] belonged would be taken away" (*Gesammelte Schriften* 1.627).

II

The city as text; its uses and practices as forms of reading, of operating such a text—we encounter this figure repeatedly, in works of literature, of criticism, and also of what may be classified as "urban disciplines." The city represents one of those nodes or points of confluence where the status of textuality is today being articulated and tested.[2] It is tempting simply to accede to this metaphor (if it is one) and follow out one of its possible variants. But we have not yet determined what it is we are looking for in a "city text," what kind of use (whether operational, hermeneutic, or cognitive) might be gained from such an investigation. The textual model is often put forward as a guarantor of meaning without consideration of its specific applicability to a given phenomenon. As Roland Barthes wrote in 1967, "the problem is to make an expression like 'the language of the city' move beyond the purely metaphoric level."[3]

City is one of those aggregate and totalizing concepts that challenges textual articulation. It induces a kind of vertigo, a blockage at the level of representability. Who writes the city? How are we to define and classify "city texts"? And what kind of disciplinary or thematic criteria are in play—formalist, historical, political, aesthetic, impressionist? What allows one to posit a core phenomenon prior to the multiple denotative and representational practices that lay claim to it? In social theory a number of thinkers have recently begun to challenge analyses that assume a natural or neutral basis, an "empty arena," as the condition for social and political practices.[4] But the work of revising traditionally accredited forms of spatiality at a pragmatic level involves a prior insight into the constructive function of narrative and discursive forms.[5] As Michel de Certeau has written, "Every story is a travel story—a spatial practice. . . . These narrated adventures, simultaneously producing geographies of actions and drifting into the commonplaces of an order, do not merely constitute a 'supplement' to pedestrian enunciations and rhetorics. . . . They make the journey, before or during the time the feet perform it."[6]

In literary studies we have been used to dealing with the *theme* of the city. This generally means to work on a selection of texts—for the most part already well classified—that are in some way "about" cities. But such an approach raises a new set of problems. There is little agreement what the "aboutness," the referential factor, means.[7] Is theme in this context a topos in Curtius' sense? Could we then delimit a category "the city as text" on the analogy of "the world as book"? In thematic studies the key topic or concept—whether name, image, or narrative matrix— is drawn from the content level (the semantic repertory) of a literary work or corpus with little concern for its analytic potential.[8] Thematics is predicated upon an already existent distribution of topics, of semantic elements. It is useful when a semantic field is already saturated and no longer in a formative state. But for *city* the problem is precisely that we do not know where we might cut the thematic pie. We do not even know whether it is a single pie.

Furthermore thematics suspends the issue of the relation of observer to observed, of the investigator to the subject matter. At most, thematics adopts a form of *Einfühlung* (empathy, appreciation) that derives from the *Geistesgeschichte* tradition. But insofar as city is allied to the phenomenon of the quotidian, the everyday, it will elude thematic classification. Henri Lefebvre has made this point forcefully in his studies of quotidian existence:

> To know the quotidian is to wish to transform it. The mind cannot seize or define it except insofar as it attaches itself to a project or program of radical transformation. To study quotidian existence and use it as guiding thread in understanding modernity means that one must seek for what is capable of metamorphosis and then pursue in thought the stages or decisive moments of this possible metamorphosis; it is to understand the

real by conceiving it in the name of the possible, as implying the possible. For "man will be quotidian or will not be."[9]

A transformative potential, an intervention at the level of praxis, seems to be a constant, though often implicit, component in the analysis of the city.

An approach by way of architectural semiotics might serve as a corrective to a thematic approach. Architecture has a special status for our topic since it not only is a primary subject matter in any delineation of urban systems but is already the product of a prior articulation, in accord with a semiotics that is peculiar to it. Thus Philippe Hamon, in a recent article, writes, "Perhaps since architecture seems to be especially dependent on vision, it has been considered particularly apt—like all iconic schemas, diagrams, maps, and so on—to concretize abstractions, to be a kind of universal descriptive metaphor, a privileged metalanguage in the production of meaning" ("Texte et architecture," p. 4). This remark bears some elaboration. What Hamon terms the iconic characteristic of architecture consists in the fact that function and appearance coincide. In describing a building a writer need interpose no metacommentary to explain its uses. The description itself, in tracing a path or articulating a given stratification, spells out a narrative that is already inherent in the architectural construction. Instead of considering architecture primarily as a nonlinguistic, pictorial medium, Hamon stresses the extent to which it is in its nature a semiotization of space. This allows him to posit an underlying cognitive modality that is articulated analogically in both architecture and narrative.

And yet this conception of architecture as a privileged metalanguage by virtue of its iconicity, its affinity to vision (although, one should add, only a certain kind of vision—diagrammatic or panoramic) must be strongly qualified, as must also be the conception of an architectural narrativity, of a spatial schema that plots a linear traversal.[10] Donald Preziosi, a historian and semiotician of architecture, challenges the application of such a model to the visual arts, a model that he characterizes as "an essentially linear or transitive chain of semiosis wherein the object or message is taken primarily as a trace of the intentions of an active fashioner, whose intentions and conditions of production are to be reconstituted by users or beholders" "Between Power and Desire," p. 242). Cities, Preziosi argues, are constructs for which neither fashioner nor user (sender/receptor in a communications model) can be unequivocally specified. And he continues, "Cities and their parts endlessly ostensify, replicate, and palimpsest the differences by which solidarities and individualities are cued and construed. . . . The truth of the city is that it is forever false. A city is not a city unless it occludes the laws of its composition and the rules of its game" (p. 237). When Preziosi writes, "It has become imperative to study together the history of the road and the history of writing," he is in line with Calvino's suggestion in *Invisible Cities* that "the city must never be confused with the words that describe it. And yet between the one and the other there is a connection" (p. 51). To specify this connection, to work out the homology between topographies and texts, is one of the tasks before us.

One cannot escape the conclusion—and Raymond Ledrut has argued it persuasively—that "if there is an urban semiology, it is dependent on an urban anthropology" ("Speech and the Silence of the City," p. 122). There is no single code that could generate a systematic meaning for city, that could provide something like an urban morpheme (on the model of morphemes for apparel or for furnishings). And if the city is to be conceived as speaking to us it is in the mode of a work of art, "as an object charged with meaning by the production and the use men make of it" (p. 120). Although this represents little more than a negative conclusion, Ledrut's argument puts us on guard against those who claim a special right to speak *of* the city or *for* the city, who claim a privileged status as its mouthpieces. Often such claims are made by city builders of various kinds—architects, planners, designers, and then, deriving from them, urban theorists. It is tempting to accede to their vision, to consider that those in control of the skills and resources of material production are therefore especially endowed to define the ends for which a construction should serve. This represents, in fact, a tenet of the ideology of technocracy.[11]

In this connection Françoise Choay, in *La règle et le modèle*, has argued that the modern urban theorist—and she singles out Le Corbusier as a preeminent instance—is in essence a utopist following in the tracks of Sir Thomas More's *Utopia* (1516), that is, a planner-builder who, however benevolent his or her intentions, wants to impose a material institution upon a human collectivity in order to augment its well-being and also, not incidentally, to make humanity better, but better according to a plan—the plan, precisely, of the new edifice or city— "the radiant city" (Le Corbusier), "the living city" (Frank Lloyd Wright), and so on. Choay contrasts this utopist ideal with that of the builder elaborated by Alberti in his *De re aedificatoria* (1452). This builder is in the service of fundamental human needs. Before anything else, he must be capable of grasping the social structure for which he works as a structure composed of history, locale, and customs. The rules that this builder-philosopher devises are not authoritarian (in contrast to those of the utopist) but adapted to an array of needs, conveniences, and desires derived from the existent life forms of the community.

Choay and Ledrut, then, represent a type of urban theory that would resist the essentializing tendencies of those who claim to read the city or to speak for the city in order to justify certain pragmatic ends, to justify their right to control the material construction or transformation of cities. Their work may be connected to a type of critical urban theory of recent date (see Gottdiener and Lagopoulos, Soja, Deutsche, Davis, and Shapiro) that, in various ways, challenges aesthetic, phenomenological, organicist, and functionalist conceptions of space—conceptions, it is argued, that tend to inhibit social and political reforms in the name of an absolute ("natural," transcendental) standard of some kind.

Michel Foucault's work represents a pioneering effort in developing a linkage between spatial organization and the exercise of power. He recognized the difficulty of conceptualizing this issue. Thus he stated in an interview, "for me, architecture, in the very vague analyses of it that I have been able to conduct, is only taken as an element of support, to ensure a certain allocation of people in space, a *canalization* of their circulation, as well as the coding of their reciprocal relations" (*The Foucault Reader*, p. 253). With the study of the Panopticon, the mechanism of observation and control that is central to *Discipline and Punish*, Foucault provided an important insight into the paradigmatic cognitive function of an architectural model: "But the Panopticon must not be understood as a dream building: it is the diagram of a mechanism of power reduced to its ideal form; its functioning, abstracted from any obstacle, resistance or friction, must be represented as a pure architectural and optical system: it is in fact a figure of political technology that may and must be detached from any specific use" (p. 205).[12]

In a brief late essay, "Des espaces autres" (translated as "Of Other Spaces"), Foucault undertakes a characteristically provocative classification of what he terms *heterotopias*: "The space in which we live . . . [is] a heterogeneous space. In other words, we do not live in a kind of void, inside of which we could place individuals and things. . . . We live inside a set of relations that delineates sites which are irreducible to one another and absolutely not superimposable on one another" (p. 23). In opposition to what he sees as a modern conception of space predicated on sites as elements of a systematic organization of data (demographic, digital, etc.), Foucault wants to invoke a neglected dimension that is closer to the experiential and the phantasmatic. Yet this is not to be taken as a continuation of the exploration of internal space in the sense of Bachelard and the phenomenologists. Rather, Foucault suggests a catalog of countersites, sites linked to but at the same time operative as deformations of typical, culturally valorized loci. It is a question not of classifying utopias or dystopias but of uncovering a cultural phantasmatics as the basis for a systematic contestation of social space. As in his analysis of the Panopticon as a "figure of political technology," here too Foucault helps us avoid the traps of a thematics, which must work in terms of a preestablished repertory, and points to a more hidden and indirect dimension of what I would term *cultural territoriality.*

The problem we face in articulating this notion is that space is both the framework of our analysis (the schematic construct we require as operators of relation, as indicators of placement) and the topic of the analysis (objects and places). The former draws us to a metatheory of representation, where space is understood as the condition of the apprehension of phenomenal reality.[13] The latter runs the risk of being no more than a catalog of lived spaces, on a phenomenological model. What we require is an intermediary level of conceptualization to deal with the conversion of space into territory, to investigate the ways that space is subjected to the constraints of human needs and cultural norms.

III

Beginning with the early nineteenth century the experience of the city replaced the sense of nature that had been embodied in the preromantic and romantic concept of landscape. As Joachim Ritter makes clear, landscape in this sense is not merely a genre of painting related to a view, to a piece of nature, but a central component of aesthetics itself as the category of the reception and experience of art works:

> The history of landscape is the process whereby successively specified elements of the earth are aesthetically discovered and made visible . . . What does it signify that, in the modern period, a hitherto unknown form of representation of Nature, mediated by aesthetics, can be realized by means of landscapes? It is only by the cultivation of the aesthetic category that something like a "piece of Nature" comes to be constituted as landscape and to stand, in works of pictorial art as well as literature, for the whole of Nature. This is something that was unknown both to the Middle Ages and to Antiquity. It may also be said that landscape, in the sense we have developed, implies the presence of the whole of Nature.   (*Landschaft*, p. 42)

Following Ritter's claim that landscape is to be taken not simply as an instance of the aesthetic but as a constitutive factor in the construction of the aesthetic, it may be argued that the emergence of a new city sensibility in romanticism is far different from the substitution of one image system for another, one thematic cluster for another. What is at issue is the status of aesthetic experience and judgment itself, a development exemplified most powerfully in the emergence of the city as an alternative to landscape, more radically, as an antinature (adumbrated in Wordsworth and then made explicit in Hugo, in Baudelaire, and then in the fiction of the midcentury).

It is in its resistance to thematics, or, to put it another way, as a critical thematics that the city text as I understand it may be productive for literary studies. Raymond Williams' *The Country and the City* makes an important contribution in this connection. He argues that behind the valorization of the country and rural life in English literature there has been, ever since the postfeudal period, a powerful economic interest, the interest of an established class, based in country holdings but essentially managing them in terms of an agrarian capitalist system. The sharp contrast of city and country, the myth of rural simplicity and rural virtues are to be taken, in this argument, as elements of an ideology that have masked the real motives of a historical process.

Dickens has a special place in the argument since he is one of the few major writers who did not subscribe to the traditional valorization of country in relation to city. Williams develops this point in contrasting Dickens to George Eliot. In Eliot he finds novels of "knowable community," a term that echoes Georg Lukács' idea (in *The Theory of the Novel*) of the cultural integrity and homogeneity typical of the epic. George Eliot's attempt to imagine the knowable community had to proceed retrospectively, as the reconstruction of a lost ideal. She yearned for, but was incapable of identifying with, a homogeneous, "naive" community and so ended by representing it not from the inside, as a knowable community, but from the outside, by means of local color and in a vein of nostalgia.

One virtue of Williams' work is that it leads us to examine the country-city binarism more critically, in both historical and formalist terms. Within the literary system the emergent response to the city, to the urban phenomenon as a whole in the nineteenth century, prompts us to reconsider the mode of pastoral. Pastoral, in this light, is not "about" rural existence. If it is about anything it is about a displacement—whether that be a temporary exile as in *As You Like It* or a state of nostalgic reversion as in *Adam Bede*. Pastoral situates us in the place *to which* one flees, or would like to flee, when the conditions of ordinary existence become insupportable. We do not have a correlative term for the place *from which* one flees (*urban* is a thematic or content term and not a literary mode or genre). Perhaps this is to be explained by the deep-seated cultural valorization that has been accorded to the rural within our tradition, a valorization well expressed in William Cowper's line "God made the country, and man made the town."[14] This kind of opposition, by its very structure, manifests the dynamics of a binarism that necessarily incorporates what it rejects. Wordsworth, at the end of book 7 of *The Prelude*, "Residence in London," characterizes city dwellers as follows:

> The slaves unrespited of low pursuits,
> Living amid the same perpetual flow
> Of trivial objects, melted and reduced
> To one identity, by differences
> That have no law, no meaning, and no end;
> (lines 700ff., 1805 version)

and evokes, by contrast, the country setting of his own early life: "The mountain's outline and its steady form / . . . the forms / Perennial of the ancient hills." Yet book 7 as a whole, although a negative example within the moral framework of *The Prelude*, gives an early but incisive characterization of what may be termed the modern urban consciousness. It belies its own assertion (in the preceding passage) and contributes to the process of differentiation that establishes a new *law, meaning*, and *end* for the phenomenon in question. The narrator's passionate gesture of rejection at the end as he turns back to the natural setting takes its place in a topos that gains in urgency in the succeeding century. Robert Frost's line "Back out of all this now too much for us," [15] conveys something of its anxiety-ridden, frantic tone in the present century.

Dickens, in Raymond Williams' argument, did not aspire to anything like a knowable community in Eliot's sense. In his type of novel the fragmentation in the social structure is acknowledged, in fact, radically thematized. According to Williams, Dickens' form of the novel took upon itself the task of exploring the new kind of social structure embodied in the city:

> What [Dickens] saw, and what in a new kind of novel he learned to embody, went to the heart of the problem. For what London had to show, more fundamentally, even to modern experience, than the uniform cities of the early Industrial Revolution, was a contradiction, a paradox: the coexistence of variation and apparent randomness with what had in the end to be seen as a determining system: the visible individual facts but beyond them, often hidden, the common condition and destiny.   (*The Country and the City*, p. 154)

What eludes William, however, is a way of conceptualizing what he terms "a determining system" otherwise than merely as a representation of experiential data. Thus, although he claims that "Dickens's ultimate vision of London . . . lies in the form of his novels," his analysis does not offer new insights into what I have termed the representational protocols appropriate to the city. Williams' work poses again the issue raised earlier: Can "the city" as theme or as referent also constitute a genre? Few modern writers have pursued this issue as searchingly as Walter Benjamin. His work does not merely offer a varied and highly differentiated representation of modern urban experience; it also, more significantly, explores the possibility and conditions of any such representation.

IV

Benjamin's work represents a powerful and innovative model in a number of ways. First, his focus on the historicity of the aesthetic as a category of reception and cultural valorization made him a pioneer in exploring the mutations of the aesthetic in contemporary forms of experience and communication. Then, his approach to nineteenth-century literary history—notably in the Baudelaire studies—turned away from the traditional valorization of symbolist and modernist poetics and concentrated instead on the symptomatic status, in cultural terms, of the figure of the writer and of his production. Finally, experimenting with a variety of textual practices, he sought to make the city a preeminent analytic instrument of and for modernity. (This is reflected in the title projected for his unfinished *Arcades Project*, "Paris Capital of the Nineteenth Century.")[16]

In charting the collapse of the hegemony of the aesthetic after romanticism Benjamin was intent on avoiding the methodology of history of ideas and sensibility (essentially, of *Geistesgeschichte*). His manner of characterizing the new sense of objects, of locales, of material reality in this period proceeds not by way of description and enumeration but by focusing on new forms of response and interest, forms that both implicate and transgress aesthetic categories. These include the shock phenomenon, the loss of aura, and the flaneur. It is the last of these that I want to examine here.

In relation to the sphere of commodity the flaneur is neither a creator nor a user but an incipient version of the bourgeois consumer who endows objects with an imaginary exchange value. Yet, like other marginal figures (prostitute, gambler), the flaneur provides a more unobstructed access to the sphere of commodity, since he is attached to them not like the bourgeois consumer in a relatively rigid fixation but in a floating, inconstant manner that cannot suppress traces of phantasmatic desire: "Fundamentally, empathy with the commodity is empathy with exchange value itself. The flaneur is the virtuoso of this kind of empathy. He parades the concept of mercantilism itself" (Benjamin, *Das Passagen-werk*, p. 562). Thus flaneur is to be understood not so much as a social *type* but as an agency of reception posited in order to facilitate the analysis of a coordinate system of reality.

In a sense the flaneur and the arcades function as alternative and complementary operators in relation to the street, articulating its new status in the modern city. Each serves, though in different ways, to turn the street into an *intérieur*: the flaneur by the way he uses it and sees it, the arcades by literally covering and encasing the street. The flaneur gives over to the associational current of his environment and thus makes himself into a registering sensibility for the relics of the past as they are spread out in the décor of the streets. Benjamin relates this stance to what he terms the "colportage phenomenon," a fascination with the surface glitter of the world, with the indiscriminate aggregate of appearances, a "category of illustrative seeing" (p. 528). Thus the flaneur embodies a form of archival consciousness very different from the kind of interiorization and accretion of memory data that characterized the subject of historicism.

But the flaneur, or more generally the stance of *flânerie*, is to be identified not only with the street but also with the gigantic public architectural structures characteristic of the middle and later nineteenth century—railway stations, exposition halls, wholesale establishments, arcades—structures that seem to anticipate "the appearance of the collective on the historical scene" (p. 569). This constitutes the scene of the flaneur's leisurely strolling, his loitering. He treats these public spaces as an *intérieur*, a sphere of privatization and retreat and thus raises to a level of self-consciousness the confusion of inner and outer, of street and home, that becomes characteristic for the urban collectivity in this period.[17] While the flaneur seeks to maintain a sense of privacy amid the collectivity, the masses, his whole identity consists in a parasitic attachment to this collectivity.

Benjamin was strongly impressed by Friedrich Engels' account in *The Condition of the Working Class in England* of the isolation and dehumanization of the individual amid the teeming city crowd and saw here an adumbration of Marx's conception of the proletariat (*Gesammelte Schriften* 1.619f.). But what interests Benjamin is not so much the issue of class as a political-economic entity but rather the urban collectivity as a potent preternatural force, a force that had traditionally been mobilized by the call of *Volk* or race but that may equally become subject to manipulations of the marketplace and totalitarian rule (cf. 1.565). Hugo and Baudelaire are cited as the most prescient nineteenth-century chroniclers of this phenomenon, but their impressions, Benjamin makes clear, do not in themselves constitute an analysis of the historical conditions: "The masses had become so much a part of Baudelaire that one looks in vain for a description of them in his works. . . . Baudelaire describes neither the Parisians nor their city. Forgoing such descriptions enables him to invoke the ones in the form of the other" (*Gesammelte Schriften* 1.621; English translation, modified, from *Illuminations*, pp. 167f.). What Benjamin undertakes, then, is to treat the masses not in a traditional thematic sense, as a subject-matter or referent, but as a subject of reception, as an entity accessible only by way of certain reactive phenomena such as the shock experience or *flânerie*.

In one of Poe's tales, "The Man of the Crowd," Benjamin found a striking demonstration of the enigmatic convergence of flaneur and collectivity. And more generally the detective story provides him with a model of urban existence where individual identity has shrunk to mere traces (*Spuren*) that are recoverable only at the level of crowd phenomena. "The fundamental social content of the detective story," Benjamin writes, "is the erasure of the traces of the individual within the urban crowd." Benjamin has in mind stories like "The Mystery of Mary Roget" and "The Man of the Crowd" which focus on the determination of a path through the city—a path that, in a sense, incorporates and supplants character entities. (In the case of "Mary Roget," the character of the title has been murdered, and the narrative deals with Dupin's deductive reconstruction of her whereabouts in the city at a time when no witness could be found to verify this information. "The Man of the Crowd" is treated more fully in what follows.) When Benjamin writes, "The concept of the trace finds its philosophical determination in opposition to the concept of the aura" (letter to Theodor Adorno, December 9, 1938; cited in *Gesammelte Schriften* 1.1102), he indicates the resistance of a trace structure to any responsive acknowledgement, to anything like a returning gaze. For the experience of aura means that one imputes to a phenomenon the capacity to return a gaze ("To perceive the aura of an object we look at means to invest it with the ability to look at us in return" [1.646f.; English translation, *Illuminations*, p. 188]). Trace, by contrast, testifies to a constitutive barrier, the definitive incapacity of a phenomenon to assimilate human affect. This does not mean that the trace lacks cognitive potential. But the determination of a meaning will require the projection of a figure determined by the trace, a figure conceived as existing in the wake of the trace. It is along these lines that we may follow Benjamin's discussion of "The Man of the Crowd," a text in which the detective-story model is, in Benjamin's view, assimilated to a fluid conception of the flaneur. He characterized this tale as something like "an X-ray of a detective story." And he continues, "Its enveloping garb, represented as the criminal act, has fallen away. Nothing but the skeletal structure remains: the pursuer, the crowd, the unknown figure who makes his way through London in such a manner that he always remains in its center. This unknown figure is *the* flaneur" (1.550).

The story begins with a description of a London street scene viewed by the narrator through the window of a coffeehouse. He has before him a central thoroughfare of the city and focuses on it at an evening hour when the crowd is at its thickest. Although the initial impression is of a dense, pressing mass, the narrator soon enough provides an orderly, indeed a carefully graduated account of the elements that make up the crowd, arranging these according to profession and class and proceeding systematically from the genteel to the semirespectable and further down to the criminal, the vagrant, the utterly destitute and outcast.

In the introductory remarks the narrator had stressed the exceptional alertness and buoyancy of his mood ("one of those happy moods which are so precisely the converse of *ennui*—moods of the keenest appetency" [p. 283][18]), a feeling that passes over into his powers of observation ("I felt a calm but inquisitive interest in every thing" [p. 285]) and is immediately associated with a leisurely but attentive perusal of the newspaper. The narrator's acuteness of observation is akin to a kind of deductive ratiocination that is characteristic of an investigator or detective, akin to Dupin. He notes with some complacency, for example, his ability to see through the masquerades of certain types of gambler, or to discern the significance of minute physical peculiarities in passers-by. The stress throughout is on his skill in reading the codes of dress and behavior and thus on his ability to provide a transparent but rich articulation of what seemed at first a tumultuous, confused aggregate.

Thus far, in its focus on types and its confident characterization of classes and callings, the account has a marked sociological cast. But at a given moment the speaker's interest changes. He then focuses on individual faces in the crowd, and though his placement prevents him "from casting more than a glance upon each visage, still it seemed that, in my then peculiar mental state, I could frequently read, even in that brief interval of a glance, the history of long years" (p. 287). This illusion of being empowered to read individual faces in the crowd, the fruit of a "peculiar mental state," is what is to be tested in the episode that follows. He picks out from the crowd a single face, "that of a decrepid old man." And the narrator's initial impulse is to devote himself to the study of that single figure, "to form some analysis of the meaning conveyed" by this extraordinary countenance. It is a face that conveys to him the most contradictory and extravagant impressions, from "vast mental powers" to "malice" and "blood-thirstiness," from "merriment" to "despair." He feels, though, that its meaning may be reached, is somehow accessible. " 'How wild a history,' I said to myself, 'is written within that bosom!' Then came a craving desire to keep the man in view—to know more of him" (p. 287). Fascinated, well-nigh mesmerized, by this figure he hurries out of the coffeehouse and proceeds to follow the old man through a long, labyrinthine circuit that moves through many districts of the city and its outskirts. Throughout this perambulation the old man, unconscious of his pursuer, seeks out and immerses himself in whatever crowd the neighborhood offers.

What is notable about the second part of the tale is that the history of the old man never comes to be written. What we have instead is an account of the quest, the narrator's pursuit of the mysterious figure through a whole night and day. Finally abandoning his pursuit, the narrator exclaims that this old man "is the type and the genius of deep crime. He refuses to be alone. *He is the man of the crowd.* It will be in vain to follow; for I shall learn no more of him, nor of his deeds. The worst heart of the world is a grosser book than the 'Hortulus Animae,' and perhaps it is but one of the great mercies of God that '*es lässt sich nicht lesen*'" (p. 289). This phrase ("it can not be read"), cited at both the beginning and the end of the story, functions like the motto of an emblem, a moral or didactic tag appended to an illustration. A pictorial model had been invoked elsewhere in the story—in a reference to an engraving of the devil by Retzsch and in one to the "Hortulus Animae," a Renaissance emblem book. In analogy to the emblem form, the narrative of the old man may be taken as the illustrative matter for which the motto serves as moral. This textual element, however, is hardly enlightening. Its purpose, on the contrary, seems to be to point up an unresolved, and unresolvable, enigma. The phrase "es lässt sich nicht lesen" functions as one of those self-canceling statements that is designed either to mystify or to mark a shift in the signifying process, a move to a different kind of logic or legibility.

In one sense, of course, it is perfectly clear what will not suffer itself to be read—the "history" of the old man "written within that bosom." The narrator leaves us in no doubt as to what that history would signify—"the type and the genius of deep crime." But the justification for this judgment is hardly conclusive. Explicitly we are told, "He refuses to be alone. *He is the man of the crowd*" (p. 289). But what constitutes his crime? Is it the eccentricity of his appearance, the wildness of his manner, the inexplicability of his behavior? These hardly represent sufficient grounds for the kind of absolute judgment that is rendered. It may be said that the figure functions symbolically as an embodiment of the tumult, the filth, the corruption of the neighborhoods through which he passes and in which he evidently feels at home. Certainly, if these traits are projected onto the old man's person, he may well be deemed monstrous. Furthermore, he seems incapable of bearing what has, in certain traditions, been considered a distinctive feature of personal consciousness—privacy and solitude (cf. another motto, this from La Bruyère, given at the beginning of the story "Ce grand malheur, de ne pouvoir être seul"). The man of the crowd is characterized precisely by a contrary impulse, an avoidance of the isolate state with something like panic terror.

Yet what about the narrator? As the story proceeds something changes in him. He can no longer remain ensconced behind a window, smoking a cigar, and dividing his attention between the view outside and the contents of a newspaper. He has been drawn by curiosity out into the street and then held by a fascination that leads him into the midst of the throng that earlier had been for him merely a diverting spectacle. If the story is anticlimactic in offering, at its conclusion, no revelation, no "truth" about the old man, it has done something else: it has dramatized the transformation of the narrator. From observer he has turned into investigator, to quester—a frustrated, failed quester. The motto "es lässt sich nicht lesen," although at first sight applicable to the old man, is more revealing for its acknowledgment of failure, its expression of resignation on the part of the investigator. The judgment rendered of the old man—"the type and genius of deep crime"—is perhaps more appropriately to be taken as a projection of the investigator's failure: what does not lend itself to explanation, what is not susceptible to rational analysis and energetic investigation, whether old man, crowd, or city, will inescapably be judged as criminal.

Benjamin's differentiated conception of the flaneur role allows him to apply it alternately to the old man and to the narrator. Thus he writes, "The man of the crowd is not a flaneur. Instead of [the flaneur's] relaxation of manner one finds in him a manic tendency. For that reason one may rather see in him what would become of the flaneur when the context in which he belonged would be taken away" (Gesammelte Schriften 1.627). But turning to the function of the narrator, he characterizes the emergent urban consciousness through the relation of flaneur to the crowd:

> The city is the realization of man's ancient dream of the labyrinth. This reality the flaneur pursues without knowing it. Without knowing it— nothing, on the other hand, is more absurd than the conventional thesis

which wants to rationalise his [the flaneur's] manner . . . , the thesis, namely, that he has devoted himself to the study of the physiognomic manifestations of men, so as to enable him to read nationality and class, character and destiny on the basis of [an individual's] stance, bodily dimensions, and facial expressions.   (*Das Passagen-werk*, p. 541)

As Benjamin knew very well, physiognomy constituted a widespread tenet of popular psychology in the nineteenth century and its impact on forms of character representation in fiction, for example, are significant. But he firmly rejects the idea of the flâneur as a master of physiognomy, an expert reader of the urban crowd. On the contrary, the flaneur (here identified as the narrator) testifies to the constitutive impenetrability of the city mass to mere spectatorship. The flaneur is himself caught in the mystery that he presumes to master—both the labyrinth of the city and the faces of the crowd. Initially a residual aesthete of the city spectacle, the flaneur is shown finally as himself an object of mystification, and it is his sense of the city that is expressed in the motto "es lässt sich nicht lesen."

V

The city text as I have tried to develop it—a critical discourse of the city that manifests in some manner the problematic of textuality—goes back at least to Rousseau and Wordsworth and then proliferates in the early and middle nineteenth century. It is related to a decisive change in the cultural valorization of the city in this period. On the one hand, the aesthetization of landscape in romanticism and after inaugurates a new category of *Stadschaft* as both a reaction and an alternative to *Landschaft*. The preeminence of landscape as a sheltering precinct, a site for work, leisure, and sustenance that seemed to offer direct evidence of a divine providence came to be supplanted by the metropolis or cosmopolis, based on a principle of human agglomeration and cultural sophistication. (Jean-François Lyotard's contrast, in a recent essay, between *domus* and *mégapole* parallels the distinction I am drawing.[19]) Beginning with the early part of the nineteenth century a large-scale industry of publication and dissemination came to be devoted to this phenomenon, to what may be termed the production of the city as spectacle. This, in fact, may be viewed as a central focus of Benjamin's *Arcades Project*. Baudelaire, as Benjamin has demonstrated, articulated a devastating critique of the iconization of the city. As poet of antinature he did not simply register the image of the desolate, degrading urban environment but served as exemplar and witness of a sensibility that was bred in but at the same time radically resistant to this environment, a sensibility that became a formative element of modernity.

The status of the crowd in Poe and Baudelaire marks the emergence of a collectivity that represents a radical threat to the idea of an autonomous, self-conscious subject. And Benjamin's investigations of nineteenth-century Paris disclose the illusionary aspect of the city as a sphere of human possibilities, an arena for personal self-realization. Through his experimentation with textual forms Benjamin sought to deal with the phenomenon of the city in ways that would move beyond history of ideas and traditional narrative or aesthetic constructs. Godard's *Deux ou trois choses que je sais d'elle* too may be taken as an effort to transcend a merely interpretive or analytic discourse, one that presumes to master and elucidate a phenomenon while it is, in fact, one of its symptoms.

What makes a work like Godard's a city text—and one could cite comparable examples by artists in various media: filmmakers like Wim Wenders and Michelangelo Antonioni, writers like Uwe Johnson or Saul Bellow, artists like Christo, Jenny Holzer, or Richard Serra[20]—is that it elicits a kind of reading, or processing, that is in many ways isomorphic with the experience of living in the contemporary urban environment. To read the city in this way complicates the cognitive presumption of certain semiological and functionalist trends in urban studies, but it throws light too on the motivation underlying such efforts. The kinds of city texts considered here indicate the complexity of relating a pragmatic with a cognitive intention. The city text by its nature implies a constructive process—what Lefebvre terms a work of transformation, an appropriation of space directed to the formation of a cultural territory. Indeed many of the artists I have just named are doing just that—fashioning a discourse that is responsive to, but at the same time oriented toward an active intervention in, contemporary urban existence.

Notes

1. Walter Benjamin saw prostitution as a paradigmatic instance of what he termed the *dialectical image*. The prostitute, being both saleswoman and

wares, embodies the bifurcation of commodity as an object of desire that reflexively exposes its presumed worth: "Commodity attempts to look into its own face. It celebrates its human incarnation [*ihre Menschwerdung*] in the figure of the whore" (*Gesammelte Schriften* 5.55 and 1.671).

2. Klaus R. Scherpe writes, "The older metaphorical narrative discourse ('the city as . . .') has not died out and is not to be (and why should it be?) eliminated. But the newer questions and answers to the problem of the 'narrativity of the city' lead away from the metaphoric and toward a description of significations. . . . The literary narrator of cosmopolis turns into an urbanist. And as urbanist he has the same task as the other investigators of the city: the structural articulation of the complexity of cosmopolis" ("Nonstop nach Nowhere City?" pp. 148f.; translations by the author except where indicated otherwise).

3. Barthes, *L'aventure semiologique*, p. 265 (the citation is from "Sémiologie et urbanisme," 1967). It is worth inquiring whether, twenty-five years later, this metaphoricity has been overcome, or at least complicated, made more conscious of itself. In his later work, as in the book on Japan, *L'empire de signes* (1970), Barthes demonstrated that structures of differentiation, operators of semiosis, can never be mechanically transferred from the field of language to that of image or behavior. Barthes' value is to have helped us understand that reading, textuality are themselves disputed concepts, entangled in a metaphoricity that we ignore at our peril.

4. Cf. Shapiro, *Reading the Postmodern Polity*, esp. chap. 1, "Language and Power: The Spaces of Critical Interpretation" and chap. 6, "Spatiality and Policy Discourse: Reading the Global City." The concept of "empty arena" is discussed on p. 88. See also Soja, "Taking Los Angeles Apart."

5. Cf. "Premises of a Theory of Description," in Gelley, *Narrative Crossings*.

6. De Certeau, *The Practice of Everyday Life*, pp. 115f.

7. In surveying a number of recent studies of the city as a literary theme Jef Bogman, in "La Ville Obsédant," concludes that they generally make too uncritical a link between a presumed experiential reality and the textual form of the literary work and proposes instead a more rigorous intertextual approach: "Contact with the city is to a large extent fashioned by way of texts—texts of all kinds . . . Consciously or not, every new text represents a reaction to this ensemble of texts" (p. 134).

8. Klotz's *Die erzählte Stadt*, one of the most informed and wide-ranging thematic studies, states from the beginning its intention of exploring in an inductive manner the premise "that there exists an affinity between city and novel, between an extra-literary object and a literary form" (p. 11). But this premise is supported by little more than the fact that the novel as the most "empirically oriented genre" is best-suited to illustrate the "historical mutation

of literature" through the "historical mutation of the phenomenon of the city" (p. 11).

9. Lefebvre, *Critique de la vie quotidienne*, pp. 102f.

10. Michel de Certeau reminds us (*The Practice of Everyday Life*, p. 129) that the Greek sense of narration, *diegesis*, is more a *topological* operation, manipulating and deforming schemas and maps, than a *topical* one, concerned with defining places.

11. As in Ayn Rand's *The Fountainhead*.

12. Cf. also Foucault, *Power/Knowledge*, pp. 159f. and 164f.

13. A Kantian model. Cf. "Metonymy, Schematism, and the Space of Literature" in Gelley, *Narrative Crossings*.

14. Cited in Welsh, *The City of Dickens*, p. 5

15. Cited in Marx, "Pastoralism in America," p. 55.

16. The *Arcades Project* refers to the materials (some 950 printed pages; see Benjamin, *Das Passagen-Werk*) that Benjamin had collected during the 1930s in preparation for a book on Paris and nineteenth-century culture. It consists largely of citations drawn from contemporary sources, although Benjamin left considerable commentary as well, both in his manuscripts and in essays published during this time. For further information see Gelley, "Thematics and Historical Construction in Benjamin's 'Arcades Project.'"

17. Baudelaire's remarks in *L'art romantique*, which Benjamin noted, are especially relevant here: "Pour le parfait flâneur . . . c'est une immense jouissance que d'élire domicile dans le nombre, dans l'ondoyant . . . Etre hors de chez soi, et pourtant se sentir partout chez soi; voir le monde, être au centre du monde et rester caché au monde, tels sont quelques-uns des moindres plaisirs de ces esprits indépendants, passionnés, impartiaux [!!], que la langue ne peut que maladroitement définir." Cited in Benjamin, *Das Passagen-Werk*, p. 556. The bracketed exclamation marks are Benjamin's.

18. Citations, indicated in the text, are from *The Short Fiction of Edgar Allan Poe*.

19. See Lyotard, "*Domus* et la mégapole." Of course, in proposing this binarism Lyotard is in no sense suggesting a valorization on either side. There is no question of going back: "Not that the *domus* is the figure of community which might serve as an alternative to the megapolis. It's all over with domesticity, and undoubtedly it has never existed, if not as the dream of the ancient child who woke and destroyed it in waking" (p. 213). And as for the megapolis: "Baudelaire, Benjamin, Adorno. How to inhabit the megapolis? In being witness to the impossible work, in testifying to the lost *domus*" (p. 212). David Carroll's essay in this volume discusses Lyotard's critique of any normative communitarian principle that might be derived from the Kantian *sensus communis*. In the discussion of *domus*/megapolis, Lyotard, it seems to me, continues this critique with specific reference to the ways that domestic and urban constructs have been invested with a transcendent value.

20. Urban or street art of the last two decades represents a significantly new potential. For a penetrating discussion of one instance see Deutsche, "Uneven Development."

Works Cited

Barthes, Roland. *L'aventure sémiologique*, Paris: Seuil, 1985. The articles cited are "Sémantique de l'objet" (1964), pp. 249–60, and "Sémiologie et urbanisme" (1967), pp. 261–71.

Benjamin, Walter. *Gesammelte Schriften*, vol. 1. Frankfurt: Suhrkamp, 1974.

—— *Illuminations*, ed. Hannah Arendt. New York: Schocken Books, 1968.

—— *Das Passagen-Werk (Gesammelte Schriften*, vol. 5). Frankfurt: Suhrkamp, 1982.

Bogman, Jef. "La Ville Obsédant: Le Thème de la Ville dans la Critique Littéraire." In *Avant Garde*, 1(1988): 117–41.

Calvino, Italo. *Invisible Cities*. Reprint. London: Picador, 1979. Original Italian version published 1972.

Choay, Françoise. *La règle et le modèle: Sur la théorie de l'architecture et de l'urbanisme*. Paris: Seuil, 1980.

Davis, Mike. *City of Quartz: Excavating the Future in Los Angeles*. London: Verso, 1990.

de Certeau, Michel. *The Practice of Everyday Life*. Berkeley and London: University of California Press, 1984.

Deutsche, Rosalyn. "Uneven Development: Public Art in New York City." In *October* 47 (Winter 1988): 3–52.

Foucault, Michel. *Discipline and Punish: The Birth of the Prison*. New York: Vintage, 1977.

—— *The Foucault Reader*, ed. Paul Rabinow. New York: Pantheon, 1984.

—— "Of Other Spaces." In *Diacritics* (Spring, 1986): 22–27.

—— *Power/Knowledge: Selected Interviews and Other Writings, 1972–1977*, ed. Colin Gordon, New York: Pantheon, 1980.

Gelley, Alexander. *Narrative Crossings: Theory and Pragmatics of Prose Fiction*. Baltimore: Johns Hopkins University Press, 1987.

—— "Thematics and Historical Construction in Benjamin's 'Arcades Project.'" In *Strumenti Critici*, n.s. 4(1989): 233–51.

Godard, Jean-Luc. *Deux ou trois choses que je sais d'elle*. Paris: Seuil, 1971.

Gottdiener, M. and Alexandros Ph. Lagopoulos, eds. *The City and the Sign: An Introduction to Urban Semiotics*. New York: Columbia University Press, 1986.

Hamon, Philippe. "Texte et architecture." In *Poétique* 73 (1988): 3–26.

Klotz, Volker. *Die erzählte Stadt: Ein Sujet als Herausforderung des Romans von Lesage bis Döblin*. Munich: C. Hanser, 1969.

Ledrut, Raymond. "Speech and the Silence of the City." In *The City and the Sign: An Introduction to Urban Semiotics*, ed. M. Gottdiener and Alexandros Ph. Lagopoulos, pp. 114–34. New York: Columbia University Press, 1986.

Lefebvre, Henri. *Critique de la vie quotidienne*. Paris: L'Arche, 1961.

Lukács, Georg. *The Theory of the Novel*. Tr. Anna Bostock. Cambridge: M.I.T. Press, 1971.

Lyotard, Jean-François. "*Domus* et la mégapole." In *L'Inhumain: Causeries sur le temps*. Paris: Editions Galilee, 1988.

Marx, Leo. "Pastoralism in America." In *Ideology and Classic American Literature*, ed. Sacvan Bercovitch and Myra Jehlen, pp. 36–39. Cambridge: Cambridge University Press, 1986.

Poe, Edgar Allan. *The Short Fiction of Edgar Allan Poe*, ed. Stuart and Susan Levine. Indianapolis: Bobbs-Merrill, 1976.

Preziosi, Donald. "Between Power and Desire: The Margins of the City." In *Glyph Textual Studies*, vol. 1. Minneapolis: University of Minnesota Press, 1986.

Ritter, Joachim. *Landschaft: Zur Funktion des Aesthetischen in der modernen Gesellschaft*. Münster: Aschendorff, 1963.

Rossi, Aldo. *The Architecture of the City*. Cambridge: MIT Press, 1982.

Scherpe, Klaus R. "Nonstop nach Nowhere City? Wandlungen der Symbolisierung, Wahrnehmung und Semiotik der Stadt in der Literatur der Moderne." In *Die Unwirklichkeit der Städte*, ed. Klaus R. Scherpe. Reinbeck bei Hamburg: Rowohlt, 1988.

Shapiro, Michael J. *Reading the Postmodern Polity: Political Theory as Textual Practice*. Minneapolis: University of Minnesota Press, 1992.

Soja, E. W. "Taking Los Angeles apart: some fragments of a critical human geography." In *Society and Space* 4(1986): 255–72.

Welsh, Alexander. *The City of Dickens*. Oxford: Clarendon Press, 1971.

Williams, Raymond. *The Country and the City*. New York: Oxford University Press, 1973.

JEAN FRANÇOIS LYOTARD

The Wall, the Gulf, and the Sun: A Fable

I

I intended to take advantage of the opportunity provided by this talk to take a bearing on the current historical conjuncture. That is what I used to do in the fifties and sixties when, as a militant member of the critical theory and practice institute called "Socialisme ou barbarie," it was my turn to undertake the risky exercise we called "analyse de la situation." After selecting the events that we considered to have prominent significance in the contemporary historical context, we based our analysis on them with a view to formulating an accurate picture of the world.

While the purpose of this exercise was of course to gain as correct an understanding of "reality" as possible, it was also concerned with developing appropriate practical interventions within the complex and ever-changing network of forces making up the historical situation. Thus, theoretical analysis was closely related to potential praxis. Indeed, be-

This essay was written with the help of Thomas Cochran.

sides the task of faithfully representing the world conjuncture, the question of what could be done in such a situation also had to be addressed. "What could be done" meant, more specifically, how we could help exploited and alienated peoples emancipate themselves from exploitation and alienation, and what kind of practice would enable us to realize this goal, here and now.

To begin by recalling what "situation analysis" was for me in those days is not a matter of nostalgia. It helps me to realize just how different the circumstances and expectations for situation analysis are today. Unlike a critical practice institute, we are of course not required to outline the direction of interventions. The only interventions we may envisage take form in the publication of papers and collections. This is not to say that it is a small matter to intervene in this manner; it is something else. And change does not come from what a critical group is called. Rather, the difference emerges from a change that effectively affects the historical situation and subsequently the state of criticism itself.

Briefly, and generally speaking, let us say that militant praxis, in our countries at least, has become defensive praxis. We are constantly having to assert the rights of minorities, women, children, homosexuals, the environment, animals, citizens, culture and education, the South, the third world, and the poor. We have to sign petitions, write papers, organize conferences, join committees, take part in polls, and publish books. In doing so, we assume the regular responsibilities attached to the position of intellectuals. I say "regular" because these practices are permitted and even encouraged by the law—or, at least, by the implicit or formal rules of our positions. Western society not only allows us to participate in these practices; it in fact requires us to take part in them— it needs the specific contributions that we are able to provide for the development of the system as a whole.

In these conditions, we may keep alive the feeling that we continue to fight for emancipation. And it is true. Nevertheless, there is a sign that the nature of the struggle has changed. The price to pay for assuming it—the quantity of energy and time that must be spent in order to actualize critical practices—has been reduced. This reduction clearly indicates that our strategy has changed from an offensive one, as it formerly was, to a defensive one. According to Clausewitz, the amount of time and energy required for an offensive strategy to offset an adversary power is seven times greater than that needed for a defensive strategy. By moving from an offensive to a defensive strategy, we could save 86 percent of the energy previously devoted to the task of emancipation and still get the same effect!

However, we know, in fact, that the effect cannot be the same. Emancipation is no longer the task of conquering and imposing liberty from without. It no longer represents the ideal alternative opposable to reality. Rather, emancipation is taken as one goal among many pursued by the system, an ideal that the system itself endeavors to actualize in most of the areas it includes, such as work, taxes, marketplace, family, sex, race, school, culture, communication. Of course, emancipation is not always successful in each area; it is confronted with obstacles, both internal and external, that resist it. All the same, such efforts of resistance encourage the system to become more complex and open and to promote spontaneous undertakings. That is tangible emancipation. Programs that improve what already exists are inscribed in its very mode of functioning—including venture programs, which allow for greater complexity and more flexible institutions to be introduced into system's network.

I know that the idyllic picture I am painting is as trivial as political discourses, commercial messages and administrative policy documents may be and are. It is the critic's job to detect and denounce all the cases in which the system fails to improve the process toward emancipation. I am merely suggesting that the critic's position now presupposes that the system itself is understood by criticism as being put in charge of promoting emancipation and that critiques, whatever forms they may take, are needed by the system for improving its efficiency in the direction of emancipation. I would say that criticism contributes to changing differends, if such there be, into litigations.

II

Thereby, the situation might inspire observers and commentators with the feeling that the grand narrative issued from the Enlightenment has finally prevailed over the other representations that previously competed for the theoretical and practical lead in human affairs. Throughout the twentieth century, diverse attempts—imperialism, fascism, nazism, and communism—have been made to govern human communities differently. Most of them have now been put out of the competition. The oldest and most all-encompassing Western grand narrative, Christianity, stopped shaping the social, political, economic, and cultural institutions of Western communities long ago. Marxism, the last branch stemming from both the Enlightenment and Christianity, seems to have lost all its critical power. When the Berlin Wall fell, it failed definitively. By invading the shops in West Berlin, the East German crowds gave evidence that the ideal of freedom, at least of the free market, had already invaded Eastern European minds.

Thus, the practical critique of communism has been carried out. But what about the practical and theoretical criticist power of Marxism? Having been in East Berlin in June and December of 1989, I was able to observe how anxious and concerned the East German intellectuals were (even if they had been more or less compromised with the communist bureaucracy) to save, maintain, or elaborate a view enabling all of us to criticize both Eastern totalitarianism and Western liberalism. For somebody coming from the tradition of radical Marxism, this request sounded like an appeal to go backward and start again with a double-edged criticism, against both late capitalism and the so-called communist society, which we had undertaken in the fifties and sixties. Although it is attractive, the purpose is vain.

Of course, it still remains quite possible to analyze the current situation of Eastern and Western Europe in terms of the rise of capitalism and the fall of bureaucratic regimes and organizations. But, something would necessarily be missing from the picture, something that cast its tragic light over the historical stage for a couple of centuries—the proletariat. According to the rigorous Marxist notion, the proletariat was not to be confused with the labor classes. The latter are social entities that are more or less recognizable (and falsifiable) by the means of sociology and cultural anthropology, whereas the former was supposedly the name of the authentic subject of modern human history. The proletariat was the subject whose unique property, its labor force, had been exploited by capitalism on the one hand and taken by Marxism as the real mover behind all human history on the other. The proletariat was divested of its labor force in order to allow capital to appropriate the fruits of its peculiar and precious capacity: to produce more value than this force consumes in the production process (an outstanding case of "good productivity" or, rather, "good productivity" itself).

What was ultimately at stake for Marxism was to transform the local working classes into the emancipated proletariat, that is, to convert the diverse communities of workers chained up in capitalistic relationships into a unique self-conscious and autonomous collective subject capable of emancipating all humanity from the disastrous effects of the injury it had suffered. Something sounded tragic in this vision: society was viewed as being possessed by a *mania*, haunted by a ghost, doomed to a tremendous catharsis. For the injury was a wrong that, unlike mere damage, was not redeemable by litigations since the court required equitably to hear the two parties—work and capital—did not exist. The rights of the workers were the rights of mankind to self-government, and they should be fought for through class struggle. By this I mean "class against class," with no reference to nation, sex, race, or religion.

The mere recall of these well-known guidelines of Marxist criticism has something obsolete, even tedious about it. It is not all my fault but is also because the ghost has now vanished, dragging the last critical grand narrative with it off the historical stage. The regimes that have pretended to be representative of the hero have fallen into appalling buffoonery. They collapse one after the other, allowing the stage to be opened up to rebuilding according to Western models. It can take years and years and bring about tremendous convulsions. Nevertheless, the process of rebuilding in this way (an unexpected, practical way of critique) cannot be resisted. And, in this process of practical critique, the working classes have played, do play, and will play no role as such. The international labor movement has been dissipated into local institutions that claim only to defend the rights of specific groups of workers. Local class struggles work in the same way as the other efforts of resistance I have mentioned, that is, as parts of the impediments with which the system is confronted and needs to improve itself.

Thus, the discourse that Marxists called the bourgeois discourse of emancipation and the communal organization connected with it, that is, liberal late capitalism, now look like the only survivors and winners of a bicentennial struggle that sought to impose another way of reading and leading human history. This system has good reasons to claim to be the very supporter of human rights and freedom, including the right and freedom to critique. How could the demand for radical criticism, as formulated by the East German colleagues, be satisfied if criticizing, questioning, and imagining, as Castoriadis and Lefort would say today, actually require the openness that only an open system provides?

III

In terms of the current situation, the fall of the Berlin Wall is a significant event implying many historical consequences. It also has a crucial
influence on the scope of critical approaches. The Persian Gulf crisis,
which, as I write (October 19, 1991), still remains in a state of suspense,
is no less significant, though in a different way. It is not the first time,
and perhaps not the last, that the Western system as a whole is severely
challenged by the direct and indirect effects of its imperialist policy.
Obviously, the aggressive Iraqi dictatorship is a consequence of the situation created by the presence of Western powers in the Middle East for
two centuries. They divided up the area according to their respective
interests, reciprocal power relations, and common attempts to "solve"
the contradictions that affected them, especially on the occasion of the
crisis that gave birth to the First and Second World Wars. Saddam Hussein has literally been produced by the Western chancelleries and business firms in a way even more cynically flagrant than the way Hitler,
Mussolini, and Franco were produced by the "peace" policy adopted by
the winners after the First World War. By "produced," I mean that they
were the result of the imposition of the capitalistic system's aporias to
either less developed, defeated, or, in any case, less resistant countries.

Of course, there are many differences between the situations I am
comparing. Let me point out two of them, which are of great concern
to my purpose. The first is that the challenge faced by the Western system comes at a moment when the extension of its power has reached
the greatest lengths ever known (especially with the opening of the communist areas). In this regard, it seems that Saddam Hussein has not
taken a good look at this worldwide change symbolized by the fall of the
Berlin Wall. In contrast, the crisis that struck Germany and Italy during
the interwar years affected American and all other European societies
as well.

As to the second difference, I would like to linger over it a bit, since
it merges with the general idea of this paper. What forms the basis for
and makes possible the dictatorships to which I have referred is obviously linked to social and economic distress. Such distress is accompanied by the feeling of resentment resulting from humiliation, a feeling of which most contemporary Western minds hardly have an
appropriate representation for lack of experience. A necessary condition
for humiliation is that the community and culture to which one belongs

be judged at least as eminent as the community and culture of the adversary. When it is only a matter of a recent and casual defeat, humiliation remains episodic and resentment can be overcome. This is what
we expect in the case of a unified Germany.

Here is the difference that I want to emphasize. The Arab populations living in the Middle East belong to a long, brilliant, and worldwide civilization, Islam. They are aware of this, thanks to the Muslim
tradition. And they know that Islam and Arab culture have been subjected to humiliation by the West for centuries. Undoubtedly, the Desert Shield policy has awakened once again the resentment the Islamic
peoples permanently experience. Moreover, as divided as the Arab
states may be—an effect of the Western policy—the Arab populations
do and will undoubtedly react as belonging to the ancestral community
that they recognize as their own, the Islamic *Umma*. And they are undoubtedly ready to invest in any Arab figure they see as being capable of
making the names of Islam and the *Umma* recognized and honored all
over the world.

It is here that the force of Saddam Hussein lies, not in his military
weapons. It is not by chance that this leader of the secularized Arab
movement, the Baas, appeals to the *Umma* to resist the violation of
Muslim holy places. And it is also here that the very challenge posed by
the Gulf crisis lies. In the short term, the Baghdad dictator will undoubtedly be defeated in one way or another. In the midterm, the
Middle East map, including Lebanon, Israel, and Palestine, will undoubtedly be revisited. However, the point is whether, in the long run,
Islam can continue to resist the wholly secularized way of life that prevails in contemporary Western and Western-identified societies,
whether it will still be able to oppose the secularized West with the
spiritualization or, let us say, the symbolization that completely encompasses the details of everyday life and makes Islam a total civilization
rather than a specific religious belief. It represents a way for human
beings to be together, one that is completely extraneous to the Western
way. Like God's voice, a voice heard by Abraham and Muhammad long
ago, the muezzin's voice sounds over cities and deserts recalling that the
Law itself is the unique source of authority in human affairs.

Let us take the position of authority as a touchstone in order to separate the two parties facing each other in the Middle East conflict and to
consider what is actually at stake there beyond the noise of the declara-
tions and weapons. In the modern or, rather, postmodern system, au-

thority is a matter of arguing. It is only attributed or lent, as it were, to an individual or group that comes to occupy its place for a period of time. In principle, this place of authority remains vacant. Thus, although it is the ultimate voice of the Law, authority is designated by contract. This is the paradox of democracy in that the supreme agency or foundation for making decisions concerning the whole community is based on the decision of the community. In this sense, the transcendence or Otherness attached to the notion of the Law, which is considered as the ultimate appeals court, remains immanent to the community's sameness. The vacancy of the space of authority that I have just mentioned is a perfect example of the blankness or looseness that the open system preserves within itself in order to allow it to criticize, correct, and adjust its own performances. To the extent that authority may be analogically represented by the father's figure, it could be said that the father is elected by the sons and daughters among themselves.

In the Islamic tradition (like the Jewish one), however, the "father" elects his people, designates his representatives and prophets, and dictates the Law to them. Posited as unfathomable, the transcendent Law is accessible only by reading the letters (the voice itself is unheard except by the prophets) that have been inscribed in the Book by the first witnesses and passed on to further generations. Authority is a matter of interpretation rather than of argumentation—an interpretation of a special kind that adds nothing to the letters but only attempts to "fill up" the blank spaces between them—something like the Talmudic reading.

In fact, the notion of authority as pure Otherness is common to Muslims and Jews. The difference lies in the way the moral content formulated by the reading of the Book is to be actualized. And this difference in actualization stems from the fact that the Hebrew tradition had already been crossed over by the Christian message when the Koranic Law was laid down by Muhammad. The "good news" brought by Christianity is that, thanks to the mystery of the incarnation, that is, the sacrifice of God's son, and thanks to the reading of it, which Paul of Tarsus elaborated and imposed, the Law of Obedience is turned into the Law of Love, and the spiritual community linked by the reading of the Book may itself embody a concrete—first political (the Empire), then economic (protestant capitalism)—community. Although a theology of incarnation is missing from it, Islam retains the message that the political actualization of its Law is required as its evidence. Thus, it is concerned with the task of manifesting the authority of the Book by fixing the significance of the Koranic verses and inscribing it into the worldly reality (as does Christianity, with analogous dogmatic and political consequences). As such, authority becomes a matter to be testified to by secular achievements—and when such achievements are lacking, humiliation ensues. And this has not failed to be the case. When confronted with the modern and classical West, Islam was defeated because the Koranic Law did not allow the Muslim political states to develop economic power, whereas the West was authorized to do so by the dogma of the incarnation, a dogma that could legitimate success in all secular areas. In the last analysis, such was the reason for the failure of the powerful medieval caliphates. In the modern, postmodern, and even classical Western age, the Holy War seems inappropriate while wars are only economic conflicts carried on by other means. (As for the Jews, they, or perhaps their circumstances, have prevented the Jews from the attempt to form political communities, at least for a very long time. Humiliation is impossible when the Law only requires subtlety in reading, humbleness in realizing, and humor in judging. But the price is having to suffer at the hands of other political, social, and economic communities.)

The previous description, which is too brief and too ambitious in its scope, can be concluded in the following way: neither the liberal nor the Marxist reading can account for the current historical situation marked by both the fall of the Berlin Wall and the Gulf crisis. As to the latter, the good conscience of the West appears miserable in asserting that Saddam Hussein is a tyrant, that Arab people are hysterical and fanatical, that international rights are being violated, and so on, as if the West was exempt from the same sins, even recently. On the other hand, if the Marxist reading could legitimate its own discourse, it would not have to confuse the third world, the South, or the Middle East masses who were and are wretched by imperialism with the figure of the proletariat—a confusion that is absurd in theoretical and practical terms and shameful with regard to the responsibility of thinking. As concerns the fall of the Berlin Wall, things are clearer and can help us to gain a better understanding of the current situation. For the fall of the Wall, on the one hand, provides evidence that the more open the system, the more efficient it is; while on the other it shows that closed and isolated systems are doomed to disappear, either by competition or merely by entropy (Brezhnev should have studied thermodynamics a bit). In the context of the Gulf crisis, the issues are predictable, though for different reasons. However respectable Islam is as a sample of spirituality, it cannot match the concrete performances achieved by the Western system and is therefore obliged either to change its positioning (for example, by turning into a mere religious faith and practice among others) or to disappear.

Therefore, the important aspect seems to be the openness (or looseness) of systems competing with each other. With this point, two questions arise. First of all, does this mean that the whole situation should be thought of in terms of utilizable forces, that is, in terms of the notions drawn from dynamics? Second, why is it necessary for systems to compete? In Leibnizian metaphysics, which was also a systems theory, there was nothing like a struggle for victory between monads. What, then, is the mover of the competitive process?

IV

To these metaphysical questions is it necessary to give metaphysical answers? Perhaps. But the metaphysical avenue is closed—or has, at least, become the object of critique. This critique has developed in the empty interior space that the open system maintains and protects within itself. The system no longer needs to be legitimated on a metaphysical basis. Rather, it only needs the free space. Critique is and will always be possible and desirable. But, it must be remarked, its conclusion will always be the same: there is no conclusion; the conclusion is deferred; some "blanks" always remain in the "text," whatever text it is. This blank is the critique's resource. It is also the trademark that the open system affixes to the works (*oeuvres*) of the mind.

And yet this blank allows something besides critique: imagination. For example, it allows for a story to be freely told. I would like to describe the present historical situation in a way that is hardly critical. In fact, I would like to describe it in a manner that, quite frankly, is "representational" in the sense of being referential, imaginative rather than reflexive—in a word, naive, if not to say childish. It could be taken for a Voltairian tale, if I had some talent. My excuse is that this "story" is reasonably well accredited in the very serious milieus that the communities of physicists, biologists, or economists represent. It is accredited in an informal, somewhat timorous way, as if it were the unavowed dream that the postmodern world dreams about itself. It could be said that this tale represents the grand narrative that this world stubbornly tries to tell about itself, even though the grand narratives have obviously failed. This much could be said about this tale, if it were not for the fact that the hero is no longer mankind.

The teller told

In the incommensurable vastness of the cosmos, it happened that energy dispersed in random particles was gathered together here and there into bodies. These bodies constituted closed, isolated systems, such as galaxies and stars. The finite amount of energy with which they were provided was used by them to maintain themselves in aggregate systems, with the result of transforming the particles—a transformation called work. As a result of this work, energy was partly released into unusable forms, such as heat and light. However, since additional energy could not be imported, the isolated systems were doomed to collapse after a certain period of time; for they lost their internal differentiation. Energy that had previously been gathered together into bodies was subsequently dispersed all over space. Entropy is the process by which isolated systems are led toward the most probable distribution of their elements—random distribution.

In a very small part of the incommensurable cosmos, there was a small galactic system called the Milky Way. Amid billions of stars, there was a very small star called the sun. Working like any other closed system, the sun emitted heat, light, and diverse radioactive waves toward the bodies, or planets, that it had attracted to itself. Furthermore, like all closed systems, the sun also had a fixed life expectancy. At the moment that this story was being told, it was in its middle age. The sun still had four and a half billion years before it would collapse.

Among the planets was Earth. And it happened that something unexpected occurred on its surface. Thanks to the contingent constellation of various energy forms—molecules constituting terrestrial bodies, water, the atmosphere selecting solar radiations, and temperature—it happened that molecular systems were gathered together into more complex and improbable systems called cells. Here lies the first enigmatic incident whose occurrence was the condition for the continuation of this story as well as its narration. With the advent of the cell, the evidence was given that systems with some differentiation were capable of producing systems with increased differentiation according to a process that was completely opposite of that of entropy.

What was especially amazing was the ability of unicellular bodies to reproduce themselves by spontaneously dividing into two parts, both of which were identical to the original body. Technically referred to as *scissiparity*, this process of cell division seemed to ensure the perpetuation of this kind of cellular system.

Thus, birth was born and death with it. Unlike molecules, these "living" systems were required regularly to consume external energies for survival. On the one hand, such a dependence made them very fragile because they were threatened by a lack of energy. But on the other, it "spared" them the misfortune of being doomed to collapse like isolated systems; as a result their life expectancy was not mechanically predictable.

Then, another event occurred among the "living" systems: sexed reproduction. In addition to being immensely more improbable than scissiparity, this way of reproducing also allowed the offspring to be distinguished from their progenitors (thanks to the association of two different genetic codes). Hence, the "space" for unexpected events to interfere in the process of reproduction became wider, and the chance for mutations ("misreadings") also increased.

Thereafter, the story has already been told by Darwin. Remarkable, however, is the point that "evolution" did not imply purposiveness. New systems appeared fortuitously. They were mechanically confronted with the existing context, that is, the existing set of systems. The challenge that thus arose was how to provide oneself with energy. Given that the available amount of energy was finite, competition was unavoidable. War was born. As a result, the most efficient or productive systems were statistically selected.

After some time (quite short in relation to astronomical time), the system called mankind was selected. This was extremely improbable for the same reason that it is improbable for a superior monkey to remain upright on its hind legs. The vertical position freed the hands and allowed for the extension of the brain pan. Both manual techniques and those that operate by symbols called languages began to develop. Such techniques constituted additional prothesis, enabling the human system to overcome the extreme weakness that was concomitant with its improbability.

As with unicellular systems, something just as unexpected had to happen with mankind. Like the unicellular system's capacity to reproduce themselves, mankind's symbolic language had the peculiar characteristic of being recursive, that is, of being able to bring together diverse linguistic elements indefinitely (while still making sense). In addition, symbolic language had the particularity of being self-referential, of taking itself as an object. Having enjoyed similar benefits thanks to these peculiarities of language, material techniques likewise underwent a mutation. Because of language they could be referred to, improved upon, complexified, and accumulated.

Language also allowed individual human beings to inflect the rigid modes in which they had been living together in "primitive" communities. Various improbable forms of human aggregation arose and they were selected according to their ability to discover, capture, and save sources of energy. In regard to this ability, there were two noteworthy "revolutions": the Neolithic and the Industrial Revolutions.

For a long time ("long," that is, when calculated in terms of human time) techniques and communities appeared at random. The probability for improbable and fragile systems to survive remained out of control. Sophisticated techniques could possibly be neglected as curiosities and fall into oblivion. Politically and economically differentiated communities could be defeated by simpler but more vigorous systems.

Nevertheless, because of the previously mentioned particularities characterizing language, the ability to reproduce and anticipate unexpected events—including failures, which had been introduced by language itself—was developing on its own. Thus, the task of controlling unexpected occurrences, be they external or internal, became the primary task for systems to fulfill if they wanted to survive. In addition, a number of authorities began to appear in the social, economic, political, cognitive, and representational (cultural) fields.

After some time, it happened that systems called liberal democracies came to be recognized as the most appropriate for the task of controlling events in whatever field they might occur. By leaving the programs of control open to debate and by providing free access to the decision-making roles, they maximized the amount of human energy available to the system. The effectiveness of this realistic flexibility has shown itself to be superior to the exclusively ideological (linguistic) mobilization of forces that rigidly regulated the closed totalitarian systems. In the former (the liberal democratic systems), everybody could believe what they wanted, that is, organize language according to whatever system they liked, provided that they contributed to the system as energetically as they could.

Given the increased self-control of the open system, it was likely that it would be the winner in the competition among the systems all over the Earth. Nothing seemed able to stop it or even to direct it in ways other than contributing to its development. Incidents such as the collapse of the communist societies and the Gulf crisis were, on the one hand, the opportunity for the system to increase its influence while preventing it from reducing its "blank" internal space as bureaucratic regimes had already done and, on the other, the occasion for the system to improve its control over other energy resources. Moreover, the system had also started to moderate its victory over other terrestrial systems by extending its ability to regulate the ecosystem so as to ensure its survival.

Nothing seemed able to stop the development of this system except the sun and the unavoidable collapse of the whole solar system. In order to meet this predictable challenge, the system was already in the process of developing the prosthesis that would enable it to survive after the solar sources of energy that had contributed to the genesis and maintenance of the living systems were wiped out.

All the research that was in progress at the time this story was told—that is, taken at random, research in logic, economics, and monetary theory, data processing, physics of conductors, astronomy and astronautics, biology and medicine, genetics, dietetics, catastrophe theory, chaos theory, strategy and ballistics, sports, systems theory—all this research was devoted to problems of adjusting or replacing human bodies so that human brains would still be able to work with the only forms of energy left available in the cosmos—and thus preparing for the first exodus of the negen-tropic system far from Earth, with no return.

What mankind and "its" brain—or, better, the brain and its man—would look like in the days of this final terrestrial chal-lenge, the tale did not tell.

ERNESTO LACLAU

Power and Representation

The aim of this essay is to explore some of the consequences that follow—for both political theory and political action—from what has
been called our "postmodern condition." There is today the widespread
feeling that the exhaustion of the great narratives of modernity, the blur-
ring of the boundaries of the public spaces, the operation of logics of
undecidability, which seem to be robbing all meaning from collective
action, are leading to a generalized retreat from the political. I would
like to try to explore this claim and shall do so by considering, as my
starting point, some of the most fundamental assumptions of the modern approach to politics. From the point of view of the *meaning* of any
significant political intervention there was in modernity the generalized
conviction that the former had to take place at the level of the *ground* of
the social—that is, that politics had the means to carry out a *radical
transformation* of the social, whether such a transformation was conceived as a founding revolutionary act, as an orderly set of bureaucratic
measures proceeding from an enlightened elite, or as a single act opening the way to the operation of those mechanisms whose automatic

unfolding would be sufficient to produce a "society effect." There is, in addition, the question of the *framework* that allows a conceptual grasp on such a political intervention. This was provided by the notion of *social totality* and by the series of causal connections that necessarily followed from it. As has been pointed out,[1] if we take Machiavelli and Hobbes as opposite poles in the modern approach to politics—the first centering his analysis in a theory of strategic calculation *within* the social, the second in the mechanisms-producing society as a totality—it is the Hobbesian approach that has constituted mainstream modern political theory. This leads us to a third feature of political action as conceived in the modern age: its radical *representability*. It could not have been otherwise; if there is a ground of the social—which is a condition of its intelligibility—and if, as a result, society can only be considered as an orderly series of effects, that is, as a totality, then an action whose meaning derives from such a ground and such a totality has to be fully transparent to itself and thus endowed with limitless representability. As well, this transparency and representability had to be necessarily translated to the *agent* of the historical transformation. A limited historical actor could only carry out a universal task insofar as he was denied access to the meaning of his actions, insofar as his consciousness was a "false" one. But as both Hegel and Marx knew very well, a social totality that lacks the mirror of its own representation is an incomplete social totality and, consequently, not a social totality at all. Only the full reconciliation between substance and subject, between being and knowledge, can cancel the distance between the rational and the real. But, in that case, representation is a necessary moment in the self-constitution of the totality, and the latter is only achieved so long as the distinction between action and representation is abolished. Only a limitless historical actor—a "universal class"—can make this abolition actual. This dual movement, by which the ground becomes subject through a universal class that abolishes all "alienation" in the forms of representation and by which the subject becomes ground by abolishing all external limitations posed by the object, is at the center of the modern view of history and society.

These four features converge in a fifth one that could perhaps be considered as the true horizon of the modern approach to politics: once the last foundation of politics is made fully visible, power becomes a purely appariential phenomenon. The reasons for this reduction are clear: if one social group exercises power over another, this power will be experienced by the second group as irrational; but if history is, however, a purely rational process, the irrationality of power must be purely appariential. In that case, either historical rationality belongs to the discourse of the dominant groups—and the claims of the oppressed are the necessary but distorted expression of a higher rationality that generates, as its own condition of possibility, an area of opaqueness; or the discourses of the oppressed are the ones that contain the seeds of a higher rationality—in which case their full realization involves the elimination of any opaqueness (and therefore any power). In the first case coercion and opaqueness are indeed present; but as the power of the dominant group is fully rational, the resistance to power cannot be external but only internal to power itself; in that case the coercion and opaqueness of the brute fact of domination can only be the necessary appariential forms through which the rationality of power takes shape. If a system of domination is rational its repressive character can only be appariential. This leaves us with only two alternatives: either the gaze of the dominant group is fully rational, in which case that group is a limitless historical actor, or the gazes of both the dominant and the dominated groups are partial and limited ones, in which case the attributes of full rationality are automatically transferred to the historical analyst. The important point is that in both cases reality of power and representability of history are in an inverse relationship.

These distinctive features of modernity are so deeply entrenched in our usual forms of conceiving society and history that recent attempts to call them into question (what has been called, in very general terms, "postmodernity") have given rise to a tendency to substitute them for their pure absence by a simple negation of their content, which continues inhabiting the intellectual terrain that those positive features had delineated. Thus, the negation that there is a ground out of which all social contents obtain a precise meaning can be easily transformed into the assertion that society is entirely meaningless; questioning the universality of the agents of historical transformation leads quite often to the proposition that all historical intervention is equally and hopelessly limited; and showing the opaqueness of the process of representation is usually considered equivalent to a denial that representation is possible at all. It is, of course, easy to show that—in a fundamental sense— these nihilistic positions continue inhabiting the intellectual terrain from which they try to distance themselves. To assert, for instance, that something is meaningless is to assert a very classical conception of meaning, adding only that it is absent. But in a more important sense it is possible to show that these apparently radical reversals can only acquire whatever force of conviction they can carry by a clearly detectable inconsistency. If I conclude—as I will later on in this text—that no pure relation of representation is obtainable because it is of the essence of the process of representation that the representative has to contribute to the identity of what is represented, then this cannot be transformed without inconsistency into the proposition that "representation" is a concept that should be abandoned. For in that case we would be left with the nude identities of represented and representative as self-sufficient identities, which is precisely the assumption that the whole critique of the notion of representation was questioning. In the same way, the critique of the notion of "universality" implicit in the idea of a universal agent cannot be transformed into the assertion of the equally uniform limitation of all agents—because in that case we could ask ourselves, Limitation in relation to what? And the answer can only be that it is in terms of a structure that equally limits *all* agents and that, in the same sense, it assumes the role of a true universality. Finally, in order to be radically meaningless, something requires, as its condition of possibility, the contrastive presence of a full-fledged meaning. Meaninglessness grows out of meaning or, as has been asserted in a proposition that states exactly the same, meaning grows out of nonmeaning.

Against these movements of thought, which remain within the terrain of modernity by simply inverting its fundamental tenets, I would like to suggest an alternative strategy: instead of inverting the contents of modernity, to *deconstruct* the terrain that makes the alternative modernity/postmodernity possible. That is, instead of remaining within a polarization whose options are entirely governed by the basic categories of modernity, to show that the latter do not constitute an essentially unified block but are rather the sedimented result of a series of contingent articulations. To reactivate the intuition of the contingent character of these articulations will thus produce a widening of horizons, insofar as other articulations—equally contingent—will also show their possibility. This involves, on the one hand, a new attitude toward modernity: not a radical break with but a new modulation of its themes; not an abandonment of its basic tenets but a hegemonization thereof by a different perspective. This also involves, on the other hand, an expansion of the field of politics instead of its retreat—a widening of the field of structural undecidability that opens the way to an enlargement of the field of political decision. It is here that "deconstruction" and "hegemony" show their complementarity as the two sides of a single operation. It is these two sides that I shall discuss now.

Let me start by referring to one of the originary texts of deconstruction: the analysis of the relation between meaning and knowledge in Husserl (the "formalist" and the "intuitionist" sides of his approach), as presented by Derrida in *Speech and Phenomena*. Husserl, in a first movement, emancipates meaning from the necessity of fulfilling it with the intuition of an object. That is, he emancipates meaning from knowledge. An expression such as "square circle" has indeed a meaning: it is such a meaning that allows me to say that it refers to an impossible object. Meaning and object fulfillment, as a result, do not necessarily require each other. Moreover, Derrida concludes that if meaning can be strictly differentiated from knowledge, the essence of meaning is better shown when such fulfillment does not take place. But, in a second movement, Husserl quickly closes the possibilities that he had just opened by the breach established between knowledge and meaning.

> In other words, the genuine and true meaning is the will to say the truth. This subtle shift incorporates the *eidos* into the *telos*, and language into knowledge. A speech could well be in conformity with its essence as speech when it is false; it nonetheless attains its entelechy when it is true. One can well *speak* in saying "The circle is square"; one speaks *well*, however, in saying that it is not. There is already sense in the first proposition, but we would be wrong to conclude from this that sense *does not wait upon* truth. It does not await truth as expecting it; it only precedes truth as its anticipation. *In truth*, the telos which announces the fulfillment, promised for "later," has already and beforehand opened up sense as a relation with the object.[2]

The important point—the deconstructive moment of Derrida's analysis—is that if "meaning" and "object intuition" are not related to each other in a teleological way, in that case—from the point of view of meaning—it is undecidable whether the latter will or will not be subordinated to knowledge. In this respect the path followed by Joyce, as Derrida points out, is very different from Husserl's. But if Husserl subordinates meaning to knowledge, and if this subordination is not required by the essence of meaning, it can only be the result of an intervention that is contingent vis-à-vis meaning. It is the result of what Derrida calls an "ethico-theoretical decision" on the part of Husserl. We can see how the enlargement of the field of structural undecidability brought about by the deconstructive intervention has, at the same time, widened the terrain to be filled by the decision. Now, a contingent intervention taking place in an undecidable terrain is exactly what we have called a *hegemonic* intervention.[3]

I would like to explore in some more detail this relation of mutual implication between deconstruction and hegemony. What the deconstructive move has shown is not the actual *separation* between meaning and knowledge, because the two are closely linked in Husserl's text—in fact, the unity of the latter results from this double requirement by which meaning has to be both *subordinated* to and *differentiated* from knowledge. So, the deconstructivist intervention shows, first, the *contingency* of a connection, and second, the contingency of a *connection*. This has an important consequence for our argument. If only the dimension of contingency was underlined, we would have merely asserted the synthetic character of the connection between two identities, each of them fully constituted in itself and not requiring anything outside itself for that full constitution. We would be in the terrain of a pure dispersion, which would be a new and contradictory form of essentialism given that each one of the monadic identities should be defined in and for itself (first extreme) and that because dispersion is, however, a form of *relation* between objects it requires a terrain that operates as ground or condition of possibility of that dispersion (second extreme)—in which case the identities could not, after all, be monadic. So, that connection to something else is absolutely necessary for the constitution of any identity, and this connection must be of a contingent nature. In that case, it belongs to the essence of something to have contingent connections, and contingency therefore becomes a necessary part of the essence of that something. This leads us to the following conclusions. That if having accidents is an essential feature of a substance—or, if the contingent is an essential part of the necessary—this means that there is a necessary undecidability inscribed within any structure (by "structure" I mean a complex identity constituted by a plurality of moments). For the structure requires the contingent connections as a necessary part of its identity, but these connections—precisely because they are contingent—cannot be logically derived from any point within the structure. So, the fact that only one of the possible paths is followed, that only one of the possible contingent connections is actualized, is undecidable from within the structure. The "structurality" of the structure, so far as it is the actualization of a series of contingent connections, cannot find the source of these connections within itself. This is why, in Derrida's analysis, Husserl's ethico-theoretical *decision* must be brought into the picture as an external element in order to establish the subordination of meaning to knowledge. An *external* source of a certain set of structural connections is what we will call *force*.[4]

This is exactly the point at which deconstruction and hegemony cross each other. For if deconstruction discovers the role of the decision out of the undecidability of the structure, hegemony as a theory of the decision taken in an undecidable terrain, requires that the contingent character of the connections existing in that terrain is fully shown by deconstruction. The category of hegemony emerged in order to think the political character of social relations in a theoretical arena that had seen the collapse of the classical Marxist conception of the "dominant class"—the latter conceived as a necessary and immanent effect of a fully constituted structure. The hegemonic articulations were from the beginning conceived as contingent, precarious, and pragmatic constructions. This is why, in Gramsci, there is a sustained effort to break with the identification between hegemonic agencies and objective social positions within the structure. His notion of "collective will" tries precisely to effect this break, so far as the collective wills are conceived as unstable social agencies, with imprecise and constantly redefined boundaries, and constituted through the contingent articulation of a plurality of social identities and relations. The two central features of a hegemonic intervention are, in this sense, the *contingent* character of the hegemonic articulations and their *constitutive* character, in the sense that they institute social relations in a primary sense, not depending on any a priori social rationality.

This, however, poses two problems. The first refers to the external instance that takes the decision. Is this not to reintroduce a new essentialism via the subject? Is it not to replace an objective closure of the structure by a subjective closure through the intervention of the agent? The second problem concerns the conditions of visibility of the contingency of the structure. For reasons that will become apparent in a moment, these two problems must be tackled successively, in the order just presented.

Regarding the first point, it is obvious that the matter cannot be solved on the basis of simply asserting that the trick is done by a subject who rearticulates around its project the dispersed elements of a dislocated structure. There is, in fact, a far more complex relation between subject and structure than the one that this simplistic version of what is involved in a hegemonic articulation suggests. For the obvious question arises: who is the subject and what is the terrain of its constitution? If we want to avoid facile deus ex machina solutions this question must be answered. A first answer would be in terms of a well-mannered and "enlightened" Marxism: there is a primary terrain on which social agencies are constituted—the relations of production—and a secondary terrain on which the dispersed elements to be hegemonized operate. In that way we are in the best of both worlds: we can assert the full role of agency in doing the articulating job without falling in any *demodé* subjectivism; we can maintain the notion of a fundamental agent of historical change without renouncing to the multiform and rich variety of social life; we can give some free rein to the intriguing game of historical contingency knowing that we have the disciplinary means to bring them back—"in the last instance"—to the stern world of structural constraints. What a beautiful and tidy little world! The drawback of the picture is, of course, that if the separation between the two levels has any validity at all, then we have to make explicit the totality within which that separation takes place; and if there is such a totality, contingency cannot be true contingency. For if the *limits* of the contingent are necessary, then these limits are part of the contingent identity. Conversely, as the necessary limits are limits of the contingent variation, the presence of that variation is absolutely necessary for the existence of the limits and in that case, as we asserted earlier, contingency becomes necessary. The world is, after all, more wild and unforeseeable than the tidy blueprints of our *bon pensant* Marxist.

So, let us mix the cards and start the game again. The hegemonic subject cannot have a terrain of constitution different from the structure to which it belongs. But, however, if the subject were a mere subject position within the structure, the latter would be fully closed and there would be no contingency at all—and no need to hegemonize anything. The terms of our problem are the following: hegemony means *contingent* articulation; contingency means *externality* of the articulating force vis-à-vis the articulated elements; and this externality cannot be thought as an actual separation of levels within a fully constituted totality because that is no externality at all. So, how to think an externality emerging within the structure in a way that is not the result of a positive differentiation of its constitutive levels? This can only happen if the structure is not fully reconciled with itself, if it is inhabited by an origi-

The lack & the constitution of the subject through the act of identification

nal lack, by a radical undecidability that needs to be constantly superseded by acts of decision. These acts are, precisely, what constitute the *subject*, who can only exist as a will transcending the structure. Because this will has no place of constitution external to the structure but is the result of the failure of the structure to constitute itself, it can be formed only through acts of identification. If I need to identify with something it is because I do not have a full identity in the first place. These acts of identification are thinkable only as a result of the lack within the structure and have the permanent trace of the latter. Contingency is shown in this way: as the inherent distance of the structure from itself. (This is, in fact, the matrix of all visibility and of all representation: without this distance no vision would be possible.)

This leads us to our second problem: what are the conditions of visibility of the contingency of the structure? Part of this question has actually been answered: so far as no specific content is *predetermined* to fill the structural gap, it is the conflict between various contents in their attempt to play this filling role that will make visible the contingency of the structure. But this leads to another consequence, which is of greater importance for our argument. The visibility of the contingent character of the content that closes the structure requires that such a content is seen as indifferent to the structural gap and, in that sense, as equivalent to other possible contents. This means that the relation between the concrete content and its role as filler of the gap within the structure is purely external—that is, precisely where the contingency lies. But in that case, the concrete content that does the filling will be constitutively split: on the one hand it will be its own literal content; on the other— so far as it fulfills a function that is contingent vis-à-vis that content—it will represent a general function or filling that is independent of any particular content. This second function is what, in another text, I have called *the general form of fullness*. Thus, the complete answer to our second problem would be that the condition of visibility of the contingency of the structure is the visibility of the gap between the general form of fullness and the concrete content that incarnates that form. In a situation of great disorder the need for *an* order becomes more pressing than the concrete content of the latter; and the more generalized the disorder, the greater will be the distance between these two dimensions and the more indifferent people will be to the concrete content of the political forms that bring things back to a certain normality.[6] This is what differentiates our approach to the lack inherent in all social forms from a dialectical transition. For the latter there is also no possibility for any content to remain in its own being. But the march forward from this impossibility proceeds through *determinate negation*; that is, the lack preannounces the concrete forms of its own filling. No contingency is involved in this process.

We can draw now some general conclusions about this split. It is easy to see that were a total closure of the structure to be achieved, the split would be superseded, because in that case the general form of the fullness would be immanent to the structure and it would be impossible to differentiate it from the concrete—literal—content of the latter. It is only if the fullness is perceived as that which the structure lacks that general form and concrete content can be differentiated. In that case we would apparently be left with a simple duality by which we would have, on the one hand, the (partially destructured) structure, and on the other, the various and—as we have seen—partially equivalent attempts to fill the structural gaps, to introduce new restructuring discourses and practices. There is, however, a sleight of hand in this way of presenting the matter, by which something essentially important is concealed. Let us examine the matter carefully. Everything turns around the status of this category of "equivalence," which we have introduced to characterize one of the dimensions of the relationship between the various discourses that try to fill the structural gap. What is the condition of possibility of such an equivalence? Let us think of the well-known example of people who live in the neighborhood of a waterfall. They live hearing, all their lives, the noise of the water falling—that is, the sound is a permanent background of which they are normally unaware. So they do not *actually* hear the noise. But if for any reason the fall of the water suddenly stops one day, they will start hearing that which, strictly speaking, cannot be heard: silence. It is the lack of something that has thus acquired full presence. Now, let us suppose that this silence is intermittently interrupted by noises of different origin that the fall of the water had made inaudible before. All these sounds will have a split identity: on the one hand they are *specific* noises; on the other, they have the equivalent identity of *breaking* the silence. The noises are only equivalent because there is silence; but the silence is only audible as the lack of a former fullness.

This example, however, misses one dimension of the communitarian lack: the latter is experienced as deprivation, while I can be perfectly indifferent to the presence or absence of the noise of the fall. This is why the *social* lack will be lived as disorder, as disorganization, and attempts to supersede it exist via identifications. But if social relations are discursive relations, symbolic relations that constitute themselves through processes of signification, then the failure of this process of constitution, the presence of the lack within the structure, itself must be signified. So the question is, Are there specific discursive forms of presence of the lack? Does this split between concrete content and general form of fullness have specific ways of showing itself? The answer is yes, and I will argue that the general form of fullness shows itself through the discursive presence of floating signifiers that are constitutively so—that is, they are not the result of contingent ambiguities of meaning but of the need to signify the lack (the absent fullness within the structure). Let us suppose a political discourse asserting that "Labor is more capable than the Tory Party to ensure *the unity of the British people.*" In a proposition like this, which is fairly common in political argument, we have an entity—"unity of the British people"—that is qualitatively different from the other two—Labor and the Tories. First, this unity is something to be achieved, so that, contrary to the other two entities, it is not something actually existent but the name of an absent fullness. But second, the kind of political unity that Labor and the Tories would bring about would be substantially different, so that if the term *unity* meant a concrete entity at the same level of the two political forces, the proposition would be almost tautological—it would be equivalent to "Labor is more capable than the Tories to ensure a Labor kind of unity of the British people." But obviously the original proposition does not intend to say *that.* So on the one hand, the various political forces provide the concrete content of the unity, without which the unity cannot exist, but on the other hand that unity is not fully exhausted by any of these alternative concrete contents. "Unity" is a floating signifier because its signifieds are fixed only by the concrete contents provided by the antagonistic forces; but at the same time this floating is not a purely contingent and circumstantial one, because without it political argument would be impossible and political life would be a dialogue of deafs, in which we would only have incommensurable propositions. The basic split mentioned earlier finds the form of its discursive presence through this production of empty signifiers representing the general form of fullness. In another essay[7] I have shown that if an expression such as "the fascist succeeded in carrying out the revolution in which the communist failed" made any sense in Italy in the early

1920s, it is because the signifier "revolution" was an empty one, representing people's feeling that the old order coming from the Risorgimento was obsolete and that a radical refoundation of the Italian state was needed.

Let us take one last example. In an article published some years ago[8] Quentin Skinner takes issue with the way Stuart Hampshire presents an imaginary dialogue between a liberal and a Marxist.[9] According to Hampshire the disagreement convolutes the meaning of the term *political*: the Marxist gives to it an extensive application while the liberal use is far more restricted. For Skinner, however, much more than the meaning of the term is involved in the dispute, given that it is not at all clear why incommensurable meanings attributed to a term would establish a criterion for preferring one to the other. And he concludes:

> If the Marxist is genuinely seeking to persuade the Liberal to share or at least acknowledge some political insight, he needs in effect to make two points. One is of course that the term *political* can appropriately be applied to a range of actions where the Liberal has never thought of applying it. But the other, which his application of the term challenges the Liberal to admit, is that this is due not to a disagreement about the meaning of the term but rather to the fact that the Liberal is a person of blinkered political sensitivity and awareness.[10]

I agree with Skinner's two points, but I would like to add something concerning the kind of dialogical process that the two operations involve. To convince the liberal that the term *political* can be applied to a range of actions that it had not encompassed before is something that can be done, as Skinner himself points out, only if the Marxist should be able to claim with some plausibility that he or she is employing the term in virtue of its *agreed* sense.[11] Now, if the liberal does not perceive that this agreed sense encompasses the kind of situation that the Marxist is referring to, this could be for one of two reasons: either because of a *logical* mistake or, more plausibly, because of a "blinkered political sensitivity and awareness." So Skinner's two points are not really different from each other; to apply a term to a new range of actions on the basis of an agreed sense requires, as a sine qua non condition, a *redescription* of a given situation in terms that do away with the blinkered political sensitivity. But with this we have advanced very little. For why would a redescription be accepted at all? If somebody is perfectly happy and well-installed in a description A, he or she has no reason whatsoever to move to another description B. The only way out of this impasse is if the description B does not come to replace a full-fledged description A but provides *a* description to a situation that had become increasingly undescribable in terms of an old paradigm. That is, the only way the process of conviction can operate is if it moves from lack of conviction to conviction, not from one conviction to another. This means that the function of a new language is to fill a gap. So, Hampshire is correct in thinking that there is no possibility of choice between two separate worlds of thought; but Skinner is also correct in sustaining that the dispute is not just about the meaning of the terms but about wider redescriptions. If we agree that the condition of a successful redescription is that it not only replace an old one but also fill a gap opened in the general describability of a situation, then the valid redescription will have a split identity: on the one hand, it will be its own content; on the other, it will embody the principle of describability as such—that is, what we have called the general form of fullness. Without this second order of signification, without what we could call the hegemonization of the general form of describability by a concrete description, we would be in Hampshire's "separate worlds of thought," and no interaction between political discourses would be possible.

The previous developments provide some elements to address our initial question: how to transcend the historical horizon of modernity without falling into the trap of an exclusive alternative modernity/postmodernity in which the purely negative character of the contents of the second pole means that those of the first continue dominating unchallenged? How to go beyond a nihilism whose very logic reproduces precisely that which it wants to question? Our argument will be, first, that it is the structural undecidability discussed in the preceding, when accepted in all its radical consequences, that makes it possible to go beyond both modernity and its nihilistic reverse; and second, that this going beyond modernity consists not in an abandonment of all its contents but rather in the loss of its dimension of horizon (a category that I must explain). I shall discuss the first point in connection with the operation of the logics of representation and power in contemporary societies and shall move later to the question of the crisis of the basic horizon of modernity.

Representation first: what is involved in a process of representation? Essentially the *fictio iuris* that somebody is present in a place from which he or she is materially absent. The representation is the process by which somebody else—the representative—"substitutes for" and at the same time "embodies" the represented. The conditions of a perfect representation would be met, it seems, when the representation is a direct process of transmission of the will of the represented, when the act of representation is totally transparent in relation to that will. This presupposes that the will is fully constituted and that the role of the representative is exhausted in its function of intermediation. Thus the opaqueness inherent in any substitution and embodiment must be reduced to a minimum; the body in which the incarnation takes place must be almost invisible. This is, however, the point at which the difficulties start. For from neither the side of the representative nor that of the represented do the conditions of a perfect representation obtain— and this is a result not of what is empirically attainable but because of the very logic inherent in the process of representation. So far as the represented is concerned, if he or she needs to be represented at all, this is the result of the fact that his or her basic identity is constituted in a place A and that decisions that can affect this identity will be taken in a place B. But in that case his or her identity is an incomplete identity, and the relation of representation—far from being a full-fledged identity—is a *supplement* necessary for the constitution of identity. The crucial problem is to determine whether this supplement can simply be *deduced* from the place A where the original identity of the represented was constituted, or if it is an entirely *new* addition, in which case the identity of the represented is transformed and enlarged through the process of representation. It is our view that the latter is always the case. Let us take a very simple example, in which the contribution of the representative to the constitution of the "interest" to be represented is apparently minimal: a deputy representing a group of farmers whose overriding interest is maintaining the prices of agricultural products. Even in this case the role of the representative far exceeds the simple transmission of a preconstituted interest. For the terrain on which this interest must be represented is that of national politics, where many other things are taking place, and even something apparently as simple as the protection of agricultural prices requires processes of negotiation and articulation with a whole series of forces and problems that far exceeds what is thinkable and deducible from place A. So, the representative *inscribes* an interest in a complex reality different from that in which the interest was originally formulated, and in doing so he or she constructs and transforms that interest. But the representative is thus also transforming the identity of the represented. The original gap in the identity of the represented, which needed to be filled by a supplement contributed by the process of representation, opens an undecidable movement in two directions that is constitutive and irreducible. There is an opaqueness, an essential impurity in the process of representation, which is at the same time its condition of both possibility and impossibility. The "body" of the representative cannot be reduced for essential reasons. A situation of perfect accountability and transmission in a transparent medium would not involve any representation at all.

So, the idea of having a perfect representation involves a logical im-possibility—but this does not mean that representation is *entirely* im-possible. The problem, rather, is that representation is the name of an undecidable game that organizes a variety of social relations but whose operations cannot be fixed in a rationally graspable and ultimately uni-vocal mechanism. Representation has been criticized very often in democratic theory for the difficulties it poses for an accountability that is considered essential in a democratic society. But most versions of this criticism are ill-grounded. To see the danger only in the possibility that the will of a constituency is ignored or betrayed by its representative is a one-sided view. There are of course many cases in which such will is ignored and many cases of systematic distortion. But what this criticism ignores is the role of the representative in the constitution of such a will. If, as I stated, it is a gap in the identity of the represented that requires the process of representation to fill it, it is simply not true that the reduc-tion of the social areas in which representative mechanisms operate will necessarily lead to more democratically managed societies. We live in societies in which we are increasingly less able to refer to a single or primary level as the one on which the basic identity of the social agents is constituted. This means, on the one hand, that social agents are be-coming more and more "multiple selves," with loosely integrated and unstable identities; and on the other, that there is a proliferation of the points in society from which decisions affecting their lives will be taken. As a result, the need to "fill the gaps" is no longer a "supplement" to be added to a basic area of constitution of the identity of the agent but instead becomes a *primary* terrain. The constitutive role of representa-tion in the constitution of the will, which was partly concealed in more stable societies, now becomes fully visible. The level of national poli-tics, for instance, can operate as one on which the discourses of the representatives propose forms of articulation and unity between otherwise fragmented identities. This means that we cannot escape the framework of the representative processes and that democratic alternatives must be constructed that multiply the points from and around which representation operates rather than attempts to limit its scope and area of operation.

We have seen what is involved in a situation in which the discourse of the representative must fill a gap in the identity of the represented: that discourse will have the dual role, to which I referred before, of both being a particular filler and symbolizing the filling function. But this means that the gap between the two terms of this duality will necessarily increase in present-day societies and that the role of the "representatives" will be ever more central and constitutive. Is that really so bad; are we increasingly distancing ourselves, through that developing gap, from the possibility of having democratically managed societies? I do not think so. The situation is rather the reverse. In a situation in which concrete content and general form of fullness cannot be differentiated—that is, in a close universe in which no representation is required—no democratic competition is possible. The transparency of a fully acquired identity will be the automatic source of all decisions. This is the world of the Homeric heroes. But if there is a gap in the identity of social actors, the filling of this gap will necessarily generate the split between filling content and filling function, and because the latter is not necessarily associated with any content there will be a competition between the various contents to incarnate the very form of fullness. A democratic society is not one in which the "best" content dominates unchallenged but rather one in which nothing is definitely acquired and there is always the possibility of challenge. If we think, for instance, in the resurgence of nationalism and all kinds of ethnic identities in present-day Eastern Europe, then we can easily see that the danger for democracy lies in the closure of these groups around full-fledged identities that can only reinforce their most reactionary tendencies and create the conditions for a permanent confrontation with other groups. It is, on the contrary, the integration of these nations into wider ensembles—such as the EEC—that can create the bases for a democratic development, and that requires the split from oneself, the need to be represented outside oneself to be a proper self. There is democracy only if there is the recognition of the positive value of a dislocated identity. The term *hybridization* aptly proposed by Homi Bhabha and other writers is fully applicable here. But in that case the condition of a democratic society is constitutive incompletion—which involves, of course, the impossibility of an ultimate rational grounding. We can see that this is a degrounding that escapes the perverse and sterile modernity/nihilism dichotomy: it confronts us not with the alternative presence/absence of a ground but with the unending search of something that has to give a positive value to its very impossibility. Gayatri Spivak has spoken of "strategic essentialism." Although I do not particularly like the formula I think it tends, in some way, in a direction similar to this logic of undecidability whose contours I am trying to define.

We are in the same situation if we refer to power. The traditional notion of an emancipated society is that of a fully rational society from which power has been entirely eliminated. But as we have seen, power must be, for the rationalistic conception of society on which the notion of emancipation is based, purely appariential. This presents to us the terms of an antinomian situation. If emancipation is to be possible as a *real* event—that is, if it is to have an ontological status and not be just the lived content of the false consciousness of people—then power must also be real. But if power is real, the relation between power and that which emancipates itself from it must be one of radical exteriority—otherwise there would be a rational link leading from power to emancipation, and emancipation would not be truly so. The difficulty lies in the fact that a relation of radical exteriority between two forces is a *contingent* relation, and consequently if emancipation eliminates power through a contingent process of struggle it must itself be power. Could it not be said, however, that once emancipation has destroyed power it ceases to be power? No, because full transparency and rationality cannot logically proceed from the opaqueness inherent in a contingent act of power. It is only if the overthrowing of power had been the expression of a higher rationality that had transformed it into a *necessary* step that emancipation would be rational through and through. But in that case, as we have seen, it would have ceased to be emancipation. So the very condition of emancipation—its radical break from power—is what makes emancipation impossible because it becomes indistinguishable from power. The consequence is not, however, the nihilistic result that emancipation is impossible and that only power remains, because what our conclusion asserts is that power is the very condition of emancipation. If all emancipation must constitute itself as power, there will be a plurality of powers—and, as a result, a plurality of contingent and partial emancipations. We are in the Machiavellian situation of a plurality of struggles *within* the social, not in an act of radical refoundation that would become the source of the social. What is displaced is the logically impossible idea of a radical dichotomy that makes emancipation synonymous with the elimination of power. But, as in the case of the impurity inherent in the process of representation, the dimension of power that is ineradicable and constitutive of all social identity should be seen not as a burden but as the source of a new historical optimism. For if a total elimination of power were attainable, social relations would be entirely transparent, difference would become impossible, and *freedom* would be a redundant term. We would reach, effectively, the end of history.

This leads me to my last point. What we are witnessing in our contemporary experience is the end of modernity as a horizon but not necessarily of the particular objectives and demands that have conformed to its contents. We call *horizon* that which establishes at the same time the limits and the terrain of constitution of any possible object—and that, as a result, makes impossible any "beyond." Reason for the Enlightenment, progress for positivism, communist society for Marxism—these are the names not of objects within a certain horizon but of the horizon itself. In this sense, the basic features of the modern conception of politics that I pointed out at the beginning of my text are firmly rooted in the main dimensions of modernity conceived as a fundamental horizon. Now, generalizing the main conclusions of my argument, I could assert that the crisis of that horizon, which has been pointed out from many quarters, has—far from leading to a generalized implosion of the social and to a retreat from participating in public spheres—created instead for the first time the possibility of a radically political conception of society. Let us go briefly to our five features and see in what way the "postmodern" turn helps to liberate politics from its limiting modern ties.

Radical transformation, in the first place: if this transformation is conceived as taking place at the level of a rationally graspable ground of the social, then the transformation is the work of reason and not of ourselves. A rationality transcending us fully determines what is to happen, and our only possible freedom is to be conscious of necessity. It is in this respect that a universal class can be only a limitless historical actor who abolishes the subject-object duality. But if there is no ground of the social, any historical intervention will be the work of limited historical agents. This limitation, however, is more than compensated for by a new freedom that social agents win as they become the creators of their own world. As a result, the notion of radical transformation is displaced: its radical character is given by the overdetermination of partial changes that it involves, not by its operation at the level of a fundamental ground. This explains why the second and fourth features that we had found in the modern approach to politics are also displaced. The category of "social totality" certainly cannot be abandoned because, so far as all social action takes place in an overdetermined terrain, it "totalizes" social relations to some extent; but totality becomes now the name of a horizon and no longer of a ground. And, for the same reason, social actors try to overcome their limitations but, to the extent that the notion of a limitless historical actor has been abandoned, this overcoming can be only the pragmatic process of construction of highly overdetermined social identities. What about representability? It is clear that if there is no ultimate rational ground of the social, total representability is impossible. But in that case we cannot speak of "partial" representations either, which, within their limits, would be more or less adequate pictures of the world. If radical contingency has occupied the terrain of the ground, any social meaning will be a social construction and not an intellectual reflection of what things "in themselves" are. The consequence is that in this "war of interpretations," power, far from being merely appariential, becomes constitutive of social objectivity.

Three conclusions follow from the preceding developments. The first is that politics, far from being a superstructure, occupies the role of what we can call an *ontology of the social*. If politics is the ensemble of the decisions taken in an undecidable terrain—that is, a terrain in which power is constitutive—then the social can consist only in the sedimented forms of a power that has blurred the traces of its own contingency. The second conclusion is that if the movement from modernity to postmodernity takes place at the level of their intellectual and social horizons, this movement will not necessarily involve the collapse of all the objects and values contained within the horizon of modernity but, instead, will involve their reformulation from a different perspective. The universal values of the Enlightenment, for instance, do not need to be abandoned but need instead to be presented as pragmatic social constructions and not as expressions of a necessary requirement of reason. Finally, the previous reflections show, I think, the direction into which the construction of a postmodern social imaginary should move: to indicate the positive communitarian values that follow from the limitation of historical agents, from the contingency of social relations, and from those political arrangements through which society organizes the management of its own impossibility.

Notes

1. S. R. Clegg, *Frameworks of Power* (London: Sage, 1989), ch. 2.

2. Jacques Derrida, *Speech and Phenomena* (Evanston: Northwestern University Press, p. 98.

3. Ernesto Laclau and Chantal Mouffe, *Hegemony and Socialist Strategy* (London: Verso, 1985).

4. This is, to some extent, the direction in which Derrida is moving in his essay "Force and Signification," in *Writing and Difference* (Chicago: University of Chicago Press, 1978).

5. In the first essay of *New Reflections on the Revolution of Our Time* (London: Verso, 1970).

6. On the basis of this argument I have tried to establish a contraposition between Plato and Hobbes in ibid., pp. 68–72.

7. In "Community and Its Paradoxes: Richard Rorty's 'Liberal Utopia,'" Miami Theory Collective, *Community at Loose Ends* (Minneapolis: University of Minneapolis Press, 1991), pp. 83–98.

8. Q. Skinner, "Language and Social Change," in J. Tully, ed., *Meaning and Context: Quentin Skinner and His Critics* (London: Polity Press, 1988), pp. 125–26.

9. S. Hampshire, *Thought and Action* (London: Chatto and Windus, 1959), p. 97.

10. Skinner, "Language and Social Change," p. 126.

11. Ibid.

Index